THE BLUE HARD LINE

R. E. LIVINGSTON

Copyright © 2025 R.E. Livingston

EBook ISBN: 979–8–9927069–1–8

Print ISBN: 979–8–9927069–0–1

Cover art and design:

Alexander P

Editor:

Sarah Grace Liu

www.threefatesediting.com

Formatter:

Liz Steinworth

www.theartofliz.com

All rights reserved.

No part of this book may be reproduced or transmitted in any form or by any means, electronic or mechanical, including photocopying, recording, or by any information storage and retrieval system without the written permission of the author, except for the use of brief quotations in a book review.

This book is a work of fiction. Similarities to people, places, events, or things are entirely coincidental.

Writing a novel is never a solitary journey, no matter how many quiet hours are spent scribbling notes in the dark or typing into the early hours of the morning. Inspiration may strike from within, but it's the unwavering support of family that makes the work possible.

To my loving wife Dana, who patiently endured my late-night musings, scattered notebooks, and the countless moments when I was present in body but lost in a world of words—thank you. Your love, understanding, and encouragement have been the foundation beneath every page. Without you, this story could never have been told.

In loving memory of my mother, Alyce M. Belknap, though you are gone, you are always with me.

In loving memory of my father, Robert Dwain Livingston, you wearing the badge inspired me to become a cop, thank you Pop, I love and miss you!

In memory, my Uncle, James Patrick Belknap, you were like a second father to me growing up and your years in law enforcement inspired me to pursue that career! You are the reason I named the Chief in this series after you.

H.P. Payne, your friendship and guidance to me as a young man growing up has been influential in so many ways, thank you!

Lou Picarone, Robert A. Jacobs, Frank Mares, Jim Downing, Russell Walker, Lewis Judson, Jeffrey Hunter, your friendships mean the world to me, the memories are the best and revealed here! Thank you for always being there!

Mentors who have left this world for another, Cecil Cook, "Bondo" Bob Brown, Charlie Ide, Phil Brabrooks, Chet Herbert. May you all continue to rest in peace, you may be gone, but never forgotten.

CHAPTER ONE

Friday morning, March 27, 1987, 0800, hours after working graveyard, Nikolai Drew was sitting in traffic court in the back of the room waiting to be called to testify. He had been subpoenaed by this notorious crazy lady he'd written a ticket to six weeks before for applying makeup while driving her car; with her knees, no hands on the steering wheel and the visor down. Clearly she had pushed it out as long as she could, hoping Nikolai would have no independent recollection of what happened. She had no idea that he learned long ago from his father and uncle that if you ever write a citation, always write notes on the back of your ticket so when a court appearance is required, your memory is jogged. He had done just that.

At 0810, the woman walked into the courtroom. She was dressed and made up for battle in a low-cut top, short skirt, big fake eyelashes, and makeup that would make Paris Hilton look like an amateur. She scanned the room, looking for Nikolai, but he had infiltrated the courtroom wearing a blue suit, white shirt, matching blue tie and sat in the very back so as not to be accosted by anyone. He could see her grin, clearly thinking he wasn't going to show. Nikolai was also grinning because the defendant, who seemed to be planning to portray herself as the victim, is about to be in front of Judge Sylvia Castillo, a working-class woman who made her way through college on a wing and a prayer—a woman who has no tolerance for manipulators, male or female.

Nikolai had the pleasure of running into Judge Castillo at B.B. King's located at Universal CityWalk in Hollywood one evening after his shift ended. They were sitting at the bar in front of the stage and struck up a conversation. The judge was sixty at this point, though she looked thirty, and she was single and happened to know Nikolai's uncle who was a detective sergeant for LAPD around the time she was interning. The conversation was quite interesting, and the judge didn't let Nikolai know what or who she was until well into an hour of their conversation. Since then, they had been great friends, but Nikolai, being only twenty-three, was young enough to be her grandson.

The bailiff entered the court. "All rise, the honorable Judge Castillo is presiding today, please,

THE BLUE HARD LINE

everyone raise your right hands and repeat after me, I solemnly swear that my testimony today will be the truth, the whole truth, and nothing but the truth, so help me God!" They all repeated it, including Nikolai. He always got goosebumps reciting this oath! The bailiff instructed everyone to be seated, and then the moment came, when Judge Castillo entered the court.

You could have heard a pin drop, and Nikolai saw his defendant's head drop when the judge entered.

Three cases were called and judged. Two of them had no officers present, and thus, charges were dropped, and bail was returned. Next up was Nikolai's case. Castillo called the defendant's name, she stood, and Castillo had her approach the defendant's table.

Now, normally the judge merely asked if the officer in the case was ready. Not today. "Officer Nikolai Drew, are you present and ready to proceed?" she asked.

Nikolai stood up and approached the customary desk. "I am, Your Honor." Nikolai opened his notebook and removed the copy of his citation, which had his notes. The judge recited the citation number and stated that the defendant had been cited for unsafe speed for conditions following up with, "How do you plead, young lady?"

The defendant looked over at Nikolai scowling "I plead nolo contendere Your Honor"!

The judge smiled. "Young lady, do you realize

that this plea is the same as a guilty plea, you simply are not admitting guilt"?

The defendant stammered, looking at her notes. "No, Your Honor, I thought that meant something else entirely. Then I plead NOT GUILTY. I wasn't speeding at all. This officer is just a jackass and clearly hates women!"

Judge Castillo smirked. "Not Guilty. Officer Drew, present your case."

The defendant interrupted. "Don't I get to speak, judge? Are you just going to railroad me?"

Judge Castillo raised her gavel and slammed it on the sound block. "Order, young lady, if you have watched the last group of people address the court, you will have noticed that the state of California, that is the officer who wrote this citation, will testify first. Once he has completed, then you are permitted to cross-examine, bring forth witnesses, and give your side of the story, understood? If you lash out again, I will have no choice but to find you in contempt of court and have the bailiff take you into custody, is that understood"?

The defendant lowered her head and replied, "Yes, Your Honor. I'm sorry."

Judge looked to Nikolai. "Officer Drew, do you have an independent recollection of this incident?"

Nikolai, standing at attention like a soldier, eyes fixed on the judge, stated, "Yes ma'am. After reviewing my notes, I have a clear recollection of the encounter."

The judge motions with her hand. "Proceed, officer."

Nikolai stated, "On Friday, February 27, 1987, I was working uniformed patrol in a marked black and white police vehicle 1/A/22 for the City of Los Angeles sitting at the red light on westbound Rinaldi at Sepulveda. At approximately 0645 hours, I observed the defendant's vehicle, a dark blue Nissan Sentra four-door bearing California License 1VPK656 heading southbound crossing the intersection of Rinaldi. The defendant was traveling at approximately 10 miles per hour, her visor was down, and in her right hand at shoulder height, she was holding a bottle of what appeared to be mascara. In her right hand was the mascara applicator, and she was intently applying it as she was looking in the visor mirror.

"I pulled into traffic and worked my way into position behind her and effected a traffic stop on southbound Sepulveda at Maclay Streets. I identified myself and asked for her license and registration and asked if she knew why I was stopping her.

"She placed her mascara applicator back in the tube and began fishing through her purse for the information I requested and asked me why I was stopping her. I explained that I was stopping her for unsafe speed and asked her if she had any warrants.

She handed me her information and stated she had no warrants. I told her I was happy to hear that and explained that I would return to her momentarily. I returned to my patrol unit so I could run her for warrants and write her the citation, at which time, the defendant exited her vehicle and followed me back to my car where she began pointing her finger at me, chastising me for pulling her over when she was at best only doing 10 miles per hour in a 40 zone. I had given dispatch her driver's license information, and while awaiting dispatch's response, I was writing the citation. I paused for a moment and asked the defendant what she thought the safe speed for applying makeup would be while she had no hands on the wheel and her visor down. She continued to argue with me. The citation was written, and dispatch responded that she had no warrants for her arrest. It was at this time that I set my citation book on the hood of the car and mentioned to the defendant that I personally witnessed her nearly collide into the rear of the car in front of her three times while I was trying to get in position to effect a traffic stop. I followed up with a request to sign the bottom of the citation where the red X is located, told her it is merely a promise to appear, not an admission of guilt, etc., at which time, she adamantly refused to sign the citation with a lot of colorful expletives. I then removed my handcuffs from their case and explained that if she refused to sign, I had no choice but to place her into custody, impound her vehicle, and get her before a magistrate as soon as feasible. Needless to say, she decided to sign the citation, Your Honor, and here we are, before you today."

Judge Castillo had been placing her hand over her mouth to cover her desire to break out laughing as Nikolai told the story. In her mind, she didn't know what was worse, that he had actually written the ticket, or that the driver had actually managed to survive this long driving like she had been. After all, it takes years to develop these habits. It didn't start today! She looked over at the defendant. "Young lady, your response"?

The defendant looked at Nikolai, clearly upset, and responded, "Your Honor, the officer clearly stated that I was not speeding. I was only doing about 10 miles per hour in a 40 zone, and that is only because traffic was horrendous, like it is most mornings, I stand by my not guilty plea."

Judge Castillo looked at the defendant again. "Alright, let me ask you a couple of questions young lady. First, did you have your visor down, and were you applying mascara while your car was in motion?"

The defendant replied, "Yes, judge, but—"

The judge interrupted the defendant. "No buts, young lady, is it true that you were using your knees to manipulate the steering wheel while you used both hands to apply the mascara"?

"Yes, but, judge, I had—"

"Young lady, it is clear that you were driving the vehicle at an unsafe speed, because there is no safe speed for driving while performing your makeup regimen while your car is moving. There is simply no cause to put pedestrians, other drivers, or honestly yourself in danger while operating a 3,000 pound vehicle in this capacity. Court finds for the state, bail is forfeited, you are guilty young lady, points apply to your record. This is a moving violation, you may apply for traffic school. Let me warn you, don't let me see you in my court for this again. You will not like what happens if I do!"

The defendant stomped off and headed to the court clerk. Nikolai saluted the judge, smiled, and said, "Until the next time, Your Honor, enjoy your day!"

She smiled. "Same to you officer, great testimony by the way!"

As Nikolai walked through the back alley of the courthouse to the station building, he was nearing the back door when he was approached by Victor Denofrio, a reserve police officer that had befriended Nikolai after the rookie shooting. Regular sworn police officers did not think much of the reservists. The basic opinion was that they always wanted to be cops when they grew up, and instead of signing up to do the job as a career, worked their normal jobs and worked part time so they could say they were cops as a punch line at parties. Nikolai never felt this way. He was raised with an understanding that those who served as reserves loved the badge and position so much that they would sacrifice their free time to work for free just for the honor of wearing the badge. Nikolai always took on reserves who wanted to work patrol and helped them become better. This way, they could truly be relied upon in a bad situation, rather than getting one of their partners killed or hurt. This philosophy came from his father and uncle who had been reserves themselves before becoming regular sworn police officers back in New York.

Victor had a frustrated and angry look on his face and asked Nikolai, "Do you mind if I talk to you alone for a moment? I am about to punch in for my shift for today, but I need your advice about something."

Nikolai put his arm around Victor and walked him back by where the personal vehicles were parked. "I'm always here to bounce shit off of, Denofrio. I'm honored that you would consider me someone you can do that with."

Victor began, "Look, I had a fundraiser at my house last night for Councilman Melendez. I had about 120 people over, predominantly Hispanic people from the community and some of my pals from Hollywood."

Nikolai laughed. "Yeah, you communists all like to get together and talk about taking over the country."

Victor punched him in the shoulder. "Do you want to listen or run your mouth? Stop being a dick head. Anyway, his rhetoric was all about getting rid of Chief Belknap and replacing him with a Hispanic chief. Then went off on a tangent about how we need to restore the power to the Mexicans who lost California to the White Man and so on and so forth. This diatribe went on throughout the evening. Most thought he was a nut and didn't like the way he was speaking, but others were all fire and brimstone over this shit."

Nikolai looked at him, confused. "So what advice do you want from me on this Victor?"

Victor looked at him and looked around. "What do you think I should do, talk to the chief? Take it to the Police Officers Association? What, who? This guy is a racist and bigot himself. I want nothing more to do with this guy. The chief has been nothing but good to everyone!"

Nikolai put his arm around him again, consoling him. "Don't do anything, tell no one. As for distancing yourself, don't do that. Stay close to this wingnut. Friends close, enemies closer, get it."

Victor burst in. "Fuck that and fuck this guy, Nik, he's bad news!"

Nikolai made a motion with his left hand as his right arm was still around Victor's shoulder. "You want to protect the chief and the department, right? The best way to do that is through developing intelligence, Victor. Stay glued to this guy and report to just me about whatever you hear, and I will make sure you don't get burned, fair enough?"

Victor smiled. "Okay, Nikki, I agree. You make total sense. It's the best way to learn what this guy has planned. You can count on me." By the way, did anyone from *Call the Cops* get in touch with you yet?"

Nikolai laughed. "Not yet, Victor, I am sure they will then they get around to it." The two men parted ways, but Nikolai was concerned about this political shit show he had learned about from Victor. He figured he'd talk to Bedo to sort it all out. No way can this be as big a deal as Victor made it out to be.

CHAPTER
TWO

Nikolai and Diamond Dave had found a house in Northridge with the assistance of Detective Bedo's contact. They couldn't move in for another few days, which put them into the house by April first. Luckily, it was Nikolai's day off. This meant that he was going to have to spend the next few days packing all his crap and somehow find time to get a moving truck rented for that day. He got back to the station. It was now 1030 hours, so he got out of the Monkey Suit and into shorts and a t-shirt and made his way to the cot room, letting dispatch know he was sleeping there in the event they needed him for any reason. He set his alarm for 1800 hours.

The alarm went off, and Nikolai jumped out of bed, not immediately knowing where he was. He sat there a moment to get his bearings, put on his baseball cap, and walked into the breakroom. He poured himself a cup of coffee and sat at the table alone in an attempt to wake up. He was not really good at being one of those who wakes up bright eyed and chipper. He was best left alone until the first cup of coffee took effect. As he sipped his coffee, the chief's secretary walked by with a blonde guy in a suit who stood about six foot. It appeared he was a new recruit by the look on his face, wide eyed, overwhelmed, and also excited. Nikolai remembered that feeling and more than likely that look. Nikolai got another cup of coffee, walked into the dispatch area, and began reading over the daily look from the last shift. Just then, he noticed the blonde recruit walking toward him through the dispatch windows like he was on his way to the back door of the station. Nikolai stopped what he was doing and cut the guy off. He stuck out his hand with a grin. The rookie stopped and shook his hand.

"Nikolai Drew is the name, you a new guy?" he asked.

The blonde said, "Yes sir, just got sworn in and starting tomorrow on day shift, name's Jordy Baker."

Nikolai asked him if he was interested in a cup of coffee and motioned toward the break room. The two sat down, and Nikolai poured the rookie a cup of coffee. "Cream and sugar?" Nikolai asked.

Baker said, "Just black, sir."

Nikolai laughed out loud. "Don't call me sir, I'm a FNG (Fuckin New Guy) just like you, brother. Call me Nikolai or Drew and no, I'm not Russian." He handed Baker the cup of coffee and sat down. Nikolai asked the standard battery of questions one asks a rookie: *Where are you from? What drove you to this line of work? Where do you live?*

Baker smiled. "I'm from Montebello, still live there and my parents were both teachers. I just couldn't work in that field. This felt natural to me."

Nikolai told him how he could relate as his mother was a twenty-five-year employee of the Riverside County Office of Education. He asked Baker what his first shift was and who his first training officer was going to be. Baker told him that he was beginning his shift this very next day from 1600 hours to midnight working with FTO Hunter. Nikolai told the rookie that he was going to be in for fun because Hunter was a great FTO who specialized in Officer Safety and was very patient. Baker stood up and walked with his coffee and dismissed himself as he had a lot of things to get together before he started his shift the next morning. The two men shook hands. Nikolai thought that the rookie was wound way too tight and stand-offish!

Nikolai walked to the locker room, got out his gym clothes and his running shoes and put on his twenty-pound tactical vest. He walked out the back door of the station, hit the stopwatch start button, and began his three-mile run down MacNeil to First St. East to Brand and headed north, up to Glenoaks

Boulevard then headed east. He sang cadence along the way and increased his pace considerably as he continued. He hit Maclay Street and headed south back down to First Street and back to the police station. Nikolai looked down at his watch. Three miles with a twenty-pound pack in twenty minutes, an excellent time he thought to himself!

He hit the gym afterward and got in his two-hour workout. In between sets, he made his pre-workout energy shake in his blender, which he kept in his locker. The regimen he put himself through was strenuous. This was a push/pull day, meaning chest and back, two huge muscle groups, and he chose to do 300 repetitions, which meant 60 reps and 5 sets per muscle group. Nothing fast and sloppy about this routine either, each set met with full movement, coupled with a full contraction at the extension of each rep, One has to have the right kind of fuel in the system to handle such a pounding, which usually means eating or drinking copious amounts of carbs during the workout.

After two hours of physically abusing himself, Nikolai went back to the cot room, it was 2030 hours, so he set his alarm for 2230 hours, he thought to himself, 'It's hard to believe it's still Friday!' He needed to get a couple hours rest before having to shower up, suit up, and show up! His head hit the pillow, and he was out.

The alarm went off, and Nikolai got up, walked

down the hallway, and poured another cup of coffee. He sipped it slowly and headed to the locker room. He opened his locker and retrieved his razor, soap, and shampoo. He liked that Aussie Mega Shampoo. He thought it smelled nice, and for some reason, he thought it worked well on what little hair he had.

Fifteen minutes later, out of the shower, he wrapped his towel around his waist and shaved his face, making sure to trim that ever so perfect mustache that seemed to help him look older than twenty-two. He applied hair gel to his hair, blew it dry, then got dressed. His final preparation was to use hair spray to keep the spiky look intact during the shift.

He pulled out his shoe-shine kit and touched up the shine on his work boots then put on his slacks, then his boots. He pulled his t-shirt over his head, then his bullet proof vest. He looked over his shirt to make sure there were no loose threads, his badge was clean, and everything was in place. He slipped the shirt over each arm and then zipped it up. Zippers were installed in the neat and tidy patrol officer's shirt to make it easier to get on and off, and all the creases were sewn in so they always looked sharp. He buttoned the top and bottom buttons, then tucked the t-shirt, bulletproof vest tails, and the uniform shirt into his underwear, pulled his slacks up, fastened them, and cinched up his pants belt. Nikolai had five keepers on his belt, always. (Keepers are leather two snap clasps that run under the patrol officer's pants belt and fasten around the Sam Browne utility belt, which holds his or her weapon, ammunition, cuff cases, and radio.) He slipped the keepers beneath the pants belt in the consecutive spots he had chosen, then placed his utility belt on, fastened the chrome buckle, then fastened the keepers, making sure everything was in its intended place and secure. All of this was to keep the patrol officers' things where they needed to be and of course, was designed with officer safety in mind. This way if an altercation ever took place, a suspect cannot move his belt from one side to another should a struggle ensue.

Grabbing his clipboard, Nikolai walked out of the locker room and set the clipboard onto the last table in the back of the squad room. It felt good to finally be off probation, he thought to himself. He enjoyed sitting in the back of the room so he could watch everyone. He had a bit of time before roll call began, so he walked into the dispatch center and looked over the daily log one more time. There wasn't much to see, a couple of report calls handled, no arrests made. He walked over to the breakroom, poured another cup of coffee, then made his way into the squadroom and took his seat before anyone even walked in.

Ten minutes before roll call began, the mob started to show up. Some were enthusiastic; others looked like they hadn't slept in a week. One could depend on the condition of the shift sergeant to see what the shift expectation was going to be like. In this case, Sergeant Brodie was known for being retired on active duty, lazy, and had the nickname "Sgt. Nutty" because one could never tell from one day to the next what team he was batting for, meaning the cops who worked for him, or trying to suck up to the chief so he could make lieutenant in the near future.

He had never been a real cop. He was a college boy who was promoted to sergeant because he had a degree, not because he knew the job.

Either way, the man treaded water as a sergeant and actually had no idea what he was doing, and most thought he should have been a computer programmer, not a cop.

Nikolai had the mindset that he would just do what was expected of him and then some and not let the mental disorder of others get in the way of enjoying his job. The rest of the officers on the graveyard shift were chatting it up, mostly about hot cars, hot women, or what promotion they were trying to get ready for. Sgt. Nutty barked and told everyone to listen up. He ran through unit assignments and told Nikolai he was assigned to X-Ray 1. An X-Ray unit can be either a blessing or a curse as the unit is designed to be a rover who picks up back up calls or overflow report calls. Since the shift prior was practically dead quiet, this could be a good way for Nikolai to stir up some excitement.

Sergeant Nutty concluded with a "Be Careful Out

There" speech, and the group adjourned. Nikolai picked up his war bag and walked to the back of the station where he loaded up and made his patrol car ready for the evening's work!

He first checked the trunk, making sure there was a complete first aid supply kit, then emergency flares, blankets, spare tire. He then checked the interior of the car for contraband, just in case the previous driver failed to catch something a dirtbag left in the unit during their arrest. He then returned inside the station, walked to the armory, and retrieved a Remington 870 shotgun, made sure the pump-action slide was open and the weapon was unloaded and walked outside. Once to the unit, he slid the action forward and loaded the weapon with double-aught buck. The high capacity magazine in the weapon held six rounds. He sat in the driver seat of the unit and slid the twelve-gauge shotgun into the rack, closed the locking mechanism, and double-checked that it was in fact locked and secure. The next thing was to check the scanner. It worked, and then he grabbed the microphone, squeezed the red button on the side, and proudly blurted over the KMA-367 Airways "X-Ray One is 10-8" (KMA-367 is the FCC issued frequency for LAPD).

He pulled out onto Brand Boulevard and headed north and began to head toward the outskirts of Pacoima near Foothill Boulevard and Arroyo. On any given day, one could park, sit in the wash, and use binoculars and watch the drug addicts either drive in or walk up on the cul de sac on Dronfield Ave. to buy crack, heroin, or even score pot. It was like a scene out of *Night of the Living Dead*, zombies just lumbering toward their fix! Then, if one was ambitious and patient, one could pick up one or two felony possession arrests.

Nikolai turned off all the lights of his unit and slowly pulled to the curb on Arroyo when out of nowhere, a motorcycle turned onto Arroyo in front of him, came right at him, and pulled a wheel stand and zoomed past him, accelerating to over seventy miles per hour. Nikolai laughed and said out loud, "Well shit, it's showtime"! He swung a U-turn then floored the unit, still blacked out hoping to sneak up on the cyclist. The bike dropped back down to two wheels and slowed just slightly as he turned left onto westbound Foothill Boulevard, completely failing to stop for the red light. Nikolai turned on the unit's headlights, slowed for the light—no traffic, so he hit the rotators but not the siren. He grabbed the mic and put out, "X-Ray One, control, be advised, I am following a vehicle at a high rate of speed westbound Foothill from Arroyo. Vehicle is a late model Suzuki, silver in color, I am unable to obtain the plate. Can you please notify air support we could use assistance; not passing Maclay Street."

The dispatcher repeated the pursuit and followed

up, "Air one, are you anywhere near Foothill and Maclay, unit to back X-Ray One identify."

The motorcycle turned to the right onto Hubbard, then immediately onto the 210 freeway heading east. Nikolai calmly put out his location before anyone could respond, "Control, be advised, I am now eastbound on the 210 freeway from Hubbard, vehicle speed is approximately 110 miles per hour, traffic conditions are light."

Backing unit Officer Rawlins chimed in, "1-L-22 to X-1, be advised, I am right behind you entering the 210 eastbound at Maclay. I will call out the pursuit from here."

Air Support chimed in, "Air One, we are supersonic from West Hollywood, comin' at ya."

The motorcycle continued to accelerate, now well over 130 miles per hour. "L-22 to all units, be advised, we are not passing the 118 freeway, continuing eastbound on the 210, still little or no traffic and at approximately 110 miles per hour." These guys knew that if they put out that they were pushing 140 miles per hour the shift sergeant would call off the pursuit, so, they fibbed a little to stay engaged.

The motorcycle exited the Sunland Boulevard off ramp. "L-22, be advised, suspect vehicle has exited Sunland Boulevard heading northbound. Traffic is still minimal to non-existent."

"Air One, be advised, we are three minutes out."

Suddenly a new voice appeared over the radio. It was Sgt. Nutty "1-L-30, be advised I am in the area. Units involved in the pursuit, monitor speeds on surface streets, we may need to terminate the pursuit if air support isn't here quick."

Nikolai and Rawlins exited the freeway and turned left in an attempt to stay with the motorcycle, and like a ghost, the motorcycle vanished. They approached Foothill Boulevard, stopped, and Nikolai exited his vehicle, hoping to hear the loud sound of the motorcycle, but there was nothing.

He grabbed the mic and put out over the air, "Control, be advised, we lost the suspect vehicle in the area of Sunland and Foothill Boulevard. We will stay in the area for a few, just in case. Again, we have lost the suspect vehicle."

"Air One, we are over you now, X-Ray-1. We will keep an eye open as well."

Nikolai and Rawlins pulled into the McDonalds parking lot at the corner of Sunland and Foothill, turned off their units, and just listened. The motorcycle had a very loud exhaust, and they knew they would hear him if he was still out there. "Well, brotha, that got my blood pumpin', this dirt bag is probably already in a garage somewhere," Rawlins said laughing.

Nikolai laughed back. "Where the hell were you when I initiated? You were on me like stink on shit."

"I was actually coming up Arroyo from Glenoaks

when I saw you make the U-turn and go after Evil Knievel. I just cruised and waited, hoping you'd get on the 210, and patience paid off today," Rawlins said with a cat-ate-the-canary grin. "I am honestly surprised Nutty didn't shut us down. He is such a paranoid sort. He probably figured we'd lose the guy."

"Air One units, no sign of your suspect vehicle, were buggin' out. Good night."

Nikolai and Rawlins got back in their prospective vehicles. Nikolai broadcast, "X-Ray One, be advised, units are 10-8, we have no sign of the suspect vehicle, thank you Air One for the assist."

"Roger X-Ray One, all units 10-8."

CHAPTER
THREE

Sergeant Nutty chimed in and asked Nikolai to meet him at the corner of Maclay and Foothill. Nikolai acknowledged the request. In a matter of a few minutes, Nikolai exited the 210 onto Maclay and found the sergeant parked with his lights off at the northwest corner of Foothill and Maclay in the vacant parking lot. Nikolai pulled alongside the sergeant's cruiser and rolled his driver side window down.

"Evening, Sarge," Nikolai said.

"That was a fun one! Just wanted to tell you that your broadcast started off a little panicky sounding, but after a hot minute or so, you calmed right down and took control. I didn't have to say a word. you did a great job letting us all know how this was progressing," Sergeant Brodie said.

Nikolai grinned and nodded respectfully. "Thank

you, sir, would have liked to get the bastard though, without killing any innocent bystanders, of course."

"What all did you have him on, out of curiosity?" Sergeant Brodie asked.

"Sarge, I was sitting facing south on Arroyo with my lights off, just watching the area for drug traffic and that knucklehead popped a wheelie heading toward me at 50 and accelerated to 70 by the time he got to Foothill. He ran the red light at Arroyo and Foothill, then again at Maclay and got up to 110 long before he got to Hubbard, just simply reckless driving, which turned into evading," Nikolai said.

Sergeant Brodie laughed. "Well, it's probably a kid who gets off on running from us. Either way, good job, catch ya later."

As Nikolai drove away, dispatch put out a call. "Control 1-L-21, respond to 1019 8th Street, 415 Family Dispute, unit to back identify."

Officer Fricassi responded, "Roger, 21 en route."

Nikolai grabbed the back-up call immediately and because he was literally one block away, put out the response, "X-Ray-One has the back. Put me in the area control. 21, I am standing for you."

Nikolai pulled into the area and turned out all his lights as well as hits the kill switch that eliminates the brake lights of the unit coming on. He rolled down his windows and pulled to a stop two doors down from the house on 8th Street, exited his patrol car, and quietly closed the door. Walking up, he could hear the man and woman screaming at one another. He was patiently waiting for the primary unit. There was no sound of physical violence, so approaching the house at this point is not worth the risk of getting hurt.

A moment later, Fricassi broadcasted that he is on scene. He pulled up on the opposite side of the residence, and he too had his unit blacked out. Nikolai covered the end of his flashlight with his hand and flashed it twice so Fricassi could see him across the street from the home kneeling alongside a parked car. Fricassi walked over to him and squatted down.

"What do you have kid?" Fricassi asked Nikolai.

Nikolai loved being called "kid," despite the fact that he was six inches taller than this guy and outweighed him by sixty pounds. "Just yelling, hard to make out what they are saying, but the husband and wife are both losin' it."

Fricassi has had ten years on the job and was a good cop, a little lazy, but a good cop. He stood and motioned Nikolai to walk with him. "Let's keep it low-key. We will separate them, turn their backs to one another. That will stop them from arguing and get them to focus on us and make it so we can see each other. You take the husband, I'll take the wife, got it?"

"You got it, brother," Nikolai said. He was excited to get in and see what the real deal was with these two. At this time of the night, it was anyone's guess, but in Nikolai's mind, someone was going to jail.

The two officers got to the front door, each standing on opposite sides. Fricassi knocked loudly, but there was silence. Fricassi knocked again and said, "LAPD, come to the door please."

The door opened, and a male Hispanic wearing nothing but boxers stood in the door with an angry look on his face and barked, "What the fuck do you want?" He looked behind him and screamed at a woman, "Did you call the cops, you bitch?" Fricassi enters the door, which is the living room of the residence, looking at the hands of the man to make sure he has no weapons.

"Sir, we're just here to check on you. We got a call from an anonymous neighbor that there was one hell of a fight going on. Are you both alright?" Fricassi moved past the man and engaged the woman in the home.

Nikolai had also entered the home and engaged the husband, keeping him facing the door. "What is your name, sir? I am Officer Drew."

The man was furious, sweating and clenching his fists. "Fuck you, I don't have to tell you nothing. No neighbor called you, it was that fucking bitch."

Nikolai lowered his voice, calmly looking down at the man with gentle eyes. "Sir, honestly, I could hear you both yelling inside my car when I pulled up. It was a little loud. Everyone is allowed to have a bad day, I get it. We just have a job to do, and that's simply to make sure you are both alright."

"My name is Rene. I am having a hard time. I was fired from my job today. I have been stressed all fucking day. This bitch only cares about herself. I am so tired of feeling like I am the only one working to keep a roof over our head."

Nikolai smelled alcohol coming not only from the man's breath, but his aura. The man was hyper, moving around a lot, and his pupils were dilated and bloodshot. He'd seen this a lot, and he started looking around the home subtly for drug paraphernalia.

Fricassi addressed a woman, who was crying. She was wearing a robe, female, Hispanic, and about 4'11". He had turned the woman so her back was to Nikolai and the man, keeping a clear line of sight of his partner. "What's your name, ma'am?"

"Freta Marquez," she said sniffling as her eyes continued watering.

"Who is he, ma'am?" Fricassi asked, motioning with his eyes at the half naked man chatting with Officer Drew.

Wiping her eyes with her robe, she mustered the ability to calm herself and speak. "He's my husband, he's having a real bad day. He got fired from his job, and he's been drinking all day and night, he's just angry."

Fricassi had been looking at her to see if he could see any signs of injury. "What does he do for a living? Has he hit you at all?"

Freta quietly replied, "He's an electrician at

PG&E. He had a drug test come back positive for something, and they terminated him. He has hit the walls, but not me. He's just not well."

Nikolai asked, "Rene, has she hit you at all today? Your eyes look a little swollen."

"Fuck no, she hasn't hit me, she knows better!" Rene was getting more agitated.

Nikolai changed the subject. "Is that your Chevy pick-up in the driveway?"

Rene looked puzzled for a moment, pauses, looked down, and then looked up smiling, "Yeah man, that's my 3500!"

Nikolai smiled. "That is one wicked rig. Did you lift it yourself and put the custom wheels and exhaust on her?"

Rene continued. "Yeah, that lift was a bitch. My buddy and I did it in my back yard last month, I got the tires and wheels not long after that, and San Fernando Muffler hooked me up with the 4" exhaust. It's a diesel so, you gotta have a killer system so it can breathe, you know what I mean, eh?"

Nikolai felt like he was making progress getting the man to calm down. He was no longer clenching his fists. "Well, I love the look of that truck, and the silver was a great choice as well. What's your last name, Rene?"

"Marquez, with a Z. Ya know what, Holmes, I wanted blue, but they didn't have one. I saw this one and settled, but it's really growin' on me."

Nikolai smiled. "I have a blue Chevelle. I love blue myself! What's your date of birth, Rene?" he asked.

Nikolai has been filling out a field interview card as they have been talking. Suddenly, the calm look in Rene's eyes turned wild, Nikolai didn't like the feeling he was getting.

"What are you writing down, Holmes?" The man looked over his shoulder at Fricassi and saw him also filling out a field interview card. Nikolai has slowly replaced the pen to its spot in the pocket of his uniform shirt and the field interview card to his breast pocket. The man quickly turned and simultaneously swung at Nikolai's face. Nikolai moves out of the way of the punch, but it caught him at the outside area of his jaw.

Nikolai didn't flinch. He went with the flow of the punch and grabbed the right wrist of the man's hand with his right hand, gripped the man's left shoulder with his left, and placed the man into a wrist restraint, locking the man's right elbow into his bulletproof vest and applying pressure to the man's wrist.

Nikolai leaned in and whispered, "Now, see, we were having a perfectly nice conversation, and you had to go and strike a police officer. Now, shit bird, put your left hand on the back of your head or your bad day is about to get worse."

The man, now angry, was trying to escape the huge right arm of Nikolai Drew. He applied a little more pressure, and the pain takes the man to his knees. Nikolai leaned in again and whispered, "See, if you don't relax and do as I ask, I am gonna snap that wrist like a fuckin twig, and you're gonna end up goin two places tonight, my friend, first the hospital, then jail, you pickin' up what I'm layin' down?"

Nikolai applied a little more pressure.

"Okay, okay, fuck, you're gonna break my wrist, ese!" The man moved the hand to his head, and Nikolai took his cuffs out of their holster and applied one to the man's left wrist, took the wrist, moved it around and behind him and slipped the other wrist into the other end of the cuffs.

In a matter of less than a minute, Fricassi witnessed the man go from combative to compliant. Nikolai stood the man up and began walking the man to his unit. He looked over his shoulder at Fricassi. "Get this man some clothes please."

As he walked the man to his police car, the man yelled at him, "What the fuck are you arresting me for! I didn't do nothing, mother fucker."

Nikolai opened the back door of the patrol car, patted the suspect's waistband down, and placed him inside the back of the car, making sure he didn't hit his head. "I am arresting you for assault and battery of a police officer and being under the influence of a controlled substance, for starters, sir. Now, remain calm. You have the right to remain silent. I would recommend you do just that."

Nikolai entered the unit and pulled into the driveway of the residence. He got out of the car and met Fricassi at the front door of the home. Both officers were keeping an eye on the patrol car and the man in custody. Fricassi laughed. "You okay? I couldn't tell if he got a clean shot to your face or not? What did you say to him to get him to go off?"

Nikolai gave him a confused look. "Brother, I haven't a clue. I thought I had him calm, he looked over at you, then the fight was on!

"Anyway, I'll take him in and start the booking if you don't mind finishing up here. Did he hit her? Do we have a domestic violence?"

"No man, he lost his job over a bad drug test, so she says, and has been drinking all day and losing his mind with her. Does he have anything other than alcohol on board?" Fricassi asked.

Nikolai smiled. "He's as high as a kite, I can't tell if it's coke or meth, but it's a stimulant. Check his car and see if you can find anything in there. See if she has the keys and if she will let you look inside to check for weapons. I'll get all the info on his intoxication wrapped up by the time you get in, and hopefully he will comply with a urine test. I'll even cut the paper if you like, chief."

Fricassi shook his hand. "See you in a bit."

Nikolai got in his unit, grabbed the microphone and broadcast, "X-Ray-1, be advised, we are code four, I have one in custody and en route 10-19."

Dispatch responded, "Roger X-Ray-1, reporting code four on Eighth Street, en-route 10-19 with one 10-15."

Nikolai pulled into the station and advised dispatch he had arrived with his prisoner. He immediately walked him into the jail, secured the prisoner in the booking cell, and placed his service weapon and backup .38 revolver in the gun locker, secured it, and placed the key in his pocket. He then retrieved the prisoner and escorted him back to the interview room where he could examine his pupils further. He asked Rene to stand against the wall facing him, removed his pupil exam card from his pocket for comparison, and turned off the lights. He removed his mini flashlight from his pocket and turned it on so he could see the pupils in different variations of light for comparison.

"What the fuck are you doing, asshole?" Rene asked.

"I am checking your pupils for a moment. Now keep your eyes open, sir." In dim light, the pupils were measured to be 7.5 millimeters, quite large, larger than normal. He moved the light closer, and the pupils hardly moved, down to maybe 6.5 millimeters. He turned the lights back on and removed one handcuff and moved Rene's hands in front of him, cuffing him again. He then pulled out a chair at the interview table and asked Rene to have a seat. Nikolai asked Rene to place his hands on the table.

"What for, Holmes?" he asked.

"Just relax, brother, this will only take a minute." Rene placed his hands on the table. Nikolai asked him, "So, what year is that Chevy truck?"

Rene relaxed a bit and told him, "It's an '86, I got it with hardly any miles on it." After a few minutes of idle chit-chat, Nikolai placed his fingers on Rene's right wrist, he looked at his watch and counted 65 beats in 30 seconds which is 130 beats per minute. The combined four symptoms. Sweaty skin even with no clothes on, rapid and repetitive speech, dilated pupils, and the elevated blood pressure substantiated that Rene was under the influence of a central nervous system stimulant.

Nikolai escorted Rene back to the booking cell and told him he'd be right back. Nikolai went to the storage room and retrieved a clean set of prisoner clothing: a pair of slippers, a blue button-down shirt, and pants that were made to fit the average person. He slid them through the holding cell door and asked Rene for his hands. He removed his handcuffs and handed him the clothes and told him to get dressed. The booking officer came in and asked him what he was being booked for. Nikolai pulled him into the hallway.

"Do me a favor, just fingerprint and photo him and hold off on the charges for a bit. We definitely have him for battery on a police officer and being under the influence of a controlled substance, but I suspect we may have more. Get his full information and we will run him through the system to see if he has warrants. We will see how this plays out when Fricassi gets in."

Nikolai walked back into the jail area, and asked Rene, "Are you thirsty? Want a cup of coffee or anything?"

Rene looked at him, puzzled. "I am hungry, Holmes. Do you have any food around here?"

Nikolai looked at him for a moment then replied, "Tell ya what, I need a urine specimen from you. If you give me that, I'll run out and get you a cheeseburger, how's that?"

"You're kidding, right?" Rene replied.

"Nope, serious as a heart attack, amigo," Nikolai replied.

Rene thought this over for a moment and replied, "If you're serious, I'll pee right now."

Nikolai lifted a hand and put up his index finger indicating he would be back in a moment. He walked to the evidence storage area, got a urine specimen jar and walked back to jail. He retrieved a pair of rubber gloves, put them on his hands, and unlocked the booking cell. He escorted Rene to one of the cells and opened the jar and told Rene to fill the jar halfway and not to piss on the jar. Rene took the jar and did as he was requested, although he managed to piss all over the jar, and handed it back to Nikolai.

With a disgusted look on his face, Nikolai took the jar, screwed the lid on tightly and said, "Thank you."

"You're gonna get me a cheeseburger, right?" Rene asked as Nikolai escorted him back to the cell.

Nikolai locked the door and said, "A promise is a promise, amigo."

Nikolai took the jar, washed it off with soap and water, and dried it with a paper towel. He then removed the rubber gloves, wrapping one inside the other, and threw them away with disgust and uttered, "'I'm sorry,' he says, fucker pissed on the jar on purpose."

He filled out the evidence label, placed it over the lit of the jar onto the glass, and walked back to the report room.

Just then he heard Fricassi over his handheld radio. "L-27 to X-Ray-1."

Nikolai removed the radio from his belt. "Go for X-Ray-1."

Fricassi sounded a little excited and responded, "Switch to frequency 2."

Nikolai switched over to the other frequency, which was done for one-on-one chatter and avoided the primary frequency being tied up with nonsense so emergency chatter would not be interrupted.

Fricassi was clearly excited, not the norm for him at all. "Drew, hold off on charging until I get there. I have something you're gonna want to see. I also have some clothes for our attacker."

"Roger that, see you in a few." Nikolai switched back to frequency one, and at that moment, Sergeant Nutty walked in the back door.

"Whaddaya got, kid, and what does Fricassi mean by our attacker?" This was one of those moments when Nikolai couldn't tell whose team the sergeant was on. He couldn't hear one bit of empathy or concern from the voice of the sergeant. Felt like he was more concerned about saving his own ass.

"Well, sarge, we got to the dispute call, and the guy was amped. During our initial interview, he, well, he took a poke at me." Nikolai pointed at his chin.

"Are you okay, son, or should I be asking how the dirtbag is?" Sergeant Brodie moved into the booking area and saw no one in any of the holding cells. "Where is he, Drew, for the love of fuck?"

Nikolai laughed out loud, "Relax, Sarge, he's being fingerprinted. I never raised a hand to the man, just a simple compliance hold to get him under control. Absolutely no medical treatment required."

Sergeant Brodie developed a relieved look on his face, even smiled. "So, what are you charging him with?"

Nikolai smiled. "So far, 243 c, 11550, and who knows what else, Fricassi is on his way in with something he thinks I need to see. It'll look good on the log, unlike the whole losing the motorcycle pursuit thing."

Brodie patted Nikolai on the shoulder. "I can't wait to read the report. Sharpen your pencil, kid. I don't wanna have to make you rewrite it." Nikolai looked at the sergeant and thought to himself, *No wonder they call this dipshit Sgt. Nutty. He talks about having officers rewrite reports when the man has never done a bit of legitimate police work in his life. What is it Dad used to say—There are those in command that think they are in control, and all the while, those who are in control are not in command.*

Nikolai sat down at the typewriter, an IBM correcting Selectric. This was an old friend. He learned to type in junior high school, and by the time he graduated high school, he was typing over one hundred words per minute not having to look at the keys. He grinned, thinking back to when his mother recommended he take a typing class and how it would help him later on. Who could have guessed how truly important this would end up being.

Fricassi walked in the back door and looked around for Nikolai almost frantically, calling his name.

"I'm in the report room, dickhead," Nikolai responded.

Fricassi walked in, took a seat next to Nikolai, and opened up a paper bag with a cat-ate-the-canary look on his face. "Look in the bag. You're gonna fuckin shit! The wife was initially upset that you took the hubby away in cuffs, but then, walked me into their bedroom and showed me where fucko kept his stash."

Nikolai looked in the paper bag and removed a plastic bag that contained twenty-two small ziplock bags each containing a small yellowish colored rock substance. "Twenty-two rocks, possession for sale it is! Tell the booking officer to add the charge of 11350 H&S, my friend! Did you get his clothes from the wife as well?"

Fricassi laughed. "Oh, yeah, clothes are in the car. I can slice off a small piece of this for labwork and book it all along with the urine specimen while you write the report."

"You got it. I need to make a food run, and I'll be right back." Nikolai walked out the back, jumped in his vehicle, and headed to the local McDonalds which was open 24-hours. He switched his unit radio to frequency two and called into the desk, "X-1 control, you hungry up there, I am makin a Mickey D's run."

The dispatcher happened to be starving and replied, "You know how to win a woman's heart. Six-piece nugget thingy, a small fry, and an iced tea please, and thank you."

"Roger that request for high-end cuisine. X-1 out, see you in 10 or 15." Nikolai hung the mic back on the dashboard of the unit and was now contemplating how to use this felony charge to turn this guy into an informant. It was going to take a bit, and it would take a conversation with good ole Sergeant Nutty to see if he was willing to entertain the idea.

Nikolai made it through the drive thru and picked up eight cheeseburgers, one six-piece McNugget, four orders of french fries, one Coke, two Diet Cokes and one iced tea for the group at the station. One burger, fry, and drink were for the prisoner he made the promise to. He returned to the station, walked into the break room. He split up the food and took the McNuggets, an order of french fries, and the iced tea to the dispatcher. He then took the burger, fry, and Coke to the prisoner, who was subsequently shocked and delighted that he wasn't forgotten.

"You're the real deal, Drew. Thanks, Holmes, I was starvin!" Rene said.

Back to the report room Nikolai went, and in less than thirty minutes, the arrest report was complete. He went over Fricassi's evidence log and request for labwork on the rocks and submitted all of the paperwork with a Post-it note for the sergeant to chat with him before the end of shift.

CHAPTER
FOUR

Nikolai walked out the back door, looked down at his watch, and realized it was now 0345 hours. As he sat down in his cruiser, he pondered what he was going to do the rest of the shift. He pulled out of the station parking lot and just as he was about to click the mic and put himself 10-8, there was a broadcast from dispatch.

"Control to 1-L-22, respond to 585 Glenoaks Boulevard, the San Fernando Swap Meet. See the man regarding suspicious circumstances."

Nikolai grabbed the mic before Officer Rawlins could respond. He felt guilty about putzing around with an arrest all night so wanted to make a gesture to buy the call; "X-Ray-1 to 22, I'm 10-8, I'll buy that call if you like."

Rawlins sounded happy in his response. "22 to X-1, copy that and many thanks!"

Nikolai arrived inside the gate of the swap meet, he noticed that the gate lock was on the ground cut off. He pulled to the back and found the R-P (Reporting Party) leaning against his car. Nikolai parked, turned off the unit, and walked over to where the man was standing.

"Good morning, sir. I'm Officer Drew, LAPD. I understand you called about something suspicious. I saw the lock cut off the gate. Was that what you were calling about?" Nikolai at that moment caught the scent of something burning. He looked at the R-P and began to walk around the building. He noticed that there was smoke coming from an area by the kitchen between the roof and the wall. There are no windows to look into. The building was an old block building used as a kitchen and food vendor for the drive-in movie theater and used much the same way for the swap meet.

The R-P told him, "There's something very wrong. The gate was cut open when I got here, and when I walked up to the front door, it was locked from the outside." The two men walked around the back of the building to the back door of the building. It, too, was locked, from the outside.

———

Nikolai told the R-P, "Do me a favor. Move your car away from this building, and follow me." They pulled their cars away, and Nikolai immediately grabbed the mic and called in, "X-Ray-1 to control, contact LA City Fire, and have them send units to my location, we have a fire burning at the swap meet building. Request an L-30 meet at my location please. Control, I have two vehicle plates to run at your convenience as well. Please advise when you're clear to copy."

Dispatch confirmed the request for the fire department and immediately requested Sergeant Brodie to respond to Nikolai's location. The dispatcher then broadcast over the radio, "X-Ray-1, go with your vehicle plates."

Settling down, he removed a field interview card and asked the R-P his name and what he noticed.

"My name is Jaime Jimenez. I am one of the coordinators for the swap meet, I got here this morning to start getting ready for tomorrow's swap meet and found the gate lock cut off, gates wide open, and I found the two cars parked where they are now. When I get here, the owner's car is usually here, but today this other one was parked next to his. The gate is always locked, and so is the door, but never padlocked on the outside."

"Do you know if the owner is in the building sir?" Nikolai asked.

"I don't know. I went to unlock the door, and the lock was so hot I couldn't touch it. This is not good, señor."

Two fire trucks arrived. They exited, and the

captain assessed the building and approached Nikolai. "I'm Captain Kline, what do you have?"

Nikolai shook the man's hand and told him that he had no idea. He told him what the R-P told him and said he saw smoke coming out of the kitchen area between the roof and the block walls of the building. The fire captain asked the R-P if he had the keys to the building. Jimenez reached into his pocket, removed his key ring containing two keys and said, "Yes sir, the Master Lock key opens both the big locks on the doors. The other unlocks the doors."

The firefighters were already removing fire hoses from the trucks, both poised at different sides of the building. One of the men was turning off the gas to the building at the same time. The fire captain handed off the keys to one of the men who unlocked the barred steel door at the front of the building.

He yelled at the men flanking him, "This fucker is hot, watch yourselves." The fireman used a seven foot long crowbar to open the steel door after it was unlocked. The fire was minimal, until the door opened and it went off like a bomb.

The fireman ran around the other side of the building and unlocked that door as well. By the time he got the door open, the building was fully engulfed in flames. Three firemen were geared up with oxygen, manning hoses, spraying into the doors of the building.

Sergeant Brodie arrived while the firefighters were working feverishly to extinguish the flames.

"Whaddya got, Drew?" Brodie asked.

"Sarge, it's hard to say. The R-P got here to go to work, found the gate lock cut off with bolt cutters, got to the building, and found it bolted on the outside. The owner's car is parked where it normally is, but the R-P has never seen the other car before. Once they get the fire under control, we can get some more in the way of answers."

Within less than an hour, the flames were out, now being 0500 hours. The fire captain walked over to Nikolai and Sergeant Brodie, shaking his head.

"Well gents, you have two dead bodies on your hands and it's not death by smoke inhalation. Whoever did this set a back draft that burned slowly. The building has no ventilation, typical of this kind of construction, so there was no air to feed the flames. It appears whoever set it used an accelerant, gasoline from what I can tell. It's not safe enough to go in there yet, but there's only a little blood around the two bodies and on the desk. You have a man and a woman in there. Both necks were slit from one side to the other. They were both sitting in chairs, bound at the wrists, behind them, and their ankles tied together. They weren't burned too badly. The bulk of the burning was from after we opened the door. The oxygen fed the flames, and it went off like a bomb. I am pretty sure they were dead long before any of us got here. Neither of them were gagged."

"Well hell, who would want to kill a swap meet operator, unless the woman fits into the narrative somewhere?" Nikolai asked.

Sergeant Brodie smiled, "Clearly they had no idea what they were doing or they would have left a door open. This building has no air circulation whatsoever. They did lock the place up tight so it would be difficult to open up. I imagine that whoever did this killed them and wanted to torch it to destroy the evidence."

He removed his portable radio and called into the dispatcher, "L-30, do me a favor please and notify David 50 and let him know we have a double 187 at our location, and we're gonna need him." (David 50 is the Detective Commander for their division and is in charge of getting the investigative team on their way for a murder).

Dispatch responded, "Roger that L-30, contacting David 50 now."

"Now we wait. Hopefully they can get here before shift change, but if they don't, the overtime is always fun, right kid?" Sergeant Brodie said to Nikolai.

"David 50 to L-30, go to frequency two," came the voice of a groggy Lieutenant McHale, commander of the Detective Bureau over LAPD Foothill Division.

Sergeant Brodie removed his handheld radio from

its holder, switched over to the other frequency. "30 go ahead."

"I have Bedo on the way to you as we speak. He'll be there in 30 or less. Who's the primary unit on this cluster fuck?" McHale asked.

"That would be Drew, sir," Brodie responded.

Lieutenant McHale responded, "Excellent, have him stand by the crime scene for Brodie. We have already reached out to the coroner. I'll join you as soon as I can."

Sergeant Brodie responded, "Roger that, Lt.," and switched back over to the primary frequency. "Well, kid, I'll get you a cup of coffee. How do you take it?"

"Black please," Drew replied.

Sergeant Brodie addressed the R-P. "Mr. Jimenez, we have our homicide unit on their way, I need you to stand by until they can speak with you, alright, sir? While I'm at it, can I bring you something as well?"

Jimenez thanked the sergeant and asked for a cup of black coffee and assured him that he had no problem waiting around.

Dispatch was heard over the radio. "Control to X-Ray-1, switch to two."

Nikolai switched over to the alternate frequency. "X-Ray-1 on two, go ahead."

"Be advised, the two vehicles come back with no hits. One is registered to Stavros Papadopoulos out of Northridge. The second vehicle is registered to

Georganne Emerson out of North Hollywood. I have the printouts for you," dispatch advised.

Nikolai responded, "Roger that ma'am, back to one."

Nikolai looked at the R-P who had overheard the radio chatter. "Is Papadopoulos your boss?" he asked.

The R-P nodded his head yes, and went on to say, "Yes, that's him, but I don't recognize the woman's name."

While waiting for Bedo to arrive, Nikolai began drawing the crime scene and placing plastic numbered cones at each of the pieces of evidence he could find. He had paid attention to Bedo and some of the senior officers and was well versed at detecting details and thought this would be a good opportunity to see if he missed anything. He knew Bedo would appreciate anything that was done to speed up the basic investigation.

CHAPTER
FIVE

Detective Bedo arrived at the swap meet building at fifteen minutes before six a.m. The fire department was still there making sure that the fire stayed out and waiting for their arson investigator to arrive. Bedo made his way out of his unmarked vehicle, a 1986 Chevrolet Caprice that was dark blue. He was wearing a white shirt, dark blue slacks, dark blue tie, and his hair was slicked back with somewhat of a five o'clock shadow. He pulled a pack of Marlboro reds out of his shirt pocket, removed a cigarette with his teeth, lit it and put the pack back in his pocket and his lighter in his pants pocket. He walked slowly over to the building, motioning Nikolai to join him.

"Well kid, you got me up before dawn. What the fuck kinda shit show do you have for me?" Bedo asked, dangling his cigarette from his grinning mouth.

Nikolai walked the detective around the crime scene and let him take it in without speaking. He also handed him a field interview card he filled out with the information he had and told him about the R-P, who was still there standing by to be interviewed. While walking around, Bedo put on rubber gloves. R-P Jimenez started to walk into the building, Bedo lifted his right hand and said, "Sir, this area isn't safe yet, but mostly, I need to examine it for evidence, so please wait outside for a bit. I'll be right with you, okay?"

The R-P sat back down on the fender of Drew's police cruiser. Drew walked around beside Bedo, just watching what he was doing, taking in Bedo's process. After looking around for about fifteen minutes Bedo spoke to Drew.

"This is interesting and nice work with the whole numbered cones thing, Nancy Drew," Bedo said, pointing at the ropes that restrained the victims' ankles and wrists. "They are both tied up with two different kinds of knots. You see that this guy has rope going around his ankles and wrists four times, then it's tied tightly with a square knot, right? Then look over here. This chick has rope tied to one wrist haphazardly, then the same with the ankle. Then the rope is wrapped two different ways around the ankles and wrists and tied with god only knows what kind of knot securing the ropes. The two victims had their throats cut, cutting the carotid arteries of both.

Whoever did it slid the knife into the side of the neck all the way to the other side, then thrust the blade outward away from the spine. This cuts the windpipe and arteries at the same time, and there is no yelling or screaming out of the victims. They were facing one another, so the suspect wanted each of them to see one another as he did the deed. I'm pretty sure that they have each other's blood all over them."

Bedo looked at Nikolai and asked him, "Do you see anything that has your attention, kid?"

Nikolai had been looking around and pointed out to Bedo, "Isn't it peculiar that one of the bodies has blood all over his mouth? There's also a rag on the floor with blood all over it."

Bedo smiles. "That's good, kid. That would lead one to believe that the last to have his throat cut bit the suspect." Bedo hit the male victim's face with his flashlight and pulled his jaw down so he could get a look at the victim's teeth. He told Nikolai to have a look, "See this, kid, there's some flesh between the teeth and blood as well."

Bedo then scanned the interior of the building with his flashlight, noticing that the fire had not fully destroyed the ceiling or interior of the building. "Whoever lit this fire was a novice. They left this place intact. You say that the doors of the building were barred and locked on the outside, right?"

Nikolai nodded his head yes and responded, "Yes sir, the R-P said he got here, found the lock, cut off the gate, and was going to open the door. He attempted to unlock the door, but it was hot. That's when he called us."

"This is so creepy. I know this guy. His parents were the owners, and when they died, they left it to him. He was offered a couple million for this twenty-acre parcel, but it's paid off. The swap meet just makes him a killing, and most of it is in cash. There has been rumors of drugs being run out of this place and stolen property for a decade since the original owner died, but no one has ever been able to nail them."

Bedo reached into the pocket of the male and retrieved the male's wallet and found his driver's license. He wrote down the name, driver's license number and date of birth and found three hundred dollars in cash. He placed them in an evidence envelope and noted where they were found. He also observed a pager on the man's belt and retrieved it and also placed it in an evidence envelope noting where he found it. The woman was another story, no purse on her or near her.

They heard the sound of two vehicles pulling up. One was the evidence technician, and the other was the coroner. The evidence technician approached Bedo, and the two men entered the building together. Bedo pointed out the work that Nikolai had done and what to take pictures of and what to collect, mainly identifying the lacerations on the necks of the victims, the different kinds of knots used to bind their feet and wrists, and to get samples of the blood found on each. He pointed out the blood observed on the mouth of the one victim as well as the rag on the ground that was soiled with blood. "You know what you're doin, kid, get to it."

The coroner approached Nikolai, introducing himself as Baxter Mane. "I'm going to check the time of death to the best of my ability for you." The coroner saw Bedo and acknowledged him, then went about his business. He made a laceration into the lower back of the male first and inserted a thermometer in him and made some notes. He announced to Nikolai that he was checking the liver temperature so he could roughly determine the cause of death. He then cleaned off the thermometer and performed the same inspection on the female.

"Detective Bedo, have you received the photos you needed of the binding of these two? I would like to remove them so I can check for rigor if you don't mind."

Bedo looked over at the evidence tech and asked, "Do you have what you need?"

The evidence tech gave him a thumbs-up and chatted with the coroner directly. "If you don't mind, doc, can we move the bodies together? I'd like to cut the ropes off and preserve the knots as much as possible."

Baxter Mane, paused briefly, looked at the two

victims and said, "Absolutely, young man. May I suggest we move them one at a time to my van. Let me get the assistance of this young officer, and I will be right back to help you carry them out one at a time."

The coroner motioned to Nikolai as he exited the building and opened his van. He reached in and grabbed a black body length plastic bag and asked Nikolai to hold on to it so it stayed in place for the men so they could bring the first body out. Baxter and the evidence technician repeated that process twice, and the evidence technician gently rolled the bodies to their side and cut the ropes off their wrists, then ankles, tagging them and bagging them accordingly to where they were for evidence. The different types of knots were bound to tell another story later on.

Baxter examined the limbs of each of the victims. "See, Officer Drew, there is no rigor mortis in the limbs just yet, nor is there any lividity. These two both died within the last three to four hours. I'll have more after I get them to the lab, but I'd imagine this is pretty close."

"Sir, can you also do us a favor? Can you examine the blood around the male's mouth and look closely at his teeth. We believe that he may have bitten the suspect and there may be skin between his teeth. The blood on the victim's mouth could all be a match."

Baxter Mane grinned at Nikolai. "Well, we have been experimenting with this whole DNA thing that has come about. We have literally been sending in all blood samples for further testing because of the large amount of unsolved crimes that exist. I'll gladly check into all of that, young man. It's like a treasure hunt of sorts! The only bitch is that it's expensive as all hell, and it takes months to get the results back."

Nikolai had been contemplating the time of death of the victims and was debating the time that the motorcycle sped by him riding a wheelie. The two incidents were literally within a block of one another. He took out his notepad and wrote down all the bullet points he could think of that would help him write the crime report, as well as linking the earlier motorcycle pursuit to the crime.

Nikolai arrived back at the station and was typing vigorously on the IBM Correcting Selectric. The narrative was coming along well, give or take the typos and punctuation errors he caught along the way. The police report requirements were pretty basic, after all. It began with the first heading, "Facts," which illustrates with words what got the officer to the location. For example, on such and such a date at such and such a time, I, (Officer Drew) responded to such and such a location in regard to a call of suspicious circumstances. Upon arrival, I contacted the R-P (Jaime Jimenez), who provided the following statement. Then comes the "Statements," which is obvious. Following that is the heading "Investigation/Observations," and in that will be the lengthiest portion of the report that requires the most detail. The last heading will be "Evidence." In that, the officer should write the brief description of what was located and label them with a number. This is regarded as the legend portion of evidence. During this process, the officer or detective or evidence tech, whoever is assigned the task will also draw the crime scene sketch, placing a number next to each piece of evidence located, bodies included which will match the legend. This will all be followed up by the crime scene photos, which will also be placed into evidence and labeled as well as duplicated for further review during the course of the investigation.

In this particular case, Nikolai was only charged with writing the initial crime report and what he observed. Detective Bedo was handling the crime scene sketch and worked with the evidence technician to label, articulate, and photograph all evidence.

It was now 0730. Nikolai got up to stretch his legs and get a cup of coffee and was joined by Sergeant Nutty. "Hey, Sarge, how ya doin?" Nikolai said gleefully. Sergeant Brodie poured a cup of coffee and looked harshly at Nikolai and responded sarcastically, "Just peachy, kid! Fuck me, I swear to all that is holy, I think my wife is intentionally trying to kill me!"

Nikolai chuckled, nearly choking on his coffee and asked, "How so, Sarge?"

Sergeant Brodie rolled his eyes up at the sky. "I don't tell anyone my personal shit, but we had a kid about two months ago. Don't go repeating this shit or I swear to God I will beat your ass and see to it you're walkin' a footbeat in the shittiest part of 77th Division!"

Nikolai wanted to laugh at the likelihood of such a thing but responded kindly instead, "Your secret is safe with me, Sarge."

Sergeant Brodie went on, "Anyway, between the two of them, I can't get a moment of sleep during the day! It's like being in hell!"

Nikolai pondered Brodie's dilemma for a moment. He decided to offer some advice that always helped him sleep during the day. "Can I offer some ideas that may help, Sarge?"

Brodie looked at him and smiled. "Kid, anything you can offer that will stop me from coming in here will be deeply appreciated. I have tried it all, but hell, who knows, maybe you have a secret that will help, spill!"

"Well, it's like this, before I go home, I run for a mile to two to get my body exhausted. I have dark sheets over my windows, so the room is literally black when I close the door, then I place a towel at the bottom of the door to help keep the light and noise out. Then, I have a cassette tape of ocean sounds that I play softly. It keeps out the sounds that we normally try to avoid. For example, I have a neighbor with a Basset hound that won't shut up. My roommates are not sympathetic either. When I did all this, it made it so I can now sleep like a baby, even when I am here at the station in the cot room, and you know how loud that room is."

Brodie looked at Nikolai, surprised. "Well, I haven't tried any of that, kid. I will give it all a shot today. How is your report coming along. Do you need overtime to wrap it up?"

As the two walked to the report room, Nikolai removed the last page from the typewriter, put all of the pages together, and handed the completed report to Brodie. "No sir, she's all done. Just look it over and tell me what you need tweaked, and I will square it away quickly so we can all get out of here on time."

The time was now 0800 hours, so Nikolai walked out to his cruiser to clean out all of his gear. As he walked in, Detective Bedo caught him in the hallway and asked him to come by the Detective Bureau before heading home. He acknowledged he would and walked into the armory to return his shotgun, slide back and unloaded to its proper location, as well as the shotgun shells, and note the exchange in the log book.

As Nikolai walked down the hall toward the locker room, Officer Sorelson nearly knocked himself out as he exited the squad room, slamming his body into Nikola's left side. "Watch where you're goin, ass kisser," Sorelson said sarcastically.

Nikolai was just about to address the attitude of the officer and was halted by the hand of Sergeant Brodie pulling on his right shoulder. "Nikolai, this is one of your best reports yet. Get your gear put away and get outta here, mister!" Brodie said. The two men went into the locker room together, put their gear away, and got into their civilian clothes. As they left the locker room, Sergeant Brodie paused and spoke to Nikolai. "About Sorelson, you did the right thing about ignoring him, kid. I don't need to tell you this, but there are cops who come to work carrying baggage from other sources. Some of them are just pissed off at the world until they get their first, or for that matter third cup of coffee in them. Be the better man. You can't control them, but you can control you."

Nikolai nodded. "Thanks, Sarge. You're right, see you tonight."

Nikolai walked back to the Detective Bureau to check in with Detective Bedo as he was asked. As he approached the detective's desk, Bedo stood up and escorted Nikolai out the back door to the parking lot. Bedo took out a cigarette, lit it, and as he exhaled he coughed and put his hand on Nikolai's shoulder. "Well, this is gonna be a fun one, kid. The woman component of the murder in this shit-show happens to be married to a cop out of Burbank. I found her purse and her ID in her car in the parking lot. When I ran the plates, they came back registered confidential to Burbank P.D. The address of the property is in her and the cop's name. I love this love triangle shit. Now I have to notify the poor bastard his wife is dead."

Nikolai displayed a disgusted look on his face. "Well, ain't love grand. I am headed home, detective. I will likely be in a couple hours early so I can hit the gym if you need me. I did have a word with the coroner. Are you working with him to run all the blood through this DNA screening thing he was talking about?"

"Yeah, I am still not sure about how this thing works. Apparently through testing, they can match DNA found or collected at past crime scenes that remain unsolved. It opens a door to solving them. The future is going to be seriously more interesting when it comes to working cases, that's for sure, kid!"

Nikolai grinned. "I love it, I have to tell you, this one has my head spinning. There is just something not right about the whole thing."

Bedo took a drag from his cigarette and laughed as he exhaled. "You got that right. Let's work closely together on this one. I think I am gonna need all the help I can get. Now get the hell outta here, will ya!"

Nikolai walked to his El Camino, fired the beast up, and began the long drive home. This last shift felt like a week's worth of work, not one day. Nikolai looked in the mirror for a moment and reminisced to one of his father's old sayings. "This day has worked my very last nerve, and it feels like it's being worked by a midget with a ball peen hammer!" All he could ponder was the thought of being able to move into the new place with Diamond Dave in a couple more days and how convenient it was going to be.

CHAPTER
SIX

Sunday morning, March 29, 1130 hours, hit Nikolai like a Mack truck. The last day of work, and now he was spending today getting a U-Haul truck, packing, and getting ready for the big move to L.A.! He woke up to the noise of the household, put on a robe, and walked out to the kitchen where Sherrie and Jake were laughing and having coffee. Apparently Jake stopped back at the house between jobs, and Sherrie was just getting up. It may be 11:30, but Nikolai had just gotten to bed at nine!

Nikolai looked at them and said sarcastically, "Ya know, you two are the worst roommates on the damn planet!" Pouring a cup of coffee, he continued. "I have had maybe two hours of sleep, for the love of God. I have a shit ton of work to do to get ready to move!"

The two laughed hysterically, and Jake smiled, saying with sarcasm, "Brother, every time you roll up in that noisy ass El Camino, you wake us all up, so call this payback! By the way, are you ready for tonight?"

Nikolai scratched his head. "Tonight?" he replied.

Jake laughed again. "Yes, tonight, our farewell party, remember? We're heading to Palm Springs to cruise and raise some hell, gonna be about eight of us heading out around 8!"

Nikolai was still groggy but replied hesitantly, "Yes, man, I remember and will be dialed in and ready to go. This will be one hell of a night! Sherrie, can you still give me a ride to the U-Haul place so I can get my truck?"

Sherrie acknowledged that she was ready whenever he was. Nikolai sipped his coffee and gave her a thumbs-up as he retreated to his bedroom so he could take a shower.

Nikolai got his U-Haul truck and spent the entire first part of the day loading the truck with everything he owned. Without the help of his roommates and his cousin, this would have never been possible! Nikolai then placed a padlock on the door of the moving rig and left it backed into the driveway before heading to the valley on Monday afternoon.

They were getting into the place a day early, and he was quite excited! It was 1800 hours, so Nikolai had his cousin Louie, his roommate Jake, and his sister Sherrie follow him to their favorite spot on Van Buren off the 91 freeway, Taco Tia, where he would buy them all a well-deserved lunch!

It was like a caravan pulling into the parking lot of the taco spot. Nikolai led the way in his '69 El Camino; Jake in his bright orange, lowered Datsun pickup with ladder rack and full complement of tools; Louie in his '62 Ford F-150; and Sherrie in the burgundy '68 Chevelle with black vinyl top! Nikolai and Sherrie's mom helped buy the car for Sherrie. It was a regular circus with the crew arriving somewhere, and Nikolai was going to miss this. Four combo burritos, four tacos, four orders of fries and drinks were devoured over chatter about their friendship, the back-breaking efforts of loading the U-Haul, and the cruise night they had planned. Nikolai shook their hands and hugged Sherrie thanking them for their help, and Nikolai confirmed the plan to meet at his place at 7 p.m. so they could all caravan to Palm Springs. They all broke, and watching the cars part in separate directions hit Nikolai like it was the end of an era.

Nikolai arrived back at the house before Jake and Sherrie. His room was empty except for his war bag, some clothes, shoes, and of course his hygiene gear in the bathroom and his bath towel. He took off his clothes and ran the water in the shower and waited for it to get hot. As he looked at his frame in the mirror he pondered how he managed to get to this place.

This 235-pound, 6'2" man was nothing like the guy who stared back at him in the mirror a mere five years ago. He got into the shower, washed off and began to shave. Suddenly, he felt himself being doused with freezing cold water and overheard the laughter of his buddy Jake! He was always a prankster. The shock of the cold water was enough to give someone a heart attack, and he yelled, "Jake, you fuck what the hell is wrong with you, man!" laughing as the warm water relaxed him. He got out of the shower, wrapped himself up in a towel, and chased the idiot roommate through the house, out the front door, and into the street! He walked back in, fixed and blow-dried his hair, and started getting dressed. He decided that red parachute pants, with his red, black, and white M.C. Hammer style shirt would show off his frame rather well. It was tight, cut off at his waist, and had literally one half a length of a shirts normal sleeve! Nikolai's twenty-inch bicep popped, and his forty-eight chest looked massive in the shirt. He put on his red, black, and white Nike tennis shoes and walked out into the family room of the place they had called home for the last two years!

Jake was also dressed provocatively, wearing black parachute pants, white short shirt, and black Nike tennis shoes. He was about 6'1" and about 190, and they looked like brothers. Sherrie walked out of her room and laughed. "You two look like you just walked out of an Oingo Boingo concert. The ladies of

Palm Springs will be chasing you two all night, that's for sure! You may also want to make sure they are real ladies by the way!"

By now, the knuckleheads had all arrived at the house. Jake and Louie, at least. Walker Hayes and Ricky Hassler had decided to drive on their own in Ricky's turd-brown lifted Jeep, which by the way, had no top and no doors, only a roll bar. The plan was to meet at the Carousel on Palm Springs Canyon Drive by eight p.m. and then cruise the boulevard from there. The plans were always put into place, but Ricky and Walker never seemed to follow through. They were always too busy letting their crotches navigate them through life. The drive was a little cramped in Nikolai's El Camino, Louie in the middle riding "bitch" as they called it, which made for a close quarters drill.

They managed to arrive on the outskirts of the city onto Palm Springs Canyon Drive, and Nikolai pulled over so they could stretch their legs. Louie immediately took up a seat on the folding chair he brought in the bed of the souped-up El Camino. Jake and Nikolai began the cruise down the famed cruise spot, and to their surprise, there were a million cars and crazy girls hangin' out the windows flirting with everyone, and some were even exposing the gifts God gave them to anyone who would pay attention. Down the entire strip, no one spotted Ricky or Walker or the turd-colored Jeep.

Meanwhile, as they lurched slowly in traffic, Louie was flirting with two girls in a red Mercedes convertible. Nikolai and Jake were laughing as they bantered back and forth. Jake looked at Nikolai laughing and said, "I swear to God, if that fucker goes off with chicks this early in this thing, I am gonna throw myself out of the car into traffic"! It was at that very moment that Louie bailed out of the El Camino's bed and jumped into the passenger compartment of the red Mercedes! As the Benz pulled alongside of the El Camino, Jake yelled at him, "We are all meeting at the Denny's on the outskirts of town no later than 2 a.m., shit-head, you don't make it, you're shit outta luck!"

Louie laughed. "Yeah, yeah. I get it. I'll catch up to you fuckers later!"

Nikolai looked over at Jake. "Now don't you go gettin' all nuts and jump out and into traffic, you crazy fuck, the night's young." Jake threw up his hands in disgust and laughed.

As they got to the end of the street they did see "The Carousel" bar, and damn if Ricky and Walker weren't standing up inside the Jeep waving their arms like mad men, trying to get their attention! Nikolai pulled an illegal U-turn and pulled in behind Ricky's Jeep. By then, Walker had jumped out and removed the large orange cones that blocked the parking spot in anticipation of the trio's arrival. They were obviously stolen and had lettering spray-painted on them that read "Riverside Public Works."

Jake jumped out of the El Camino, and they all began high-fiving one another. Nikolai finally got out and walked over to the men who were all laughing. Ricky gave Nikolai a hard high-five and then gave him a bear hug, then came big ass Walker! He was 6'5" and ripped as hell weighing in at two hundred and fifty pounds.

He could have easily been mistaken for Hulk Hogan, and yelled, "Good to fuckin see ya, Law Dog. God damn it, man, I missed ya!" Walker wrapped his arms around Nikolai's upper torso, hugged him, and lifted his 235-pound frame off the ground like he was a rag doll! Nikolai gasped and said, "Jesus, man, put me the fuck down or people are gonna think we're dating!"

Walker and Ricky jumped in the topless, doorless Jeep, and Walker made a crazy face and said Niki, we're goin' on a hunt, save our spot with the cones. We will be back in a bit!" Nikolai set the cones up, and Jake removed two folding chairs out of the bed and set them up on the street where Ricky had his Jeep parked, between the cones. Jake pulled two cans of beer out of the cooler and poured them into plastic cups and handed one to Nikolai, throwing the empty cans into a trash bag that he strategically placed between two buildings behind them. They were laughing at the cavalcade of slow-moving cars that went by and the women exposing themselves to all who would watch. Suddenly, a 1959 Vette pulled alongside of them with the top off. There were two women inside, and they looked down at Jake and Nikolai smiling. The driver, a thin brunette, hoisted herself up and asked the two if the El Camino was theirs. Nikolai smiled. "Nah, we just stole it for the night."

The driver smiled and said, "Well, you two are cute. If your stolen ride can catch us, you might collect a reward!" She dropped down in the driver's seat and sped off, spinning the tires and spitting gravel at the two men. Nikolai and Jake looked at each other, took a sip of their beer, and grinned.

Jake said in his cocky fashion, "My mother always used to say, a man chases a woman until she catches him. We will see them again!"

After thirty minutes went by, Nikolai stood up, folded up his chair, and laid it in the back of the El Camino. He stretched and looked at Jake and waved him to get up. "Let's get outta here and see what kind of trouble we can get into. I'm tired of waiting for those two." Jake got up, folded up the chair, and used a bungee cord to re-secure them in the bed of the El Camino. Nikolai fired up the El Camino and slowly inched into traffic as Jake stood in the street and got a car to let them in. Jake was simultaneously placing the cones strategically back into place to reserve the two parking spaces, knowing of course the likelihood of them doing that was slim!

Jake slid a cassette tape case out from under the seat, trying to find something that would motivate them as they were cruising. He held up two possibilities "Alright brother, what's it gonna be, Billy Squire, or Tommy TuTone?"

Nikolai laughed. "Give me some Squire, man. That will get our blood pumpin."

Jake took the cassette that was in the stereo and replaced it with Billy Squire, and the first song to come over the speakers was "Whadaya Want From Me"! The two smiled at each other, and Nikolai reached down and turned up the volume. As luck would have it, the two stumbled across the vipers in the Corvette that taunted them earlier. They were now in the lane closest to each other, going opposite directions.

The brunette driver was dangling a cigarette and grinning at Nikolai. She removed it from her mouth and grinned, "You boys better hurry up. The grand prize for capturing us is gonna expire before long!"

Nikolai smiled. "Darlin', I'm a professional driver. You can't evade us for long!" There was a break with a slight curb between the two opposing lanes. Nikolai crept slowly and made an illegal U-turn, and the oncoming '65 Mustang Fastback let him proceed! As the rear tires of the El Camino hit the pavement, Nikolai stepped on the gas, and the car drifted sideways spinning the two rear tires equally, the positraction rear end was putting the power to the ground quite well. Stuck in traffic, the two men were laughing at one another because they realized their attempt to catch up to the girls was more than likely futile as they were twelve cars ahead, and not only was the traffic a mess, but the stop lights were not working in their favor. Fifteen minutes had passed since Nikolai made the illegal U-turn, and Jake had gotten out and back in the El Camino three times to keep an eye on the Vette, maintaining its whereabouts!

After moving another ten feet, Jake got back out of the El Camino, stood on the door jam and told Nikolai, "They are turning left, brother!"

Nikolai turned the radio down. "I can't hear you, numbnuts. What did you say?"

Jake gets back in the car, shuts the door and points to the left and screams, "You gotta get over there. They are turning left at the light, we're gonna lose them!"

Nikolai laughed. "Got it, you don't need to yell. Jesus Christ, man!"

Nikolai saw the Vette as it made the turn onto the street. "Alright, they aren't doing a U-turn. They are making a getaway, we aren't gonna let that happen!"

Nikolai drove over another curb, albeit slowly. Every time they pulled an illegal move like this, they ran the risk of getting stopped, and though Nikolai had "The Brass Pass" as he liked to put it, Palm Springs Cops had absolutely no sense of humor when it came to out of town party boys, cop or not and Councilman Sonny Bono had his police department arresting anyone who got out of line to clean up the nonsense that was going on in the city. As the El Camino slowly made its way over the curb, Jake was out of the car politely asking folks to let them through. Jake was no small measure of a man, and folks seemed to appreciate his politely asking them to let them go by.

They got through the barrage of cars and were now traveling on a street parallel to the street the all-elusive Vette was driving on. They had no traffic, so Nikolai sped quickly two streets up and turned right. He stopped at the corner, turned off his lights, and waited for the Vette. Jake was watching all directions as Nikolai was fixed on the direction where the target women should be approaching from.

All of a sudden, the lifted brown Jeep with no doors or top pulled in front of them! Walker jumped out and ran to the front of the El Camino and yelled at Nikolai, "Hey man, your radiator is leaking fluid everywhere," and pulls the hood up, in the middle of traffic.

Nikolai immediately looked down at his temperature gauge, and it was acting normal at 185 degrees! Jake jumped out of the El Camino, shut the hood, and confirmed that there was nothing wrong with the radiator. Jake got immediately back in the El Camino and laughing said, "Those mother fuckers, damn it man, that fucker Walker is workin' my last nerve like a midget with a ball peen hammer! Where did those Gypsies in that Vette go?"

Nikolai laughed. "Keep an eye out, brother. They couldn't have gone far!" Just then Jake pointed up ahead. The Vette was turning down an alley, and the blonde in the passenger seat was facing them and had her top raised up, exposing her naked breasts. She removed her bra and threw it in the street, saying, "Come and find us if you can. That's better than Cinderella's magic slipper"! Jake jumped out of the car, ran and retrieved the bra, and ran all the way back to the car, which had not moved an inch!

Nikolai looked at Jake with a disgusted look on his face. "You know what this means, right?" The two men looked at one another and said simultaneously, "Revenge!"

Nikolai was looking frantically to find a driveway or any out so he could drive on the sidewalk if he had to so they could get back in the hunt! Jake patted him on the shoulder, but Nikolai ignored him, still intent to find a way out of this traffic jam. Jake patted Nikolai on the shoulder one more time and points the opposite direction from where Nikolai was focused.

Jake said in a concerned voice, "Nik, look down there for a moment. Is that who I think it is?"

Nikolai looked him in the eye. "This had better be good, fucko. We don't want to lose these chicks, damn it!"

Jake laughed. "Oh, if that is who I think it is, our night is about to get very interesting."

Nikolai turned his head, focused on a police cruiser with his yellow flashing overhead lights on, and saw an officer with a slender blonde-haired man bent over a police car buck-ass naked.

It didn't take long to realize that their pal Louie, who had jumped out of the bed of the El Camino earlier, was not being detained by local law enforcement. As a ton of questions raced through his head, the elusive Vette with the two girls slowly drove by and they were waving at them, the passenger screaming for them to follow them! Nikolai looked over at Jake and, brooding, said, "You have absolutely gotta be shittin' me. What the fuck did this idiot get himself into!"

Traffic miraculously started moving, and Nikolai put the El Camino in drive and drove by to confirm their fears, and sure as hell, they confirmed for themselves that it was in fact their friend Louie. The man was stark naked and bent over the police car being interrogated by two uniformed cops. Louie suddenly noticed Nikolai's El Camino and looked down in shame, and as they drove by slowly, Jake flipped Louie off, grinning like a Cheshire cat. Nikolai made a right turn at the next side street, shut the car off, and turned off the lights and told Jake to stay in the car. Jake laughs. "What the hell are you gonna tell them?"

Nikolai smiled. "I'll come up with something clever."

Nikolai slowly approaches the officers as they are handcuffing his friend and placing him in the back seat of the patrol car, badge in his hand, and the other up as well, both shoulder high. "Hi fellas, I'm an off-duty cop, just wanted to see if I could be of assistance with the poor naked fella you have locked up. He's a friend of mine, I'm ashamed to say."

The two officers turned and after recognizing the badge, they waved Nikolai to approach. The senior officer was 5'8". He had a crew cut, and his uniform was impeccable. The second officer was a young rookie and looked about average and was having a hard time trying not to laugh. The senior officer put out his hand and introduced himself. They shook hands and the officer stated, "Bill Loveland. Our friend here apparently got picked up by a couple of girls in a red Mercedes convertible. They cruised around with him for a bit. According to him, one jumped into the back seat with him and got rather friendly. While he was preoccupied, the other girl pulled off behind a building up the road where it is nice and dark, pulled a gun on him, and made him strip naked. They got his clothes, socks, shoes, and his wallet with all his cash and left him. Do you know anything about this?"

Nikolai bowed his head, shaking it, he replied, "Yessir, he was with us when they were picking up on him. They coaxed him into getting in the car with them. As he drove off, we made plans to pick him up at the Denny's on the outskirts of town. Is he being arrested?"

The officer looked at Nikolai and shook his head. "Frankly, I had him cuffed and was going to take him to the station to examine him further to see if he was under the influence of something or evaluate him for being a nut! I had no idea what the hell we were going to do with him to be honest. Does he use drugs at all?"

Nikolai chuckled and replied, "No sir, he's the straightest guy I know. He barely drinks. I've known him since third grade and came up through Cub Scouts, Weblows, and Boy Scouts together. He is just as naive as he appears, just a nice guy."

Officer Loveland smiled, took out his notepad, and took down all of Nikolai's info, name, Police Department, and phone numbers as well as his driver's license information. When he got done taking down all of Nikolai's information, he opened up the car door and asked the rookie to uncuff the bewildered and embarrassed man and get a blanket out of the trunk. He looked back at Nikolai and said,

"You are gonna solve a lot of problems for me tonight, brother. Just get him out of town. I have to be honest with you, the sadist in me was looking forward to making the rookie process and sort him out. Just get him out of town, fair enough?"

Nikolai agreed and escorted his buddy with the bruised ego back to his car. As they all got in, Jake sat in the middle and told Louie, "Don't get close to me, ya naked bastard!"

As Nikolai started the car and they made their way home, Louie holding his head in his hand begged, "Is there any way we can keep this between us fellas?"

Jake laughed out loud. "You're kidding right? You screw up our shot at a couple of amazing chicks in a convertible Vette, and you honestly think we're NOT going to share this everywhere we go?"

Nikolai pulled out and looked over at Louie. "Son, you're doin the walk of shame on this for a while. I only wish I had a camera so I had evidence to share with everyone! You better hope they don't call my police department and burn me with them over your little stunt, or you're in deep shit, my friend."

The drive home was full of laughter and jokes poked at Louie. He continued to try to redeem himself by repeatedly bragging about making out with a sexy brunette in the Benz convertible, but was denied any sort of victory every time they reminded him that he ended up naked with no wallet, no money, and no ID, and no key to get back in his house! When Nikolai dropped him off, it was nearly midnight. As Nikolai backed out of Louie's driveway, Louie yelled, "Hey, a little help here?"

Nikolai rolled down the window and replied, "You're on your own my friend as he drove away." As Louie walked up the driveway, three of the neighboring homes' porch lights came on, obviously alerted by the loud voices. Louie quickly ran around the back of the house praying the back door was unlocked. He looked up with a smile and said, "Praise the Maker," as he opened the unlocked door. He just knew this was gonna be a story he would never be able to live down, ever!

CHAPTER
SEVEN

Monday, March 30, moving day! Nikolai began the long journey to the police station. It was now 1700 hours. Nikolai parked the rig in the employee parking lot, double-checked the rig was secure, removed his war bag (bag full of clothes, hygiene supplies and so forth), and walked into the back door of the police station. He was exhausted and would need to get some sleep before the graveyard shift began. This was his last shift before taking a much needed two days off to settle into the new digs.

As he walked into the back door of the station, he ran into Detective Bedo and one of the swing shift patrolmen. They broke off, and Bedo approached Nikolai and asked him if he was prepared for the big move.

"You have no idea, I am so tired of this fucking commute. It's mind numbing," Nikolai said with joy.

Bedo grinned. "You are not going to believe how an extra two or three hours a day are going to benefit you personally and professionally, kid! Anyway, have you heard anything from the coroner on this nonsense?"

Nikolai and Diamond Dave met at the new property in Northridge, Nikolai with his U-Haul moving van full of his personal effects, and Dave with his parents in tow with his dad's '68 pea green, metallic Chevy pickup complete with the matching green camper shell and keystone model chrome wheels full of his bed and incidentals.

They all worked together to move the items to their prospective bedrooms and Nikolai's living room and dining room furniture. Once the heavy moving was done, they all worked to get the important items assembled like the beds and loosely fitting the couch and dining room table. Nikolai's mother and sister arrived, and the three women began feverishly giving the house a deep cleaning.

They lucked out that there was a washer, dryer, and refrigerator in the home, and Nikolai had conveniently set up an appointment with Pacific Bell to hook up the phone line as well as having the cable company set up the three cable T.V. hookups, all set for the same day. Nikolai had the majority of the heavy stuff put away. All that was left to do was unpack and organize. Rather than taking that on, he decided to run the wire from each of the television locations to the spot where the cable was already mounted to the roof's eve. He had already sized up what to do when he first looked at the property and realized that the utilities were all overhead. Being a former cable T.V. installer and technician definitely has its privileges.

Nikolai went to the garage where all his tools were located, opened up the bottom drawer of his roll away toolbox, and removed his old cable utility belt. He then grabbed his spool of cable and the caddy that held it, as well as his six-foot ladder, and walked to the back yard. Right where the cable attached to the eve was a vent that led into the attic. He removed his wire cutters from his pouch and cut away some of the mesh, large enough to run three strands of RG-6 cable through, the insulated cable that installers use to run a line from the main line, split off to run to each of the televisions. Nikolai figured he would need three strands of cable, each about forty feet long. He grabbed the end of the cable and walked off that amount, cut the cable at the correct length, then repeated this two more times. He then taped the three ends of the cable together and slid them through the hole he made in the attic vent. The next move was to get Diamond Dave to feed the cable to him once he got up into the attic.

Nikolai went into the house with the six-foot

ladder in two, set it up at the attic access door which was in the home's hallway then went about finding Dave. Dave was in his bedroom setting up furniture with his father. Nikolai interrupted. "Hey brother, can I ask you for your assistance for a moment?" Dave looked up and acknowledged joyfully. Nikolai went on. "I have three runs of cable set to run into the attic and need you to feet them as I pull them in. Before we begin, let's walk the house and confirm where we want the three televisions to be set and see where the best place is to poke a hole through the ceiling areas."

Dave smiled and replied, "So smart, this way the cable jock doesn't come in and fuck up the house. He just needs to set up the cable boxes and take the terminator off the cable port outside and fire it up!"

Nikolai laughed out loud. "You got that right!"

They spent a few minutes in each room. Nikolai poked a hole in the ceiling with his screwdriver strategically in a closet space behind each wall where the televisions would be set and stuck a piece of cable into the attic so he could find the holes once he was up there. Nikolai entered the attic with his flashlight, and Diamond Dave went to the rear of the house. Nikolai yelled from the vent area, "Are you ready, fucktard?"

Dave laughed and replied, "Yes I am, oh grand master of the mentally deranged!" Nikolai slowly pulled the cable into the attic as Diamond Dave fed it into the attic vent. In just a few short minutes, the cable was set. Nikolai cut the electrical tape off the ends, freeing the cable to be fed down into each of the areas they determined. As he did so, he reflected back to the days when he worked with Jake for D/P Communications and how Jake trained him how to install cable efficiently, cleanly, and flawlessly, and by working in the attic of a home, it would literally shave hours off of an installation and at the same time, avoid running strands of cable around the interior and exterior of a client's home.

Back then, they were, after, all on piece work, meaning getting paid by the job, not by the hour. Guys like Jake and Nikolai could install 8 to 10 residents a day, where the less ingenious technician might get 4 or 5 done. He smiled to himself and reflected about the fun and the pain of climbing a telephone in the rain with gaffs (spikes attached to one's ankles to help climb poles that didn't have spikes. There was more than one occasion when Nikolai gaffed out and fell ten or twenty feet. He smiled again thinking someone truly must be looking after him all these years. Nikolai climbed out of the attic, grabbed his six-foot ladder, and went back to the eve at the back of the house. He then took each cable and wrapped them into a safety loop. He then cut fittings and cramped them with his old crimping tool and then even attached a three way splitter to the feeder line and the three down legs that led to each of the television locations. Nikolai then walked to the telephone pole and observed that the feeder cable was screwed into a terminator that was screwed into the tap on the pole and that there were no pegs on the pole. Nikolai walked back to the garage and retrieved his old Bashlin gaffs and his lineman's belt, put them on, and made his way back to the telephone pole. With all his tools ready to go, Nikolai scaled the telephone pole, attached the safety strap around it at the top, and removed the terminator device off the port and screwed the cable into the now functioning port.

Nikolai carefully removed the safety strap, attached it to his belt, and traversed down the pole with ease. He removed his climbing gear and put it back in his roll away toolbox. He then retrieved his old drill with the two-foot-long cable drill bit and went to work carefully drilling holes through the walls from the closet areas into the rooms where the televisions would be sitting. He then slid wall bushings over the cable. These bushings created a seal and slid securely into the hole that the cable was slid through which looked cleaner than just leaving the cable in bare drywall. He then estimated the length necessary for each television of each room, cut fittings, and crimped them with his handy tool. The cable dog that came out was going to be thrilled when he arrived, Nikolai thought!

Now being four o'clock, the power was

transferred, utilities all set up, and the last part of the shenanigans was about to take place! Diamond Dave and Nikolai had no sooner placed the three televisions where they needed to be, than the cable television installer knocked at the door! Diamond Dave answered, and to his surprise, the Installer was a five foot, four inch petite female, who looked fit and ripped. She already had her tool belt on and introduced herself as Elizabeth. Nikolai came to the door just after the introduction and greeted the young lady.

Diamond Dave was already smitten, trying to act cool and so forth. Dave after all was always like that, just a charmer! They escorted Elizabeth to the rear of the house and showed her that they had already run wire from each T.V. to the exterior of the home where the wire hit the eve of the house from the telephone pole. Nikolai then walked her back in the house and showed her where the televisions were located.

She was so thrilled that the work was already done and complimented Nikolai on the clean installation work. She excused herself and went back to her truck to get the equipment she needed and returned quickly. While she installed each of the boxes, she asked Nikolai about his method of installation and where he learned it. He explained his experience and how he was trained. Elizabeth went on to say that the way she was trained was to wrap the home inside and out and that she had never thought of doing an installation the way she had just seen it done. She asked Nikolai how long it took him to run all three lines. He thought for a moment and replied, "About an hour!"

She laughed and said, "You know, it would take an hour each line if you had run them around the home, then ran the cables around the baseboard and around the doorways of each room, and it would look like shit!"

Elizabeth finished setting up the converters and took care of the additional wiring then began walking back toward the back door and said, "Now I just need to do some work on the tap, and we're all done." Nikolai smirked as he turned on the living room television, and it demonstrated the cable company test pattern.

Elizabeth was shocked, "Well, someone must have never secured the tap!"

Nikolai looked at her with a bit of pride and said, "I actually climbed the pole and removed the terminator from the tap earlier in the day," simultaneously handing the terminator to her.

Elizabeth smiled and thanked Nikolai. "You have no idea how much I hate hooking telephone poles! I almost always take the big ladder off my truck, but so many times, it's impossible to do so!"

Nikolai replied, "Trust me, I get it! I've fallen off more than a couple poles in my day!"

Elizabeth called in to the cable company, read off

the receiver serial numbers and when they were all programmed. She excused herself and thanked them again for making her life so much easier! As she departed, the local pizza delivery guy showed up, and Diamond Dave walked Elizabeth out to her work truck. Nikolai brought the pizzas into the house and said magnanimously, "Dinner is served!" They all sat around, laughed and joked about how they all hated moving as they drank a beer or two and ate the pizza that Dave's dad so kindly bought for everyone. The group was exhausted, rejoicing in the next chapter of Diamond Dave's and Nikolai's lives. It felt real, but not.

All the while, Nikolai was formulating his plan of what he wanted to do when he got back in uniform. His need to go 10-8 was growing, and his hunger to learn and take himself to another level was insatiable. This double murder case was driving him crazy with desire to catch the dirtbag responsible. He also reminded himself that he had to stay up late to readjust to the normality of his work life. He had to be at the police station Tuesday and ready to suit up by midnight for his graveyard patrol shift.

Everyone left the house by 9 p.m., and most everything was put away, so Nikolai decided to get in a late workout. He opened the garage, started the El Camino, pulled out, closed the garage, and got back in the car and headed to the Holiday Spa Health Club in North Hollywood. It was a 24-hour gym and only

15 minutes away. He checked in at the gym, secured his bag in his locker, and began his routine. His routine lasted about two and a half hours, and he now feeling exhausted, decided to head to the new home and turn in. Along the way, he was thinking that it would be different being so far away from home and all the people he knew, but also reminded himself that the job had occupied his life so much that he didn't have much time to himself anyway. No more parties at friends houses or his own. The job just wouldn't allow for it.

He arrived at the house, unlocked the garage, opened the door, backed the El Camino in, and secured the door, quietly. He went into the front door of the house. The lights were off except the kitchen night light. He went into his room, took a shower, and went to bed. It was now about 0030 hours, or 12:30 a.m for all non sworn personnel!

CHAPTER
EIGHT

The next morning Nikolai woke up on his own at 9:00 a.m. He had slept almost nine hours, certainly not the norm. He usually slept for five or six. Clearly the move had done him in, not to mention all the prep work and the workout that ended the night.

He walked out in his workout clothes and saw Diamond Dave drinking coffee, watching the news. Nikolai poured a cup of coffee, drank it black, and sat on the couch. "Well," he asked Diamond Dave, "how did you sleep, brother?"

Dave smiled as he took a sip of coffee. "I slept like the dead. I wasn't even worried about not having a job. It's nice to know I have a cushion, and I can find something out here I want to do. One more day of working at my dad's gas station, and I swear, I would shoot myself!"

Nikolai laughed. "Well, good for you. I was thinking, let's get in the gym this morning and play some racquetball. We haven't done that in years."

Dave laughed and agreed. "Okay, let's suit up and head out." Moments later, they had their racquetball gear. Nikolai had already opened the garage. Dave pulled out in his wicked 1969 Chrysler GTX powered by a 426 Max Wedge with an A-833 Mopar 4 Speed and a Dana 60 rear end! It didn't come with the wedge, or the Dana 60, but they sure made a great addition to the street rod, especially being Plum Crazy purple with black stripes! Diamond Dave fired up the Mopar. Nikolai always laughed and said that the damned starter on the thing sounded like a hyena laughing when it turned over. The car had an unmistakable sound, though! As the machine pulled out of the garage, Nikolai closed and locked the door, and they drove away.

They arrived at the gym, checked in, and began warming up and stretching. Two guys approached them with racquets in hand and asked if they were up to playing a game of two on two. They agreed and got to it. They all took a few warm-up shots and moved around the court to get the feel for how they each moved, and the game began. Ninety minutes was a long damned time of nonstop battle on the court. The first two sets played to 15 were a win for each team. Now they were playing the last round to 11 points to see who got to walk away with the win! After some time, Nicolai and Diamond Dave had scored 10 points to the other team's 4. Diamond Dave responded to a hard hit by running as fast as he could and rearing back with his racquet like he was going to pulverize the ball, then at the last second as he was two feet from the forward wall, he moved his hand close to his body, barely hit the ball, and hit it to the low right corner, an inch above the floor.

The ball bounced quickly into the adjoining wall at the corner and shot to the far left portion of the rear of the court making it impossible for the other team to retrieve. Game over. The two men were calm and gracious about the win, and the two others introduced themselves and mentioned that they would love to play again sometime. Nikolai exchanged pager numbers with the one guy, they shook hands, and Nikolai and Diamond Dave headed home. While driving, Nikolai looked at the names that were written on the paper. One was Scott Coolidge a Deputy District Attorney for Los Angeles, known for being a great advocate for Law Enforcement, and John Willis, owner operator of Black and White Garage, largest tow company in Los Angeles, servicing all Los Angeles Police Department and L.A. Sheriff Precincts. He thought to himself that this was a racquetball game that would need to continue.

Nikolai's pager suddenly vibrated, nearly giving

him a heart attack. "Jesus Fucking Christ," he exclaimed.

Diamond Dave looked over and laughed. "What, man, your pager go off and scare the shit out of you again?"

Nikolai, now holding the pager in hand, looked over with a Go Fuck Yourself look on his face and read the number. "Yeah, it's some 818 number with a 411 at the end, I'll call the number when we get home. Fucking electronic leash anyway, makes me crazy!" Nikolai heard AC/DC "Dirty Deeds" come over the radio and reached over and turned it up. Diamond Dave was pounding the steering wheel rocking his head and reciting the lyrics and down shifted the Mopar to second gear, stuck his foot to the floor, and banged it back to third gear chirping the tires. Man there was nothing like the sound of a big block Mopar to get one's blood pumping. All Nikolai could imagine was how wicked his stroker motor was going to sound, *if* he could ever get everyone to finish his '67 Chevelle!

They arrived home. Diamond Dave pulled up to the driveway, and Nikolai got out of the car and ran to the garage door, unlocked it, and opened it up so Dave could back the machine into the garage. The entire house shook as the Mopar's exhaust thundered in the confined area. Nikolai went into the house, picked up the phone, and dialed the 818 number. A young girl answered the phone and said with a cheerful voice, "Doctor's Office."

Nikolai was puzzled and thought about hanging up, but responded instead, "Yes, this is officer Nikolai Drew of the Los Angeles Police Department. Did someone page me from here?"

The voice perked up. "Oh, yes sir, Doctor Carbone paged you, hold please, I will get him for you." Nikolai was looking at Diamond Dave who just walked in the house with a bizarre look on his face.

Dave grinned looking at him as he walked over to the stereo in the living room and asked, "Who is it, Niki?"

Nikolai looked at him and said, disgusted, "I don't know, some fucking guy named Doctor Carbone!"

The phone picked up, and the heavy New York Italian accent spoke up. "Hey, douchebag, it's Pat Carbone. I heard you now live in the Valley, is that true?"

Nikolai laughed and replied sarcastically, "Yo, meatball, how the hell are you? Yeah, it's true, I have moved to the slums of the Valley with my buddy Dave, god help us! To what do I owe this call?"

Carbone laughed. "Meatball, love it, fucko! Listen, I have a gym membership at Wright's Gym in Northridge. I can get you in as a guest. The guy that owns the place loves cops, and I can get you in if you want to work out later. I know you're workin graveyard tonight, yes?"

Nikolai quickly responded, "Yes man, I am. Where the hell is Wright's Gym?"

Carbone laughed. "It's in Northridge. I am gonna work patrol tonight, so I thought we could ride together so I can get my hours in and figured we could get a workout in before we head in. I'd say let's meet at the station, but that old gym sucks ass!"

Nikolai responded enthusiastically, "Would love to get a work out in with you again. What are you working today?"

Carbone said enthusiastically, "Anything you want, man. I've been off for a few days."

Nikolai laughed. "You're off, alright. So where is this fuckin place located, Carbone, or do you want me to ask my magic eight ball?"

Carbone responded sarcastically, "Hold on to your panties, Nancy Drew, I'm checkin' the phone book. You might wanna grab one of these, they can prove to be helpful!"

Nikolai snapped back, yelling at the phone, "Hey, dick cheese, I just moved in; for the love of Gawd, it's like I'm talkin to a kid or somethin!"

Carbone yelled over the phone, "9301 Tampa Avenue, you kindergartner, see you there at 10!" and hung up.

Diamond Dave was laughing. "Who the hell was that, and why are you guys yelling at each other?"

Nikolai laughed out loud. "It's this guy, Pascuale Carbone. He's a chiropractor and also a reserve police officer. I met him a while back working out at the police station. We immediately started talking shit to each other like we had known one another our entire lives. He's a New Yorker like me, so he found out we moved out here, so we're gonna hit the gym and work out before work, and he's working patrol on graveyard with me."

Diamond Dave laughed again. Well shit, that ought to be fun. Two New Yorkers yellin' at each other in the patrol car all damned night, an experience I can live without!"

Nikolai arrived at Wrights Gym ten minutes early, and lo and behold, so did Carbone! Nikolai saw him exit the 1983 jade green Mercedes 450 SL convertible. Carbone was about 5'9", 190 pounds and well built, with a tiny waist, big chest, arms, shoulders, and thighs—his symmetry was perfect. The two men walked into the gym. Carbone checked in and had the woman working the desk allow Nikolai in as a guest. The two men agreed to work a chest and triceps day, and Nikolai offered to follow along with Carbone's workout program. Most who train regularly enjoy changing up their routines by going along with someone else's plan. Carbone suggested they go into the cardio area and use the jump ropes for five minutes, Nikolai loved the idea and followed along. They began together and worked the ropes for five minutes. When done, Nikolai found himself out of breath and sweating, very uncommon for him, but he liked it. Cabone seemed to be literally unaffected. Carbone escorted them over to the incline bench and asked Nikolai to load up the bar with a forty-five pound plate on each side. As Nikolai did so, Carbone went to the dumbbell rack and grabbed two forty-pound dumbbells and set them on the floor where one's feet would rest while using the bench.

Carbone asked Nikolai, "Are you familiar with the strategy of Super Setting??

"I have dabbled with it over the years, not really a fan, but let's go. Show me what you got."

Carbone pointed at the barbell. "We start on the incline bench, knock out 20 reps, then go to the dumbbells and do 20 reps of incline flys. I will start, and you can spot me."

The movement begins. Carbone easily accomplishes the movement as prescribed. The switch up, and Nikolai repeats the movement, struggling a little at the end.

Carbone grinned. "I can see why you aren't a fan. Okay, add twenty-five pounds and I will swap out the dumbbells." Carbone returns with sixty-pound dumbbells, Nikolai was not looking thrilled.

Carbone barked out, "Okay, kid. This time we do 10 reps of each. The last five reps are forced reps, meaning you compress the muscle tight for five seconds at the top of each rep, you get me?" Carbone begins, working the reps slowly, finishes with the barbell, then picks up the dumbbells. Nikolai moves in and does the same, again struggling at the end. Carbone spots him and directs him to slow down and make sure to get the five-second compression at the top of the rep.

"So, have you not focused on Upper Chest like this before, Drew?" Carbone asked.

Nikolai replied, "I can say I have not. Usually three sets of ten reps here and focus on flat bench for ten to fifteen sets heavy."

"Well, kid, we're going up one more time. Strip that twenty-five pound plate and add another forty-five on each side. I will get some new dumbbells." Carbone returned with two seventy five pound dumbbells and explained the next movement. "Okay, kid, so this is the last set of incline. We will do as many reps as we can get on this one. No less than seven, hoping for ten, get it? Just don't lift it for me. Just watch so it doesn't crash on my neck!"

Carbone seemed to be getting through the reps with ease. At seven reps, he began to struggle a bit, but he got to 8 before he and Nikolai realized he wasn't going to finish the repetition. He moved immediately to the dumbbells. He again seemed to be moving through the movement with ease, but started to struggle not at the sixth rep and finished with seven repetitions total. Carbone shook it off, and Nikolai moved into place.

Nikolai lifted the barbell and moved through the movement and managed to accomplish nine reps of two hundred and twenty-five and got the tenth with a little help from Carbone. The dumbbells are a little bit of a different story, however. Nikolai struggled after four reps and barely got six at the end.

Carbone laughed. "Well, you look good, kid, but the upper chest is a weak spot for you. You need to focus more on more than just the flat bench if you plan to develop even more strength, if that's your goal, that is."

Nikolai agreed, and just then two African American bodybuilders came over to the bench to say hello to Carbone. These two were about six foot tall and toned like professional bodybuilders, amazing stature. Carbone introduced them to Nikolai as the "Bash Brothers," one being Carl and the other being Pearl.

They all shook hands, and Nikolai had to laugh at their tank tops, they were white and skin tight and had iron-on letters on them both reading "The All-Right Brothers" and had white do-rags on their heads. The two men went on about their workout just as Nikolai and Carbone went along their way. Nikolai laughed. "The All-Right Brothers, I love it. These guys are a riot."

Carbone laughed and smacked Nikolai in the shoulder. "Yeah, they are a riot alright, but they are straight up Crips my friend, just watch your back."

The two men finished up their workout together in about ninety minutes, left the gym, and headed to the police station. Nikolai fired up the '69 El Camino, and as he drove to the police station he realized that the workout he performed with the forty-year-old Carbone was no joke! He felt pumped, but he also hurt like hell, which in the bodybuilding world is a good thing. As they were walking into the locker room, two other guys walking out shoved Carbone into the wall. The taller and lankier of the two raised a fist and said, "Hey, chiropractor, I still can't lift or walk right since that last fuckin adjustment! I knew I shouldn't trust a damn Wop to work on my back."

Nikolai took a step toward the two men, drawing his left fist back. Carbone saw what was coming and got between the two men, laughing. "Billy, you and your brother Paulie walked worse and looked like Quasimodo when I first started workin' on you!"

Carbone then shoved Billy into his brother Paulie. "You're lucky I worked on your Polak ass at all, by the way. How many of you retards does it take to load up a weight bar... Don't answer that. I don't want you two to have an aneurysm!"

Nikolai got it now. Gym humor, he thought. They went into the locker room, got their gear bags, and Nikolai asked Carbone, "Who are those two refugees from *Welcome Back, Kotter*?"

Carbone laughed. "That's Billy and Joe, we call Joe Paulie on account of him being as punchy as Rocky's stupid brother-in-law, get it?"

Nikolai laughed again. "Paulie, yeah, I get it, I like the feel of this place."

Carbone punched him in the arm. "Good, you aren't a dickhead like people say you are. That's a good thing."

The two men headed off to their cars, got in, and headed to the police station to get ready for their shift.

CHAPTER NINE

Monday, March 31 was coming to an end, and the graveyard shift was about to begin. The two men got suited up, went to the break room where there was a fresh pot of coffee brewing, no doubt courtesy of the graveyard dispatcher, Tony Rizzo. Tony was a calm and collected man of the trade. Under extreme circumstances, he managed to keep people calm with his stoic voice and relaxed demeanor. It didn't matter if he was handling a vehicle pursuit or handling a loud party radio call, he handled it all the same.

Carbone went to the squad room, and Nikolai went to the dispatch area and looked at the daily log from the last few shifts and didn't see anything of any importance. He went to his mailbox in the report room. Usually if there was something someone like Detective Bedo needed help with, there would be a note discreetly hidden beneath the usual papers there. After going through all of the crap in the box, he discovered not a thing.

It was 2330 hours, and Nikolai sat at the back table of the squad room as the other patrol officers slowly trickled in and found their seats. Their enthusiasm was less noteworthy. Sergeant Brodie walked to the front of the briefing area holding the clipboard with the daily look from the past shifts and set it on the podium. He looked at the room of patrolmen and began assigning officers to units. He noticed Carbone sitting at the front table and asked him, "Who do you want to ride with, Carbone? Your usual group of misfits aren't on the yard. This is irregular?"

Carbone smiles and points to the back of the room. "I'd like to ride with Nancy Drew back there, Sarge!"

Sergeant Brodie shakes his head. "You okay with that, Drew?"

Nikolai laughed. "Sure, Sarge, I can always stuff him in the trunk if he gets out of control!"

Sergeant Brodie shakes his head again. "Alright, Carbone, against my better judgment, you two can work X-Ray 1 tonight. Find something entertaining to do, will ya. As for the rest of you nitwits, it's April First, and I am no fool! I catch any of you retards trying to prank me, and you'll be walkin' a footbeat in South Central, get me!"

The rest of the watch was dismissed, and the two men headed over to the armory to check out a 12 gauge shotgun and ammo. Carbone stepped up, picked a shotgun, checked it to make sure it was empty, then filled out the log with the weapons serial number, rounds of ammo he has taken, 6 total, and the two men headed to the parking lot to acquire their unit.

They picked a plain car, and Carbone carefully loaded the 12 gauge Remington 870 Pump Action Shotgun with all 6 rounds then placed the weapon in the rack and checked the radio and all lights and siren. Nikolai called out to Carbone asking him to meet him at the trunk of the unit. As Carbone rounded the back bumper, Nikolai asked him, "What do you notice that's missing?"

Carbone said sarcastically, "A shovel and a bag of lye!"

Nikolai punched his shoulder. "You're a fuckin comedian aren't ya, meatball!"

Carbone smiled and in disgust said, "This thing is a mess, Nancy. There are no flares, blankets, and the first aid kit is missing about everything."

Nikolai motioned Carbone to follow him. They walked into the station and into the storage area, and Nikolai handed Carbone a box of flares, which weighed about 50 pounds and Nikolai grabbed a blanket, more flares, and a first-aid kit, and they walked back to the parking lot where they began stocking up the trunk of the unit they would be driving tonight.

Before they got into the car, Nikolai had a serious conversation with Carbone. "Do you ever have a conversation with the officers you ride with about officer safety and expectations before you go 10-8?"

Carbone replied, "Some yes, some no, most often not. Us reserves are not really looked at as partners, more like coffee makers and errand boys, if you know what I mean."

Nikolai looked at him intently. "Well, you're not that to me, so here's what I would like to propose. You back me up, if you're driving, I handle the radio and same you handle the radio if the role's reversed. I will drive the first half of the shift, so you're on the radio. Now, we work in unison. If we engage someone, we always have eye contact with one another, got it?" Carbone nodded, yes. He was actually excited because this was the first time he has ever been talked to like a real partner.

Nikolai went on. "If we get in a foot pursuit, stay with me, no matter what, and I'll be calling that out. If we get in a combative situation, and I pat my chest with my hand, that means when I make my move toward engaging the subject, I will take his upper body and you tackle his legs. All of that make sense?"

Carbone smiled. "Music to my ears, mister. I think I may have gotten sexually excited there for a moment!" Carbone walked over to the dashboard of the unit and got the last two VIN numbers for the shift log and noted the vehicle's condition and lacking supplies. They got in the unit and Carbone grabbed the radio. "Control, Shop 67 is X-Ray one and we are 10-8!" He released the button on the mic and laughed. "Fuck, I love this job!"

Dispatcher Rizzo parrotted Carbone. "Roger X-Ray one, showing you 10-8, God Help Us All!"

Carbone switched the radio to frequency two and sarcastically reached out to dispatch, "X-one on 2."

Rizzo responded, "Go ahead, you dago!"

Carbone laughed. "Don't make me spit in your coffee later, you wop!"

Rizzo laughed. "Keep this shit up, and I'll be sending you on barking dog calls all night, back to one!"

Nikolai looked confused at Carbone. "Issues I should know about with you two? Maybe like, I should drop you back at the station and head out on my own kinda shit?"

Carbone looked at him, smiling. "Na, just Italians fuckin with each other."

Nikolai had a puzzled look on his face. "Alright then, let's get some coffee and see what kind of trouble we can get into."

Carbone drove them to the 7-11 at 146 Hubbard and entered the store. They were greeted by Davinder with his smiling and jovial "Hello, buddy!" They got a cup of coffee and approached the register. Davinder once again tried to wave them off, refusing to take money, and once again, Nikolai laid two dollars on the counter.

As they walked out the door, one of the Valley's voluptuous badge bunnies, Cat Conroy (a paramedic notorious for being promiscuous with cops and firemen all over the Valley), had pulled in driving her Jeep with the top off; often her top was off as well.

She was wearing short-shorts and a tank top with no bra and lots of makeup. As she got out, she dangled a cigarette from her hot pink lips and approached the officers. She grinned seductively at Nikolai and grabbed his ass cheek with her left hand. She took the cigarette from her mouth and slowly exhaled smoke and as she released his cheek, grinned and said, "You still owe me a visit, Officer Drew!"

Nikolai pulled away from the woman's grasp. These were the kind of women that one should stay away from if they wanted to protect their reputation and their job and frankly the job itself, his father used to tell him. Nikolai was desperately trying to figure out a way to avoid any interaction with Cat.

Almost like a prayer answered from above, a black Chevy S-10 pickup flew by them. They instinctively jumped into the unit and left the trolling sex pot standing there. Carbone stepped on the gas and as he left the parking lot, the unit's rear tires broke loose, the car fishtailed sideways as they sped to catch up to the black truck.

Nikolai took the mic, looked at Carbone, and said, "Try not to kill us will ya. X-Ray 1 to control, we're attempting to catch a vehicle at a high rate of speed heading southbound on Hubbard crossing San Fernando Road, unknown license plate at this time, late model Chevy S-10 pickup, black in color."

The dispatcher repeated the call and vehicle information. "Units be advised, X-Ray 1 is attempting to catch a vehicle at a high rate of speed southbound Hubbard crossing San Fernando Road. Unit to back Identify."

Before anyone could respond, they caught up to the S-10 pickup, Nikolai turned on the emergency lights and siren and simultaneously informed dispatch. "Control, be advised, we are now westbound on Sepulveda crossing Rinaldi, vehicle license number is California Commercial 1-Lincoln-43657." The suspect then erratically turned the vehicle to the right and onto southbound Mission Boulevard, running a red light and sideswiping a car.

Nikolai broadcast over the radio, "X-Ray 1 to control, we are now southbound on Mission, vehicle has collided into a vehicle at Sepulveda and Mission, please send a unit to that location to assist the victim of the hit and run."

Dispatch assigned a unit, and at this very moment, the S-10 began to round a turn on Mission Boulevard at around 60 miles per hour. This turn was posted at 25 miles per hour because the sweeping turn was rather sharp.

Nikolai and Carbone witnessed the suspension of the truck flex and the vehicle losing control, rolling over onto the driver's side and eventually onto its roof. The vehicle slid for about sixty feet and hit a massive hundred year old oak tree that was in the parkway in the opposing lane of the street.

Carbone passed the truck, turned around, and parked the police car strategically so that no one would hit the truck and turned on the flashing yellow lights. The two men exited the unit, and Nikolai broadcast, "X-Ray 1, be advised suspect vehicle has flipped over, approximately one half mile south of Sepulveda on Mission, stand by for further."

The two men approached the truck cautiously. Carbone had removed the 12 gauge shotgun from the rack in the unit and fed a round into the chamber while Nikolai removed his side arm from his holster. Nikolai removed his flashlight from the special flashlight pocket in his trousers with his left hand and looked inside the vehicle.

The driver was suspended in the seat of the truck held in place by his seat belt and was bleeding from his head and face and was panicking. There was an odor of alcohol coming from inside the truck and beer cans all over the inside. Nikolai asked him, "Are you armed?"

The driver, a Hispanic male in his thirties shook his head no and pleaded, "Can you get me out of here, please."

Nikolai grabbed his handheld radio and broadcast, "Control, we need an R-A at our location, male Hispanic in his mid 30s, bleeding from the head, also roll Black and White Tow." Dispatch parroted the request. Nikolai holstered his side arm and asked Carbone to cover him. He then attempted to open the driver's door of the truck. It was pretty well bent up and wouldn't easily open, so Nikolai grabbed the frame of the door, gave a grunt, and moved the door to a position where he could see the driver clearly.

Nikolai told the man, "I am going to cut the seatbelt, so, I want you to put your hands below you on the roof of the car so you don't fall. Do you think you can do that?"

The driver looked at Nikolai and said, "Yes, just get me out of here, please!"

Nikolai removed his stainless steel Spyderco knife from his pocket, pressed the blade against the lap portion of the seat belt, and cut through it easily. The driver slowly lowered his body to the ground, and Nikolai helped him get free of the wreckage.

Nikolai helped the man up, placed his hands behind his back, handcuffed him, and then patted him down to ensure he had no weapons. Once the suspect was handcuffed, Nikolai again removed his handheld radio from his utility belt and broadcast, "X-Ray 1, were code four, one in custody."

The suspect had no weapons. Nikolai did find his wallet, which contained the man's identification. There was heavy alcohol on the man's breath, but because of the head wound, he would not have him perform any Field Sobriety Tests. He sat the man on the curb and just then, off in the distance they heard the sirens of an ambulance. Paramedics from L.A. City Fire pulled up, and just after that, so did the tow truck from Black and White Garage.

Carbone had returned the shotgun to its rack and was filling out a CHP180 form (vehicle impound report). He was also taking measurements of where the vehicle collided and its point of rest for their police report.

Sergeant Brodie arrived as the tow truck was rolling the pickup over on its wheels so it could be towed away. "Nice one, Drew. I have Officer Fricassi handling the other collision up the street. Fortunately there were no injuries. He got photos and all the measurements and info for you. Is this dipshit deuce?" (Deuce is slang for a drunk driver.)

Nikolai smiled. "Yeah, Sarge, I think so. He's pretty banged up, so I will have the R-A transport him to San Fernando Community Hospital and get blood drawn and then bring him in to book him, as long as he is cleared."

The paramedics looked the suspect over as the

tow truck loaded up the destroyed S-10. Nikolai asked the paramedic to transport him to San Fernando Community. As they cleared the scene, Nikolai rode in the ambulance with the driver and Carbone followed the ambulance to San Fernando Community Hospital.

On the way to the hospital, Nikolai chatted with the suspect who told him that he had been drinking and confessed that he ran because he couldn't afford another arrest for driving under the influence. As they pulled into the emergency bay at the hospital bay, nurses were waiting. They wheeled the driver in and began looking him over and took x-rays. Nikolai also directed the head nurse to please take a blood sample for evidence as he had evaded police and struck another car in the pursuit.

Carbone had run the subject for warrants and discovered that he had two warrants for driving under the influence of alcohol—the challenges for the subject got even worse as time went by. Nikolai and Carbone waited with the subject now identified as Gustavo Sanchez out of North Hollywood until the medical staff were able to determine if there were serious injuries or not.

Carbone asked Nikolai, "What if he is not cleared to book?"

Nikolai looked at him and pulled him to the doorway so as not to alarm the subject. In the hallway, Nikolai told Carbone, "If he can't be booked, we simply take the blood, book it in and write the report as normal, and we will have to issue him a citation here. If he is clear, which I think he will be, we will proceed as normal, transport him to the station, book him, and finish up the paper."

The head nurse came in a few minutes later and asked to speak to Nikolai privately. They walked into the hallway, leaving Carbone to watch Sanchez.

Head Nurse Claudia Aurenglia said, "Well, he has some minor contusions and cuts, but no concussion. He's clear to be booked." She handed Nikolai the blood sample, and he had her initial it with the date and time the sample was taken.

Nikolai re-entered the observation room and had the subject stand. Nikolai placed the subject's hands behind his back and cuffed him again and told him, "Well Mr. Sanchez, you are thankfully fine."

Sanchez was smiling and said, "Does that mean I get to go home now?"

Nikolai began escorting the subject out of the room and to the parking lot where their police vehicle was parked and said, "Well, you're going to the police station with us sir. We will book you, and in a few days, you will go to court for your arraignment. After all is said and done, then you will be able to go home, at some point."

The subject began to squirm a little acting like he was going to run. Nikolai moved his hand from the subject's bicep to his left wrist and applied a little pressure, twisting the wrist and hand. The pain got Sanchez's attention, and he settled down. Carbone opened the passenger rear door to the patrol unit, and Nikolai sat him in the car carefully. They drove to the police station and parked the patrol unit in the sally port. Carbone and Nikolai placed their weapons into gun lockers, then removed the subject and escorted him into the booking cell.

Nikolai looked at Carbone. "Get him dialed in with the booking officer, brother. I will begin knocking out the report."

Carbone nodded at him, and Nikolai went to the report room. Sergeant Brodie walked in, smiling. "Here's the report from Fricassi on the other vehicle collision and all the information. How is your prisoner?"

Nikolai gave the sergeant a thumbs-up and said, "He's cleared to book, and I have a blood sample. I don't have much more to do, Sarge. Should have the report done in an hour or so and will be ready to go 10-8."

Sergeant Brodie patted him on the shoulder. "I figured that would be the case, kid. Get her done, and let me know if you need anything."

Carbone walked into the report room, smacked Nikolai in the back of the head, "What do you need, rookie?"

Nikolai gave him a dirty look, handed him the blood sample, and asked, "This is labeled, can you put it in an evidence envelope and fill it out? Then, fill out the evidence report, make a copy, and place one in the evidence locker and bring one back for me to turn in with the report, Old Man!"

Carbone stood at attention, saluted Nikolai, and sarcastically stated, "Yes sir, three bags full sir!" He took the evidence and began to go about his business.

Nikolai jumped out of his chair, peered down the hallway as Carbone skipped merrily down the corridor, and said, "Carbone, damn good work today, mister!"

Carbone turned around and grinned and saluted again and said, "Yeah, I know." Carbone was truly happy that he was finally being taken seriously.

The report was completed sooner than Nikolai had promised. The shift was about over, and they walked out the back to clear the patrol unit. Carbone removed the shotgun from the secured rack and walked toward the back where Nikolai was removing gear from the trunk. Carbone fumbled with the shotgun and tried to pull the slide back in the Remington 870. It wouldn't move. He figured he had not pulled the trigger after removing the round before putting it back in the car. The gun pointed at the asphalt went off and pellets sprayed the asphalt, and buckshot and asphalt sprayed Nikolai's ankles.

All stopped; it was like an hour passed. Nikolai looked over the raised trunk lid of the unit and looked at Carbone with a mystified look on his face. "What the fuck did you just do!"

Just then, Sergeant Brodie ran out of the back of the station looking worried, "Did I just hear a gun go off?" Carbone, looking sheet-white started to mumble.

Nikolai interrupted. "Yeah, sarge, Carbone tried to clear the weapon and in all the excitement hadn't realized that it still had a round in the chamber. Luckily, it just blew a hole in the asphalt." Nikolai was not about to let on that he had been shot. It would turn this into a circus and could cost Carbone his position as a reserve police officer.

Sergeant Brodie began shaking his head and ran his hand through his hair. "Well, fuck, nobody is hurt, right?" Carbone and Nikolai looked at each other and shook their heads no.

Brodie was obviously pissed. "Well, I will write it up on the sergeant's log. You two get to work on the officer's reports." Brodie stormed back into the back door of the police station. Nikolai looked down at his pants, raised his leg onto the bumper of the patrol car, and pulled the pants up. There was blood running down his calf, but nothing serious. The pellets from the buckshot pierced his pants but barely penetrated his skin.

He looked at Carbone and in disgust said, "Get me some wet paper towels out of the bathroom. I have some stuff here in the first-aid kit. Make it quick, I need to put the pin back in this grenade before it's too late."

Nikolai got some large band-aids out of the first aid kit in the trunk of the car and rubbing disinfectant that was in the kit as well. Carbone ran back out moments later with wet and dry towels. Carbone started to wipe the blood up. Nikolai ripped the towels from his hands and snapped at him, "Don't add insult to injury, dipshit, gimme that!"

Nikolai cleaned the wound. It was very superficial; his pants however, that was another story. The wool pants were destroyed. He cleaned and dressed the three holes in his skin. There was still a pellet in his leg. He squeezed it and it popped out. He then bandaged himself up. Carbone was staring at him in disbelief.

Nikolai laughed. "Hey, dick cheese, be glad I was wearing wool pants. If I had anything else on, this would be an entirely different shit show!"

He disposed of the bloody towels, took the shotgun and his war bag into the station, and checked the shotgun in and told Carbone to go to the locker room, say nothing to no one, and he'd catch up with him shortly.

Nikolai then walked into the watch commander's office where Sergeant Brodie was leaning back in his chair at the desk. Brodie barked at him, "Well, where's my report!"

Nikolai put his hands on the desk and leaned in,

"Hey, sarge, I was thinking, no one got hurt. It was a simple accidental discharge. Can we just keep this between you, Carbone, and me, and chalk it up to a lesson learned and promise never to speak of it again?"

Brodie dropped his hands, paused for a moment. "If we write this up, he is looking at suspension and possibly getting his badge taken from him, you get that, right?"

Nikolai nodded in agreement. "Yes sir. He's a good cop, everyone is allowed a hall pass now and then, yes? Besides, no one got hurt, and no one else knows."

Sergeant Brodie bit his lip and gave in, "Alright, I swear to God, Nikolai, if this ever comes up, I will deny all and burn you both over this stupid shit, you understand me?"

Nikolai snapped to attention, saluted ,and said, "Sir, yes sir. It shall never be mentioned again!"

Brodie stood up and said, "Don't salute me, you idiot, and don't call me sir. I'm a sergeant, not some ass-kissing officer. Now get out of my office and tell that idiot what I just told you!"

Nikolai walked into the locker room; took off his uniform shirt, gun belt, and bullet proof vest; and stored his gear while everyone else did the same. He looked at Carbone, who still had a worried look on his face. Nikolai put his index finger to his mouth indicating to him to be quiet. He and Carbone walked out to their cars. Carbone looked at him concerned and asked, "So, what is the deal?"

Nikolai looked around to make sure no one was around and told him, "I spoke to the sarge. He told me to tell you to never bring this up and we can forget it ever happened!"

He looked Carbone in the face and leaned in. "You get that if you whisper this to anyone, we're all fucked, right?"

Carbone looked at him and said, "Whisper what to anyone?"

Nikolai looked at him, gave him a double-take, and said, "Get the fuck out of here before Sergeant Nutty changes his mind! Good job shooting me the second time since I've been on the job, dipshit! Go home, and I'll check in with you later today!"

The two men parted, and Nikolai fired up the El Camino, plugged in Ozzy Osborne's tape *Blizzard of Ozz*. The song "Crazy Train" came on, Nikolai turned it up, put the El Camino in drive and headed home, grateful he now lived only minutes away now. Driving home it hit him that this was the second time he had been shot at and he had only been a cop for a year. Was someone trying to tell him something?

Nikolai arrived home. It was now 0820 hours. What a difference from a ten-minute drive versus over an hour! If he were still living in Riverside, he would not have gotten home until 1030 hours! Praise Jesus, he thought. He exited the El Camino, unlocked the garage door, opened it, and then backed the El Camino into its parking place. He closed the door, locked it, and went into the house. He took off his clothes, looked at his blood-soaked "Wool" trousers thoroughly. The holes made from the double-00 buck pellets actually weren't that bad. He dropped the pant leg in his bathroom sink with some stain remover.

He removed the bandages from his ankle and got in the shower. The wounds were not bad at all. He got out of the shower, then put some hydrogen peroxide on the wounds. Nikolai covered the bedroom window with his black-out sheet and placed his towel under his door. Now the room was blacked out and soundproof. He turned on his cassette player with the seascapes soundtrack, and within minutes, he was asleep.

CHAPTER
TEN

The alarm clock went off sharply at 1630 hours. Nikolai got up slowly and walked to the kitchen thinking to himself, *Shit, it's still Wednesday April first! I am never going to get used to this shit!* The house was quiet. No one was home. He removed his blender from the cupboard and mixed his elixir of protein powder, raw eggs, fruit, and ice and blended it into a shake. He picked up his pager and drink and sat on the couch simultaneously turning on the television. Flipping around the channels, there was absolutely nothing of substance on. He came across an old *Speed Racer* cartoon, and instantly, he smiled and melted into the couch.

He looked down at his pager, which was turned off, and reluctantly turned it on. After a few moments of silence, the pager came to life with three pages. One was the Police Station, Detective Bedo's extension with a 411. The other two were an unknown number with a 411, then a 911, the last one coming in two hours ago.

Nikolai finished the protein shake and decided to call the unknown number with the 911 first. He turned the volume down on the television and called the number. A familiar voice answered, "Denofrio residence."

Nikolai laughed. "Hey Victor, just woke up and got your pages, what's with the 911, you okay?"

Victor Denofrio was a long-time reserve police officer for the department and worked as a sound engineer for the movie studios for thirty-five years. He was quite influential and had worked on such big TV shows as *Dan Tanna*, *Cannon*, *Barnaby Jones* and the like.

Denofrio had a serious tone to his voice. "I need to meet up with you to discuss something sensitive. Do you have time to meet up before you go into work?"

Nikolai leaned over the coffee table and picked up his daily calendar and opened it up. He stared at it for a moment and responded to him, "Sure, brother, how about in forty-five minutes at the Pick Up Sticks on Chatsworth in Granada Hills?"

Denofrio assured him he would be there promptly. Nikolai then called Bedo's desk. There was no answer, so he left him a voice message and told him he could call him back at home or page him. He then jumped in the shower, shaved, and brushed his teeth and got into some workout clothes. He left a note for Diamond Dave and told him he had a meeting and was getting in the gym around 9 if he wanted to meet up.

As he was about to leave the house, the phone rang. He picked it up, and it was Detective Bedo. "Hey, Nancy, how are you doing with that looooooooong ass commute?"

Nikolai laughed out loud. "Yeah, man, it's killin me! What's the scoop, Chief?"

Bedo laughed. "Stop with that Chief shit. I wanted to see how you were doin' after the incident last night?"

Nikolai thought for a moment and played dumb. "Hey, just a deuce and a pursuit man, nothing harsh at all!"

Bedo remained silent for a moment. "You know what I mean fuck-o, how's your ankle after the reserve nearly shot your leg off?"

Nikolai was silent for a bit. "What the fuck, man? How do you know about that? If that gets around…"

Bedo cut him off. "Relax, Nancy. Brodie called me today and told me all about it asking if he could trust you and Carbone to keep your mouths shut. I told him to relax! I own Brodie. He's screwed up so many times when I worked under him that I could get him busted down to a meter maid if he steps over the line. Anyway, I told him you were solid and that

Carbone is the dumbass that did the shooting and would never open his mouth."

Nikolai was relieved. He took a deep breath. "I have to go to a meeting, then I am free for a bit, have to get in at 2100 hours. Will you be around the station around 1830 hours?"

Bedo replied, "Rookie, I am buried. Do me a favor and swing by the office before you head to the gym."

Nikolai hung up, secured the house, and headed to meet the stressed-out reserve. He couldn't wait to hear that nonsense drama Denofrio had to share and pondered why it was so important to meet away from his house or anywhere near the office.

Nikolai arrived at the restaurant, parked the El Camino, and walked inside. He didn't see Denofrio yet, so he ordered an iced tea and sat down and went through his day timer as he waited. Denofrio arrived about five minutes later and sat down. Nikolai looked at him joyfully and asked, "You want something to drink, brother? You look a little freaked out?"

Denofrio leaned in and quietly told Nikolai, "There is some serious trouble coming for the chief, Nikki."

Nikolai leaned in and asked, "Well, are you planning on telling me what it is, or was that it? Sounds like some serious Cloak and Dagger or Get Smart kinda shit."

Denofrio, still keeping his voice down, said, "I am

not sure what to do here. If I say something to the wrong person, I get burned, and I have no intention of moving out of the city, you dig?"

Nikolai said, "I understand, brother, you can share this with me. You know me well enough to know that I would never burn you."

Denofrio again kept his voice down. "So, last night I hosted a fundraising event for Councilman Javier Melendez. At this party were about 100 key locals that have ties to big financiers. The idle chit-chat that was taking place as people talked was pretty typical, you know: We hate the White Devil, California belonged to us first and we need to take it back kinda shit."

Nikolai smiled. "Yes, I get it, but this is nothing new, Victor. What has you so shook up?"

Denofrio continued, with his hands about shoulder height open, palms up with a pissed-off look on his face. "I'm getting to that if you'll shut up for a minute. Anyway, he's there with his girlfriend, side hide chick, Deputy District Attorney Mai Chang. Anyway, he gets up in front of everyone and begins this rhetoric about taking back California and says that upon getting re-elected, he plans to start by removing Chief Belknap and replacing him with a Hispanic chief. This guy is certifiable man, the look in his eyes told the story, and he's on fire with this. I can't understand how they get off calling everyone a racist when they themselves are racist? This isn't the half of it."

Nikolai cut him off. "Okay, now I get it. It's April 1, and you're burning me with April Fool's Day shit right? Good one, Denofrio!"

Denofrio looked at Nikolai with a puzzled and disgusted look on his face. "No, this is not an April Fool's prank, and you can't tell anyone where you heard this shit. It will blow back on me, and it will get ugly."

Nikolai got up, patted Denofrio on the back, and reassured him, "Not to worry, mister. I will figure out how to get the information where it needs to go without any of it getting on you.

I have to wonder though, what does this Chinese Deputy D.A. see in this wingding? Power corrupts, absolute power corrupts absolutely, they say! See you later, Victor, I got this."

Nikolai looked at his watch. It was now 1800 hours, so he got into the El Camino and headed to the station so he could catch up with Bedo before he went home. All the way there he contemplated whether or not he should bring up what he learned from Denofrio. Bedo was tight with Chief Belknap after all, and Bedo was tight lipped.

He arrived at the police station and parked on the detective side of the building. He approached the side door and knocked loudly. Detective Bedo answered the door and walked outside to greet him. Bedo removed a pack of cigarettes from the breast pocket of his shirt, lit one, and told Nikolai, "Let's go for a ride, kid!" That was code for he needed a Coke and to talk away from prying ears.

As they drove down First Street toward Hubbard, Bedo told Nikolai what he had developed from the crime scene forensics so far. "Kid, this shit is super creepy. So the blood and skin we found on the lip and in the teeth of the male, Papadopoulos, was that of a female. So, we are trying to figure out who had the motive for this, ex-employee, ex-girlfriend, current girlfriend."

Nikolai usually just listened to Bedo talk, figuring there would eventually be a question or an assignment that came out of the conversation. There was a long pause, so he chimed in. "Well, what do we know about Papadopoulos's girlfriends, wives, employees, anything?"

Bedo took a drag from his cigarette as they pulled into the parking lot of 146 Hubbard, Bedo's favorite 7-11, and he parked the detective unit. "Kid, I know a lot about this guy. I worked a lot of security details at the swap meet over the years. He was a player, always had women walking in and out of the building while I was there. Even working patrol, I would catch him at all hours at the swap meet office building. We have some digging to do. Keep this DNA thing to yourself. It's new to law enforcement, and you may as well be talking about Martians from outer space landing on Earth, you know what I mean?"

Nikolai nodded in agreement as they entered the 7-11. Bedo got a Big Gulp Coke, and Nikolai got a bottle of water. Raginder was working the cash register and waved the two men off, suggesting they not pay.

Bedo put two dollars on the counter, and they walked out. Bedo put his foot up on the rear bumper of the Caprice, set his Big Gulp on the trunk, and took out another cigarette and lit it. A long pause took place, and Nikolai took the opportunity to share what he had learned today about the plans of Councilman Javier Melendez and also the fact of Deputy D.A. Chang being present.

Bedo looked at him with a pissed-off look on his face. "Well, kid, it's amazing how over the last thirteen years I have heard this same kind of rhetoric coming out of fools in politics. They are always race-baiting and trying to develop popularity by building a divide between us and them, no matter who the us or them may be. This time, the tone is a little more hateful, and the fact that they have figured out a target and putting it on the Old Man's back shows they are really getting heated up. Do yourself a favor, stay the hell out of this shit. Where did you get the intel from?"

Nikolai crossed his arms and looked pensively at the detective. "I can't say. The source is afraid of retaliation, but this guy's rhetoric seriously pisses me off. What the hell is with people being so bent out of shape over nonsense. We need to be focusing on making things better for the community, not creating anger and division."

Bedo grinned. "Well, that makes a lot of sense. We need to proceed carefully with this, however. I will get the info back to the chief. Just keep it to yourself, and you're right, brother, this kind of nonsense is petty, but getting on the wrong side of it can get you some freeway therapy or an introduction to the term Terminal Rank."

Nikolai looked at Bedo, puzzled, and said in a questioning way with his hands in the air, "Freeway therapy? Terminal Rank?"

Bedo laughed, "Yeah, kid, you know being sent to the farthest place away from where you live so you have to spend half your day driving... Freeway Therapy, and Terminal Rank means you are never promoted to anything, ever!"

They got back into the detective unit, and Bedo drove them back to the police station. They parted company and shook hands, Nikolai got into his El Camino and headed off to Wright's Gym, hoping he'd run into Carbone.

CHAPTER
ELEVEN

Nikolai pulled up in the parking lot of Wright's Gym. It was now 2050 hours. He cruised the parking lot searching for Carbone's jade green SL 450 Mercedes, and there it was! Carbone was just getting out of the car. Nikolai parked adjacent to the Benz, got out, and locked the car. Carbone looked at his multi-colored cargo pants and matching shirt and laughed. "What the fuck, man, you just walk off the set of an MC Hammer Video?"

Nikolai laughed. "Funny, coming from someone who looks like they got their workout clothes out of a dumpster at TG & Y!" They walked into the gym together, checked in with their cards, and walked to the locker room to secure their bags. Carbone asked, "What muscle groups do ya wanna train today, peckerhead?"

Nikolai shrugged. "How about back and bi's with

some ab work?" They agreed and began with a three-way move of pull downs, first behind the neck, then leaning back with the same wide grip, pulling to the chest, finishing up with a close reverse grip movement pulling down to the chest, a total of 30 reps.

Carbone looked and finally asked Nikolai, "Hey, how's the ankle by the way? I am really sorry about that, cheese dick!"

Nikolai laughed and pulled up his workout pants, displaying the ankle with no bandage. "It's excellent, just a flesh wound. It's healing well, don't give it a second thought."

Carbone asked. "Any word out of anyone?"

Nikolai was going to mention that Bedo knew, but decided not to share that little tidbit of information. "No man, all quiet. You need not worry about this thing. Put it out of your mind."

The gym was pretty quiet, then, in walked Carl and Pearl, loud like a couple of WWF Wrestlers as always and once again, wearing their signature garb. Today they had on bright yellow tank tops with skin tight long pants that were yellow, orange, and red striped. The shirts had thick black iron-on letters that displayed "The All-Right Brothers." As they got to their starting point, they looked over at Carbone and Nikolai and yelled, "Well, if it ain't Cagney and Lacey hangin' out with the men today! Bust any purse snatchers lately, officers?"

Carl and Pearl walked up with a gangster gait, then smiled and shook hands and hugged Carbone and Nikolai. They all went about their workouts. Nikolai and Carbone continued their workout with the seated row machine, a machine that focuses on the largest portion of the back. They knocked out another 30 reps, making idle chit-chat. There were all of nine or ten people in the gym, all going about their business except for Rosa. Rosa loved asking the men in the gym to help her out with spotting and with technique. She was funny and sarcastic and always had a thing for Carbone. Nikolai was in the middle of a conversation with Carbone and Rosa was next to them doing some disturbing attempt at a lower back exercise. She tapped on Carbone's shoulder and said "Carbone, what is this exercise good for?" Nikolai moved Carbone aside and with a Hulk Hogan look on his face yelled, "NOTHIN'!"

Rosa looked scared at first, then burst out laughing! Carbone took a moment and corrected her movement and advised her to never repeat it the way she had done it before, otherwise she would likely end up crippled.

While working out, Nikolai shared the information he had heard about Councilman Javier Melendez. He asked Carbone, "You have been around quite a while. Have you had any run ins with this dipshit?"

Carbone looked pensively at Nikolai. "We all

have. This guy is a horrible councilman and spends his time pointing out why everything is wrong with everyone else instead of focusing on making the city a better place. There are rumors of corruption and taking kickbacks to smooth the path for permits for business and licenses and such. He needs a cup check if you ask me, but hey, I am not a politician, I am just a chiropractor and part time law dog. Stay out of it. You don't want to get in this jackass's sights!"

Nikolai and Carbone wrapped up their workout, and as they made their way to the exit of the gym, Carl and Pearl started razzing them. Carl shouted, "Hey, Cagney and Lacey, how about next time you two come to our gym, you dress a little more manly!"

Pearl followed up, "Yeah, quit wearing your little sister's workout clothes. You two shame real men everywhere!"

Nikolai and Carbone raised their right arms behind them and flipped the brothers a middle finger as they walked out of the gym. The two men parted ways. Carbone headed home and Nikolai headed to the station house to get ready for work.

At 2230 hours, Nikolai arrived in the rear parking lot of the station. He exited and locked the door of the '69 El Camino and walked into the locker room.

He pondered for a moment and decided to take a quick run. He had an hour and a half before he needed to suit up after all, so he darted out of the rear of the station and decided that three miles would do the trick. As he ran, he sang a cadence that he had sung many times while running to the top of Mount Rubidoux in Riverside and back down, inspired by his uncle who was a Marine Corps drill sergeant.

"Mamma told Johnny not to go downtown
The Marine Corps Recruiter was hanging around;
But Johnny went downtown anyway
To hear what the recruiter had to say
The recruiter asked Johnny what he wanted to be
Johnny said I wanna join the infantry.
So Johnny caught a plane out to Vietnam,
To fight some people called the Viet Cong.
Killed a hundred men with his rifle and blade,
Only God knows how many lives he saved.
Johnny was bad and he was brave,
Johnny jumped on a hand grenade.
Saved the lives of the men he led,
But now poor Johnny was dead.
Before he died this is what he said,
To tell his momma when he was dead
Momma, momma, don't you cry,
The Marine Corps motto is SEMPER FI!"

As he sang, his pace quickened. He was thinking about all of the things going on in the department. The crap that the councilman was saying about Chief Belknap and the desire to find something exciting to do during this next shift and whether or not something would fall into his lap. Before he knew it, he was already back at the station. The seven-minute mile he thought he had set a pace for turned out to be six minutes. He had cut off three minutes without even realizing it.

Sweating and breathing heavily, he went to the breakroom refrigerator and got a bottle of water, then went into the locker room. He removed his hygiene bag from his locker, which contained his soap, razor, shampoo, toothbrush, and toothpaste.

He showered up, shaved, brushed his teeth, and blew his hair dry then got into uniform. He was quite early, so he made his way to dispatch to see what the prior shift log looked like and what kind of activity they had experienced. It was the best way to prepare for what was facing the next shift.

Dispatcher Cindy Anglin was working dispatch for the third shift, or swing shift as it's called. She was 5'1", about 55 years old, always funny and bubbly. Nikolai picked up the daily log that was constantly updated by the dispatcher, and as he read through it he asked, "So, what's up, buttercup, anything earth shattering happening out in the Valley tonight?"

Cindy laughed. "Nothing, Officer Drew, just the typical nonsense, a traffic accident, a keep the peace call, and some miscellaneous gang activity in the parks. What would brighten up my day is that picture you promised to give me of you naked getting out of the shower!"

Nikolai looked up at her with a frown. "Now, Cindy, I told you not just no, but that you got a snowball's chance in Hell of ever getting a picture like that from me!"

Cindy gave him a seductive look and replied, "A girl's gotta ask! Hey, heads up though, the Field Training Officer called in sick for your shift. There's a reserve police officer coming in, so you're probably gonna get stuck with him, just an FYI!"

Nikolai walked across the hall to the breakroom and poured himself a cup of coffee. Sergeant Brodie walked up behind him.

Nikolai looked over his shoulder and smiled, "Hey, Sarge, want me to pour you a cup while I'm at it?"

Sergeant Brodie smiled and accepted the offer. Nikolai poured the cup and handed it over to the sergeant. Brodie pulled out a chair and sat down. "Got a minute, Drew?"

Nikolai pulled out a chair and sat down and took a sip of his coffee. "Sure, Sarge, what's up?"

Brodie looked hesitant. It caused Nikolai to think something was seriously wrong. Brodie looked at him. "Look, I hate to ask, but McNimur called in sick. Looks like he's out for a week. I need help with Training Officer shit. Would you mind handling the Reserves who come in for me while he's out? I know it's not your job, but you seem to get them, and I think it could be good for you in the long run."

Nikolai stood up, took another sip of his coffee, and patted the sergeant on the shoulder. "Sarge, I'd be happy to help out, anything you need ever. I have your back."

Brodie stood up with a befuddled look about him. "Thank you, Nikolai. I always get push back from guys when I ask them to do something extra, you know, complaining that they aren't getting extra pay for that shit and comments like that. Needless to say, I appreciate your attitude."

The two men walked into the roll call area. Sergeant Brodie took to the podium, and Nikolai sat in the front row. As the room filled up with the usual players for work, a new face entered the room and approached the sergeant. Sergeant Brodie pointed at Nikolai and said, "Reserve Officer Reed, meet Nikolai Drew. he will be acting as your training officer until Corporal McNimur returns. Nikolai, try not to kill this one, will ya?"

Reed sat down next to Nikolai, shook his hand and said, "Kill me? You got another trainee killed?"

Nikolai smiled. "Nah, he got on my nerves, so I locked him in the trunk of a police car ,and they found him dead a week later, total accident." Nikolai grinned.

The sergeant barked out unit assignments, last to Nikolai, "Drew, you and Reed will be 1-A-26, get him indoctrinated, he's brand new. Then go do what you do!"

Dispatcher for the shift, Ray Huff, walked behind Drew and said as he passed, "Who did you piss off?"

Reed looked at Huff, confused. "Him or me sir?"

Huff chuckled and didn't respond. Reed said again, a little more nervous, "Hey, him or me?"

Huff looked over his shoulder. "I'll give you about thirty minutes to get the rookie squared away, Niki!"

The crowd left the locker room. Nikolai stayed seated and looked at Reed. "Okay, kid, tell me about yourself, need to know who I am working with."

Reed began with a thick New York accent, "Well, my name is Artorius Reed. I'm originally from New York, moved here, well to San Diego eight years ago to go to Law School at Western School of Law. Anway, I passed the BAR, and I'm a lawyer and started my practice in Santa Monica. I was a paramedic back east, loved it but honestly, always wanted to be a cop, so here I am. Put myself through the reserve academy at Los Angeles Sheriff's Department, College of the Canyons, went through the process, which is basically a cough and pulse check, and here I am."

Nikolai told the rookie to get out a pad of paper and write a couple of things down. "First, what the fuck kind of name is Artorius! Jesus we may be related in some way, sounds like you came from the same bent tree that named me Nikolai! Second, what is the off-duty altercation policy for our department, meaning what happens if you get into a situation where you witness a crime and what are the steps you should follow. Three, what should you do if I engage someone in a foot pursuit, and last, but not least, answer this question in writing, you get a call of a shoplifting, man enters, say a 7-11 convenience store, grabs a 12 pack of beer, walks past the register, makes no attempt to pay, then runs out of the door with the beer. We see this happen and pursue the subject and detain him. We check his wallet and pockets and find no cash or ability to pay for the stolen merchandise. What crime or crimes do you have? I'm going to get a cup of coffee, check out our unit, and I'll be back. You have 20 minutes."

Nikolai was standing in the back talking with Sergeant Brodie about the new guy when he walked out the door, it had been twenty-three minutes since Nikolai gave him his assignment.

Reed looked at Nikolai. "Sir, I have your answers for you. Do you want to read them?"

Nikolai smiled. "No, Officer Reed, why don't you read the answers to me."

Reed looked down at the notepad where he had written his notes. "Yes sir. One, when it comes to any kind of off duty conflict or witnessing a crime, we should be a good witness and not get involved unless there is no way out of it. If we do get involved, we should first notify the agency in the area where the situation occurred, then the on duty watch commander for our agency, and be prepared to write a detailed officers report of what occurred. Two, if you engage someone in a foot pursuit, I will follow you and stay with you at all costs and assist in subduing the subject. Three, with regard to the beer run subject, he is guilty of burglary sir. He entered a building with the intent to steal beer, as evidenced by his lack of cash or ability to pay."

Sergeant Brodie smiled. Nikolai clapped his hands. "Great job, rookie. Now, let's go check out a shotgun and get 10-8." The two men walked into the armory and signed out a Remington 870 pump action shotgun and 6 rounds of ammo. Walking outside, Nikolai checked the weapon to make sure it was safe, then racked the bolt closed and loaded the 6 rounds into the magazine of the shotgun. He pointed out to Reed, "Always point the weapon in the air when loading or unloading it." He got into the driver's seat of the unit, and Reed entered the passenger side.

Nikolai placed the weapon into the shotgun rack and locked it. "Now, Reed, don't ever reach into that trigger guard and pull the damned trigger of that fucker. It will be your luck there is a round in the chamber, and you will end up deafening us when it goes off and injuring us as the damn things turns our hard top into a convertible, you got that?"

"Sir, yes sir!"

Nikolai punched Reed in the shoulder. "Stop calling me sir, fucknuts. It's Nikolai or Drew, got me?"

Reed responded, "Yes sir, I mean Nikolai."

Nikolai started the unit, put it in drive, and as they drove off told Reed, "Okay rookie, say 1-A-26 10-8."

Reed mimicked the instruction. This was the first time he had handled the radio as a police officer, and it was an electric moment for him.

Nikolai drove around several residential streets and asked Reed what kind of law he practiced, as the two chatted and Reed was totally distracted, Nikolai stopped at a curb and looked over at Reed. Reed continued talking about his law practice. Nikolai then chimed in, "Alright rookie, where are we right now?"

Reed looked at Nikolai shocked with a dumbfounded look on his face. "What do you mean?"

Nikolai said, "What I mean is, we are in the middle of the shit, we are out of the car and in a foot pursuit, and you need to tell dispatch where you are so other units can find you, soooooo, where are we?"

Reed was now in panic mode. "I have no idea, sir!" he exclaimed with a bit of fright in his voice.

Nikolai chuckled. "Well then, rookie, get your happy ass out of the car, run down to the furthest corner, and get back here with a report of where we are." There was a pause, and Nikolai barked again, "That means now, rookie. Get your grabnasty ass out of this car and find out where we are, and do it now, if you ever wanna see the inside of a patrol car again." Nikolai laughed inside.

Reed jumped out of the car and ran the quarter mile down the street, read the street signs, memorized the street signs, and ran back to the patrol car to report to his temporary field training officer. Winded, he reported, "We are in the 800 block of South Workman, sir, just north of Mott Street."

Nikolai clapped his hands. "Very good, rookie, now, where exactly is that?"

Reed, still out of breath, "I have no fucking clue sir!"

Nikolai laughed again. "Well, rookie, you are in the south end of the city, about one half mile from Laurel Canyon, which runs parallel to the five freeway. You need to know where you are at all times. That means while driving, always be cognizant of where you or your partner are driving, what direction, and by god where you are headed so that when shit goes wrong, and it will go wrong, you don't find yourself lost and with no back up. From the sound of it, you need to work on your cardio a bit, brother. If you got into a foot pursuit following me, you'd be hell bent to keep up. This job is not just mental, it's physical."

Reed's eyes were wide open. "Clearly. Sir. Man, I have a lot to learn."

Nikolai said, "Well, rookie, we will get you there,

by the end of the shift, I will get you started on a path to help you. The academy teaches you basics. Our job here is to teach you the details to apply so you will stay alive. Now, let's get out there and do some police work, like, get us a traffic stop. Whoever finds the first violator gets code 7 on the other guy's dime."

They pulled away from the curb and made their way southbound on South Workman. Nikolai turned westbound onto Laurel Canyon which rounded a bend and turned into northbound Hubbard. Just then, Reed called out, "No front license plate on that piece of shit Ford pickup truck going southbound on Hubbard, sir."

Nikolai immediately pulled a U-turn and made his way behind the vehicle. He got behind the beater old Ford pickup and got on the radio. "26 control, 28-29." (28-29 is short for ten code requesting 10-28 or, Vehicle Registration info, and 10-29, a check for wants and warrants. The smart officer will usually run this before stopping the vehicle to make sure they don't get into something they aren't ready for. A lesson Nikolai learned early in his career. An expensive one as it turns out, that nearly cost him his life.)

The dispatcher responded, "1-A-26, go with your plate."

Nikolai replied, "California Commercial Frank 40125, again, F as in Frank 40125. We are currently following the vehicle eastbound on Laurel Canyon from Hubbard."

Dispatch responds, "Roger 1-A-26, Frank 40125, stand by."

Nikolai shares where he is going with Reed. "So, we're going to check out the car thoroughly, make sure it's not stolen or has warrants, take it nice and easy. Once we get the response, we will perform a traffic stop. Your job, rookie, is to get out of the car before I do, and when we light him up and he stops, get your spotlight set on the middle of the rear window so they can't get a clear view of us, got it?"

Reed nodded his head, and dispatch could be heard almost immediately, "1-A-26, no want or warrant on a 1964 Ford registered to Alonzo Mendoza out of Northridge."

Nikolai hit the switch on the Motorola control head on the unit's dashboard and activated the emergency red and blue rotators, then alerted dispatch, "Roger, control be advised, we are going to be traffic on that vehicle in the area of eastbound Laurel Canyon and Brand."

The truck came to a stop. Nikolai immediately turned off the overhead rotators and left on the forward steady red light and the rear flashing ambers and exit the patrol car and simultaneously turned on his driver side spotlight pointing it at the driver's side door and rearview mirror. Reed did the same and actually got out of the car before Nikolai did.

Nikolai told Reed, "Okay, rookie, walk up to the passenger side, use your flashlight using your non gun hand and look inside the vehicle while I contact the driver."

The two men approached the truck, and Nikolai addressed the driver. "Good evening, sir. I am Officer Drew with the Los Angeles Police Department. I am stopping you because your vehicle doesn't have a front license plate. May I see your license and registration, please?' Nikolai had his right hand on his .45 and his flashlight in his left looking cautiously inside the car.

The driver was an older Hispanic gentleman. He politely responded, "Yes sir, I have no idea where that license plate is, I never had one." He reached in his pocket and removed his wallet and handed the driver's license to Nikolai. He then leaned over and opened the glove box of the truck and removed the registration for the vehicle, handing that to Nikolai as well. Nikolai noticed that the registration was current. He also noticed that the driver's license was in the same name as indicated on the registration paperwork. Nikolai spoke again to the driver. "Alright, sir, I am going to check you out real quick and I will be right back. Please wait here and keep your hands on the steering wheel, okay. You don't have any guns in the car or small nuclear weapons, do you?"

The driver laughed and responded, "No sir, none of that."

Nikolai walked back to the passenger side of the patrol unit, looked at the rear license plate of the truck, which had current registration. Nikolai looked at Reed, "have you ever run a person for wants and warrants, rookie?"

Reed replied, "No sir, this is my very first day actually working in a patrol car."

Nikolai laughed. "Well, lucky me. Okay, so watch what I do. I want you to see how this is done." Reed nodded his head.

Nikolai got on the radio, "26 control, code 4, advise when you are clear for a code 10 on one." Code 4 means the situation is under control.

Dispatch got back immediately, "Roger 26, reporting code 4, go with your code 10 info."

Nikolai went from the top of the license, giving the license number, the subject's name, address, physical descriptors, and date of birth. The dispatcher acknowledged the transmission and advised Nikolai to stand by. Moments later, the dispatcher squawked on the radio, "1-A-26, be advised, your subject has no want or warrant, license status if valid."

Nikolai responded, "Roger, thank you. Alright, rookie, let's approach the vehicle again, I am going to advise this guy to get the plate thing squared away and we're not writing him a ticket, then we will go 10-8 and chat further."

They approached the truck again, Nikolai had the driver's paperwork in his left hand along with his flashlight and still had his hand on his side arm. "Alright sir, I am not writing you a ticket tonight, but please get your license plate issue squared away, okay? You can go to DMV, and they will give you new plates free of charge. You just can't be driving around without both plates on your car, okay?"

The driver retrieved his license and registration from Nikolai's hand and thanked him for the warning. Nikolai and Reed walked back to the patrol car, turned off the spotlights and emergency lights, and pulled away. Nikolai asked Reed, "So, did that seem pretty easy to you, rookie? Also, do you know why I put out our direction of travel for the traffic stop?"

Reed replied, "Yes, I think I have it. I think the reason you broadcast our direction of travel on the traffic stop is to avoid having officers pull up on us from the front?"

Nikolai smiled and said, "Exactly!" Nikolai pulled away from the curb and proceeded east on Laurel Canyon and explained further, "So, another important thing we do while conducting a traffic stop is keep our vehicle about half the width to the outside edge of the suspect vehicle to create a safety barrier between us and traffic coming up on us from the rear. Then we light the car up at night with what we call the curtain of light, this way the suspect or subject in the car doesn't see us easily. We don't want that person to have an easy shot at us when we approach, make sense?"

Reed replied, "Yes sir. We practiced this in the academy, but honestly, it didn't make sense like it does now. Somehow it's totally different. Doing it in real life is far more interesting because we have no idea who we are walking up on."

Within moments, a vehicle approached the two officers in the opposite direction with no lights on. Nikolai executed a U-turn and went after the vehicle. They caught up to the vehicle and Nikolai told Reed to run the plate, Reed picked up the microphone and called into dispatch, "1-A-26, 28-29 on a roller."

Dispatch responded immediately, "Roger 26, go with your plate."

Reed replied, "1XBC337, repeat, California 1XBC337, we're westbound Laurel Canyon from Brand."

Dispatch responded quickly, "26, vehicle has no wants or warrants and registered to Leticia Rivetti on Rinaldi Street in Northridge."

Nikolai looked at Reed. "Light it up and put us traffic, rookie."

Reed was excited. He was running the traffic stop. It was like a dream come true. He turned on the rotators and hit the siren for a brief second to get the driver's attention. The car pulled over quickly and slowly rolled to a stop at the curb. Reed was already advising dispatch of the traffic stop, "Adam 26, show us traffic on that plate westbound on Laurel Canyon just west of South Maclay."

Dispatch parroted the transmission, and Reed and Nikolai were already out of the vehicle turning their spotlights onto the car they stopped. Nikolai told Reed, "Get up there and do your thing, rookie."

Reed walked forward between the patrol unit and the subject vehicle. He removed his flashlight from his left rear sap pocket and shined it inside the subject vehicle using his left hand, keeping his gun hand free. He observed that the driver of the vehicle was older. She was rolling down the window of the car and he observed that she was alone.

Reed identified himself. "Good evening, ma'am, I am Officer Reed of the Los Angeles Police Department. The reason I am stopping you this evening is because you were driving with your lights off. May I see your license and registration please?"

The driver looked at him, surprised. "My goodness, you're kidding. No wonder I couldn't see worth a damn." She reached down to the dashboard and turned the lights of the car on.

Reed shook his head. "Yes ma'am, now may I see your license and registration please?"

The woman removed her wallet from her purse. Reed moved the flashlight around and observed carefully as she did so. She removed her driver's license from the wallet and handed it to him, then reached over, opened the vehicle's glove box, and removed the registration card and handed that to Reed as well. "Here you go, officer. I am so sorry about that."

Reed reviewed the driver's license. It was current and had the same name as the registered owner of the vehicle. "Have you been drinking tonight, uh, Ms. Rivetti?"

The woman smiled at him. "Of course not. I was driving home from my son's house after visiting him, his wife, and my grandkids."

Reed, realizing that this was merely academic at this point and they were not writing a senior citizen a ticket, excused himself and went back to the patrol car to run the driver's information for warrants and verify her license status. He walked backward, still keeping the flashlight on the vehicle and made his way to the passenger door of the patrol car where Nikolai was standing and waiting.

Nikolai punched him in the shoulder. "Good job, rookie, now run her info."

Reed contacted dispatch and ran the woman's driver's license for wants and warrants. He did so perfectly, and dispatch came back quickly with a response indicating that there were no warrants and Ms. Rivetti's license status was valid. Reed also let dispatch know they were Code 4.

Nikolai pointed at the car and told Reed to return the woman's license and registration. Reed returned to the driver's side of the vehicle cautiously and informed the woman that she had no warrants, her license was valid, and informed her that she would not be receiving a ticket this evening. Ms. Rivetti thanked the officer and began putting her paperwork away. Reed and Nikolai returned to the police cruiser, turned off their spot lights but remained parked behind Ms. Rivetti's vehicle until she could safely pull away.

Nikolai looked over at Reed and praised him. "Not bad for your first time, rookie. You certainly paid attention to what I was showing you. Now, put us 10-8, and let's go see if we can get into some trouble!"

Reed picked up the microphone, pressed the call button, and said proudly, "1-A-26, we're clear of our traffic, show us 10-8." Reed looked over at Nikolai as he hung up the microphone and asked, "Do you think I could drive for a bit, I used to run an ambulance and am used to this sort of thing?"

Nikolai already had the unit in drive. He kept his foot on the brake, and looked over at the rookie who looked like an adolescent teen longing to get behind the wheel of his parents car for the first time. Nikolai remembered back when he was 14 and he was visiting his Uncle Bob who was the sheriff of Hudspeth County, Texas. He had spent every summer there for three years with his Uncle Bob because his mother wanted him to have a role model to look up to. The first year his mother drove their '71 Volkswagen

Station Wagon from Southern California to Del City, which was roughly 900 miles away and about a 12 hour drive straight out the 10 freeway to Texas highway 62-180 and onto the one and only paved street in Del City. All the way there, Nikolais mother started to struggle with the drive after about seven hours. They stopped for a break at a rest stop to get something to drink and get gas. The quick stop as it was called was dingy and in the middle of nowhere. Nikolai could tell that his mother was exhausted from the drive and offered to let her rest and he would drive for a while. His mother had already let him drive about everywhere in their little town and even allowed Nikolai to drive back streets to see friends. They had a great relationship, and she trusted him not to be foolish. She knew he would never disappoint her.

She smiled thinking they were only about five hours away and it was better and safer to let him drive then for her to continue as tired as she was. She handed Nikolai the keys and told him to stay heading east on the 10 freeway until he got to highway 375 and turn left, then pointing out on the map she was following she told him to take 375 to Texas Highway 62-180 and continue west to Main Street. It would have a sign that pointed toward Del City.

Nikolai remembered arriving at the cross street of 62-180 and Main Street, he turned onto the street and arrived at a sign that said, "Welcome to Del City, population 75." Nikolai remembered that he loved being in Del City with his Uncle Bob and he enjoyed having him there as well. Uncle Bob convinced his mother to leave him for the summer and after three months, he would fly him home. While there, Uncle Bob took Nikolai on some amazing adventures, none of which was as exciting as the time they were sitting at Uncle Bob's Steak House (Yes, Uncle Bob was not only the sheriff. He was also the owner of the little town's Steak House and arcade. He was quite the entrepreneur, but realized that giving people a place to go was the world's best police man). At one point, Uncle Bob tossed Nikolai the keys to his sheriff's unit and told him to drive it up the street to his house and give the car a good washing. It was in that moment that Nikolai saw in Reed what he felt like as a kid, getting the keys and being trusted like that.

Nikolai put the unit back in park, got out and told Reed, "Okay, rookie, but I swear to God, if you kill us, I will bitch at you all the way to hell." Reed could hardly contain himself. He practically ran to the driver's door of the patrol car, put it in drive, and pulled away from the curb. Nikolai told Reed, "Get us to 776 North Maclay, I need a cup of coffee."

Reed drove them to the location. He knew where the 700 block of North Maclay was, but had no idea what was there. He imagined he would find out soon enough. As they approached the area, Reed smiled, proud of himself for getting them there. Reed backed the unit into a parking spot near the front window of the 7-11 convenience store. The two men went in and got a cup of coffee, as they returned, they got in the patrol unit and just as they closed the doors of the car, a Honda CB 750 motorcycle sped by them, loud as hell, westbound on Glenoaks through the red light at North Maclay Street, nearly colliding with a car that had entered the intersection. The two men looked at each other and Nikolai said, "Well, what the hell are you waiting for, rookie, hit it!" Pointing at the street in front of them with his hand fully extended like a Marine Corps Drill Instructor on a rampage.

Reed put the unit in drive and sped out of the parking lot in pursuit of the motorcycle. Nikolai told him, "I have the radio and the emergency equipment, you drive and don't fuckin kill us, kid." By now the speeding motorcycle was quite far ahead of them, at Harding Street. Nikolai held off on activating the red and blue lights until they closed the gap between them. Nikolai looked over at Reed laughing and yelled, "Well, mister I drove an ambulance, ya wanna punch it, this guy isn't gonna catch himself!"

Reed pushed his foot to the floor. The 1987 Caprice transmission downshifted and accelerated to 95 miles per hour. The beat to hell Honda 750 was now about a block ahead of them about to hit the light at North Hubbard.

The biker actually activated his left turn signal and turned onto southbound Hubbard at 35 miles per hour nearly colliding into an oncoming vehicle, dragging a footpeg on the street as he executed the turn. Nikolai was able to get the plate and now that they were through the turn, he activated the patrol unit's overhead red and blue lights and got on the radio. "A-26 control, be advised were in pursuit of a motorcycle southbound Hubbard from Glenoaks at a high rate of speed, California License 2- D as in David 7624."

Reed's heart was racing but felt amazingly at ease in this situation. He realized that he was finally here, doing what he was supposed to be doing. He looked over at Nikolai and said, "How do you do that?"

Nikolai holding the mic grinning like a Cheshire cat said, "How do I do what, rookie?"

Reed looking back at him and the road ahead said, "Yell at me in one breath then get on the radio and talk calmly in the next. It's like an episode of Starsky and Hutch!"

Nikolai laughed. "Practice, kid, practice!" Nikolai went back to yelling, "Now get your head back in the game before you kill someone or worse yet, me. Remember, dickhead, if you have to crash, be sure not to crash the passenger side of the car, okay!"

Reed was puzzled and asked him, "Why?"

Nikolai looked at him and laughed and yelled again, "Because it's the side of the car I'm on, shit for brains!"

Dispatcher Huff squealed back, "All units be

advised, Unit 1-A-26 is in pursuit southbound Hubbard at Fourth Street following California Motorcycle plate of 2 David 7624."

The motorcycle was traveling at about 75 miles per hour in a 35 zone and was now crossing over Fifth Street. Nikolai put out over the radio, "Control, be advised, we are continuing southbound on Hubbard, crossing Fifth." The motorcycle screamed down Hubbard and ran the red light at First Street and for some reason, stopped at the red light on Hubbard at Truman. As they approached the intersection, Nikolai broadcast, "Control, be advised, we are stopped at the red light, southbound Hubbard at Truman." Nikolai pointed out to Reed that the motorcyclist was wearing a leather jacket with a Sundowner Motorcycle Gang Patch across the back. Nikolai switched the radio over to the unit's public address system and said, "Driver, when the light turns green, pull to the left and park your motorcycle at the curb."

Looking at Reed, he laughed. "Yeah, as if that's gonna happen!"

The motorcycle immediately turned left on Truman Street, slowed down, and started to move toward the curb, Nikolai uttered, "Well, I'll be damned!"

The Bearded Biker looked over his shoulder, left his left arm up, and showed the officers his middle finger, put his hand back on the bars of the bike and took off like a bat out of hell!

Nikolai broadcast, "Control, be advised, we are now southbound on Meyer crossing San Fernando Road... Now eastbound Celis from Meyer." He looked over at Reed. "Don't get too close, rookie. If he goes down, you don't wanna end up with a K injury on your hands. That would end your career right quick and in a hurry." (K injury means someone killed during a collision.)

Nikolai continued broadcasting, "Control, we are now southbound on Kalisher from Celis. Be advised, suspect is wearing Sundowner colors, and we are in the clubhouse vicinity."

Dispatcher Huff recognized this was going to end up badly so put out a request for backup for the officers. Nikolai broadcast again, "26, be advised, we are now eastbound on Mott from Kalisher."

As they sped through the neighborhood, Nikolai yelled at Reed, "Whatever you do rookie, be careful through this area. There are lots of elderly folks always pulling in and out of driveways, don't fuckin kill anyone."

The motorcycle turned immediately to the left onto northbound Mission, and Nikolai broadcast the direction of travel calmly and succinctly. They chased the Sundowner biker in a two mile circle three times, over the period of about seven minutes.

In a matter of seconds, the motorcycle turned into the driveway on the northern end of 701 Kalisher and crashed into the wall of the building near the door which had a large sign noting "SunDowners MotorCycle Club since 1974" on the wall.

Nikolai and Reed simultaneously exited the vehicle. Nikolai got on his handheld radio and broadcast, "Control, pursuit has terminated at 701 Kalisher Street, send additional units please."

The suspect stopped the motorcycle and jumped off as it stopped. He must have thought he put the kickstand down, but the bike fell to its right side. Nikolai was in front of the vehicle approaching the suspect who appeared to be about 6'4" and about 300 pounds. The suspect turned on Nikolai and took a swing at him, lumbering about like a sloth.

Nikolai moved in close and punched the suspect with his right hand on the left side of his jaw, causing him to wobble and fall. The suspect fell and grabbed Nikolai's left leg. Nikolai responded by kicking the suspect with his right foot, trying to hit him in the chest, but missed as he lost his footing and connected with his face. The suspect regained his footing somehow and ran toward the back of the Sundowners Clubhouse building, grabbing a rain gutter downspout to use as leverage to round the corner, which went badly. The 300 pound man lost his grip and fell on the ground.

Reed was now between the suspect and Nikolai, who was just now getting back on his feet. Reed has his PR-24, an Okinawan martial arts weapon, swinging it from one side of his body to the other, yelling, "Show me your hands!" At that moment, another large man came around the building in a combative stance. Reed now moved his PR-24 from his right hand to his left and drew his Beretta 92F 9 millimeter handgun from its holster pointing at the rather large assailant, telling him in an agitated voice, "Get on your knees, do it now!"

Nikolai was looking at this hot mess and realized it was about to go bad rather quickly, uttering, "Jesus Christ, this is a shooting waiting to happen! Reed, put your toys away and help me cuff the dirtbag." Nikolai got between the combative biker and Reed and smiled at him and said quietly, "If you don't back off, fuckstick, you're goin two places."

He leans a bit closer to the man, who says in a loud and rough voice, "Oh yeah, where's that, pig?" Nikolai was sizing him up for an armbar because he was about to turn the unsuspecting biker into a human pretzel and said quietly, "The hospital, then jail, if you're lucky." At this point, three units rolled up with their overhead red and blue lights on, and four officers and a sergeant got out of their cars. The biker put his hands up and started to back up to the open door of the building and said, "We will see you soon, tough guy."

Meanwhile, Reed was bent over the suspect with one cuff on his right wrist trying to get the left arm close enough to cuff it. He wasn't having any luck. As the backup officers made their way down the alley to them, Nikolai said quietly, "For the love of fuck, I don't care if you need to use two sets of cuffs on that fucker, get him locked up."

Reed quickly removed his second pair of cuffs from his utility belt and did just that. He rolled the suspect over and helped him to his feet. Reed escorted the biker to the unit and helped him get seated in the back, no easy chore, considering the seat was hard plastic and the roll bar was in the way of his extra large legs.

Nikolai stood between the door of the clubhouse, which was open, and the police car. Another large and overweight biker walked out of the back door. He had a patch on his vest that said "Chapter President" and below it the name "Mad Mike."

He looked mean as hell, but was calm and well spoken and asked Nikolai nicely, "Officer, would you mind not impounding our brother's motorcycle? It would mean a lot to us and save him some money. He's already in enough trouble."

Nikolai paused for a moment. "I will ask him if he is alright with that, if he is, absolutely have no problem doing so." Nikolai leaned in the patrol car and asked the suspect if he would like him to leave his motorcycle with the club, or if he would like it impounded. The suspect said, "Oh, please don't impound it. Leave it with my brothers, sir, if you don't mind."

Nikolai walked up to Mad Mike. "He asked that

we leave it with you. By the way, how in the hell does a guy end up in a Harley club riding a damned Honda?"

Mad Mike grinned. "Well, he's had a hard time over the last few years. We simply couldn't kick the man to the curb like his wife did, just wouldn't seem right. Thank you, by the way, we appreciate you not impounding the man's iron horse. By the way, officer, is there any chance we can have the man's jacket and colors? They belong to the club, not him."

Nikolai replied, "Tell ya what, if he ends up having to stay with us, give me your number. I'll give you a call and release them to you, fair enough? I just don't want to uncuff the man here and go through what could be another donnybrook, ya know what I mean."

Mad Mike smiled. "That is fair enough, officer, do you have a pen and paper?" Nikolai took out his notepad from his breast pocket and took down the clubhouse number. Reed got in the driver's seat of the unit, Nikolai got in the passenger side of the unit and as they backed out of the driveway of the clubhouse and onto Kalisher Street, Nikolai got on the radio and broadcast, "1-A-26, be advised, we are clear of Kalisher and en-route 10-19 with one 10-15."

Dispatcher Huff replied, "Roger that, 26, show you clear of Kalisher and en-route 10-19 with one in custody."

As Reed drove them to the police station, Nikolai

looked at him. "Well, that was fuckin fun, you damn near ran that fucker over! Nice drivin, rookie. When we get to the station, we are going to pull in the back, remove our friend here from the unit, and before we enter the jail, we remove all guns and knives and slide them into a gun locker. Then we will turn him over to the booking officer. I would like you to back him up and be there as he is searched, fingerprinted, and photographed. I will be working on the arrest report while you do that, and when you are all done, come see me so we can go over the report, get me?"

Reed nodded with a huge grin on his face. They arrived at the station, as discussed. Nikolai first went into dispatch to get the printouts on the motorcycle and the subject. Huff was sitting in his chair, leaning back with his hands behind his head, smiling, "Well, tell me, were you driving and handling the radio?"

Nikolai smiled and replied, "No, man, I had let the rookie drive, and literally the second he took the wheel, shit hit the fan!"

Huff laughed. "How did he do? Did he fuck it up?"

Nikolai removed the printouts from the bin and smiled. "No, he did real well, kept cool and didn't overreact. He has some experience as a paramedic back in New York, so he's got a good head start."

Nikolai went to the break room and poured a cup of coffee. The pot was full, and it smelled fresh. *Thank God*, he thought! He sat down at a table and reviewed the paperwork before heading to the report room. Sergeant Brodie walked in, poured a cup of coffee, and sat across from him. Brodie said, "You had that well under control. Nice job calling it out while driving, kid, I figure you didn't want the rookie to try handling the radio on his first day."

Nikolai set the paperwork down. "Well, Sarge, the rookie was actually driving, I had just let him get behind the wheel when the biker sped by us. Gotta say, his experience as a paramedic in New York certainly prepared him for this. He did an outstanding job."

Brodie laughed. "Well, all's well that ends well. Great job to both of you, I was afraid we were gonna have a brawl on our hands with the SunDowners."

Nikolai picked up his paperwork and walked toward the report room and replied, "Yeah Sarge, no shit. I'll get this banged out right quick and in a hurry and get back in the field."

Nikolai went to work hand-writing the arrest report, and within thirty minutes, Reed had entered the report room, having completed getting the defendant, Wheeler, booked, printed, and photographed.

Nikolai handed the arrest report over to Reed and asked, "Have a look at this, counselor, and see if this lays out what you experienced as well."

A couple of moments later, Reed handed the report to Nikolai. "Reads perfectly, sir, well done."

They turned in the file, and the two men walked to the rear of the police station. Nikolai let the rookie drive the rest of the night, quizzing him on penal and vehicle codes and having him drive to specific locations. He would also have the rookie stop in the middle of the street and ask him where they were, and most of the time, the rookie knew where they were. When he failed to identify which street they were on, Nikolai made Reed exit the vehicle and run to the furthest street sign, then back and recite where they were.

It was a slow shift. No calls for service and hardly any traffic to speak of, so they drove around the rest of the night keeping a watchful eye on the city while the people slept. At the end of the shift, the men cleared out their unit and got out of their uniforms, Nikolai stored his in his locker, while Reed placed his gear into a locker he shared with another reserve officer, a guy named Roderick Toombs. Nikolai had never met this officer. In fact he had not met many of the reserve police officers. This triggered an idea. He decided that he was going to attend the next reserve meeting and asked Reed when that was.

Reed told him the date and time. Nikolai wrote on the notepad he kept to keep his thoughts straight day to day, shook Reed's hand congratulating him again on doing a fine job! Nikolai felt it was time to introduce himself to the reserve group and noted their next meeting.

Reed pulled out his calendar and told Nikolai, "The next date of our monthly meeting which is the 25th of the month, at 1800 hours. You aren't going to embarrass me are you?"

Nikolai laughed. "No, man, I want to get better acquainted with everyone is all. I haven't met most of these guys. About time I should, I think!"

The time was 0800 hours, Thursday, April second. The end of the shift came quickly, and the two men parted ways, and Nikolai got out of his uniform, walked out of the back of the station, entered the '69 El Camino, and began the short drive home.

CHAPTER
TWELVE

Ten minutes into the drive home, Nikolai's pager went off. He looked at the display screen and the number was the back line to the dispatch desk with a 411 at the end, meaning it was an information call. Rather than stop and make a call from a pay phone, Nikolai decided to turn around and return to the station.

Nikolai walked into the back door and approached the dispatch area. He entered and Dispatcher Huff was still sitting there.

Nikolai smiled at Huff. "What the hell are you doing still sitting back there, mister?"

Huff frowned. "I am here for four hours covering for the day shift dispatcher. Apparently she had an urgent kid thing she had to attend to. I paged you because L-50 is looking for you."

L-50 is the unit code for the Chief of Police.

Nikolai scratched his head. "Any idea what he wants?"

Huff shrugged his shoulders with his hands up indicating that he had no idea.

Nikolai made his way to the chief's secretary's desk. She slid her window open and told him to have a seat and she would let him know when to go in.

A couple of minutes went by, and the secretary slid the window open again and told Nikolai, "The chief will see you now, Drew."

Nikolai walked into the chief's office. "Yes sir, you wanted to see me."

Chief Belknap stood up from his desk. "Hey, Nikolai, yes, close the door and have a seat." Chief Belknap walked around to the front of the desk, shook Nikolai's hand, and motioned for him to sit as he did.

Chief Belknap began, "I am going to get right to the point, Nikolai. You were apparently at the gym, and you were talking about Councilman Melendez with your workout partner, and the topic was discussed that you had heard he wanted to oust me from the chief's position for many unfavorable reasons."

Nikolai moved forward in his chair, hands clasped together. "Yes sir, I had a friend who was at a secret meeting where they were talking about coming after you specifically. I was not happy about what was said, and my workout partner, who is also a police officer here, and I got into a topic about the councilman and how dirty he is."

Chief Belknap patted Nikolai on the hands. "Nikolai, first of all, between you and me, this guy is a piece of work. He yelled at me over the phone for a half an hour, telling me how he wanted me to fire you and so forth."

Nikolai leaned back in his chair and ran his right hand through his hair. "Damn, Chief, honestly, my words against the councilman were nowhere near as rough as what I wanted to say. Besides, I was off duty, and I am allowed to have an opinion, right? Can he demand you to fire me?"

Chief Belknap in a calming tone looked Nikolai in the eye. "First of all, sure, he can demand I fire you, but terminating a police officer off probation is much harder than that. I reminded the councilman that you have the First Amendment right to freedom of speech and also reminded him that you were not on duty and furthermore, told him that he is probably emotional and is taking the discussion he heard across the room out of context. That being said, I have an idea that can calm the situation if you are willing to hear me out. And, I have no plan to fire you, son."

Nikolai looked at the chief, concerned. "Chief, I am always happy to hear you out."

Chief Belknap smiled. "Okay, I am thinking of calling him in here this morning, if you are willing, and I mean you can say no. I won't have any hard feelings about you at all if you say no, but, if you apologize to the councilman and try to downplay this, it could work in our favor. What are your thoughts?"

Nikolai thought for a moment, then ran his right hand back through his hair again. "I'm a team player Chief. Consider it done."

Chief Belknap smiled again. "Okay, I want you to get dressed in some street clothes, nothing too nice, and hang out. Do you have something in your locker?"

Nikolai responded quickly, "Yes sir, I have something here that will work."

Chief Belknap went on. "Okay, let me see what I can do, and I will come find you in a few minutes, just hang out for a bit."

Nikolai walked to the locker room, took a quick shower, and changed his clothes thinking to himself, *What in God's name have I gotten myself into? Fuck, I am gonna get myself fired!* After a few minutes, he was dressed and smelled clean and walked into the detective bureau in search of Detective Bedo.

Bedo was leaning back in his chair at his desk, paperwork all over the place. He looked up at Nikolai, got up, and walked over to him. It was obvious by the look on Nikolai's face that he was distraught. He put his arm around Nikolai and escorted him out the back door of the bureau into the detective parking lot. Bedo removed his pack of cigarettes from his white shirt pocket, took one out, and lit it, returning the pack to the shirt pocket. "Why so glum, chum? The old man get to you about your issues with the councilman already?"

Nikolai shook his head. "Yes, man, apparently the fucker wants me fired."

Bedo looked at him, took a drag from his cigarette and exhaled. "Nikolai, you are not getting fired. You're just gonna have to suck it up a bit and apologize to the councilman. Don't overthink this shit. The man is a total jackass, and frankly, his career is living on borrowed time. You are allowed to have an opinion. Hell, you can't even be written up for this. So breathe."

Nikolai perked up. "Seriously?"

Bedo laughed. "Yes man, just breathe. You didn't do anything wrong. You may in the future want to be a little more cautious about what you say and where from now on. You don't need people knowing what you know or think, get me. Friends close, enemies closer, everyone around here has an ax to grind or hates someone who may be on their way up in the system. Remember the old saying, a wise old owl sat in an oak, the more he heard the less he spoke, the less he spoke, the more he heard, we should all act more like that wise old bird."

Just then, there was a voice over the intercom. "Officer Drew to the Chief's Office."

Nikolai walked briskly to Chief Belknap's office and peeked his head in. "Yes sir."

Chief Belknap got out of his chair. "Okay, kid, he's agreed to meet. He will be here shortly, so get a cup of coffee and get back in here and have a seat. We will wait for him together."

Nikolai went to the break room, got a cup of coffee, and returned to the chief's office. They sat on the couch at the front of the desk, and Chief Belknap reiterated, "Don't say a lot. Just be yourself. I know your heart. It will all be over shortly."

Nikolai took a sip of coffee and asked, "Chief, don't you want to ask this guy about what he said about you, what I heard, or call him out for being a racist for meeting with business owners and others for wanting to remove you from your post?"

Chief Belknap smiled. "Nikolai, best he doesn't know what I know. I have heard all of this before from other would-be politicians, and I have outlasted all of them. Best we play this loosely. We know what and who he is. That's all that needs to be done." He paused. "For now."

A few moments later, the chief's secretary escorted the councilman in and announced him. Councilman Melendez was about 5'7", with a slender build, clean cut, and he sported a thin shaved mustache and goatee. He was wearing a pin striped suit and blue tie with a white shirt underneath. He had a scowl on his face as he entered the room.

Chief Belknap and Officer Nikolai Drew stood and towered over the man. The councilman looked up at Nikolai, and his mouth was open and his eyes got big. The councilman composed himself. Chief Belknap extended his hand, and the Councilman shook his hand, looking back over at Nikolai. Nikolai extended his hand, but the councilman scowled at him, making no attempt to take Nikolai's hand.

Chief Belknap spoke first. "Have a seat, councilman. I have invited Nikolai in to meet with you personally to clear the air about what you may have heard."

The men all sat at the couch, and the councilman looked at the men and said angrily, "What I heard was your officer, who I have seen on many occasions, by the way, refer to me as a racist, a corrupt politician, and he threatened to do whatever it took to see to it I was no longer holding a position in politics. What can he possibly say to avoid him getting fired at this point, Chief? I expect you to do your job and fire this disrespectful piece of shit."

Nikolai spoke up. "Councilman, I didn't say anything like that. There were two of us having a conversation about people in the community, and yes, your name came up, but it wasn't in the way you are describing. I think you merely misheard what we were discussing, a lot of which was in jest. I want to personally apologize for any misunderstanding that came out of this, sir."

The chief sat quietly. The councilman stood up and looked down on the two men in disgust. "I know exactly what I heard, Officer Drew, and I know you are a bitter, hostile man who cannot be trusted to wear a badge as a custodian of the people of this city. Chief, I expect you to fire this son of a bitch. There is no apology that will fix this or stop me from dealing with him, or you for that matter, if you fail to deal with your subordinates."

Chief Belknap stood up and calmly responded, "Councilman, you are way out of line. Officer Drew offered to meet you like a man and apologize for any misunderstanding. He is not out of line and did nothing to besmirch the uniform he wears. I am sorry you feel this way, Councilman."

The councilman turned and walked away in anger, turned back and said, "This isn't the end of this, Belknap. You're both going to regret this."

Chief Belknap walked to the door and closed it behind the councilman. "I already regret it," he said under his breath.

Nikolai stood up. "I am sorry about this, Chief. He's a powder keg."

Chief Belknap patted Nikolai on the back. "You have nothing to be sorry for, Nikolai. If anyone should be sorry, it's that guy. If he can't accept your apology, which was heartfelt and sincere, by the way, well, fuck him. Get out of here, and get some rest. It's been a long day for you."

Nikolai walked out of the office and back to the locker room, where he disrobed again, hung his clothes in his locker, and put his workout gear back on. He walked out the back door of the police station, got in his '69 El Camino and drove home. He arrived a short time later, backed the El Camino into its spot in the garage, undressed, turned on some relaxing music, and went to bed. He shut his mind off and reminded himself that he wasn't going to please everyone in this world and drifted off to sleep.

CHAPTER
THIRTEEN

During the middle of one wicked night's sleep, the best Nikolai had gotten in years, he was startled and awoken by his phone ringing. It was 6 p.m. on Friday, and his day off. Groggy, he answered the phone. On the other end of the line was his pal and cousin by marriage Louie. "Wanted to let you know, man, Ricky Hassler got in one hell of an accident in the desert today. He was doing like 100 miles per hour and flipped that sand rail of his. He had your ex, Tina, in the car with him. She was ejected and a little banged up, but Ricky is in bad shape. They had to air lift him to Loma Linda Hospital's Trauma Unit."

It took Nikolai a moment to register what he was just told. "Damn it, man, I told him that rickety, lap belt, no harness having piece of shit was dangerous! Where are you?"

Louie replied, "I just got home from dropping off all of his shit at his house. I am gonna take a shower and get some rest. The report is that he's in an induced coma due to the severity of the injury."

"Alright, man, I'll get into the hospital tomorrow and see how he's doing."

"Two things, don't bother, they won't let you in. You'll end up in the lobby sitting on your thumbs, buddy. Also, be careful. Tina was all emotional when I saw her and was begging me for your number so she could call you. When I refused, she begged me to call you. She is broken up with whoever the hell she was dating, so watch out, she's lookin for a place to land."

"Good info. I'll pass until he's awake. As for the queen of rebound, thank you, I'll pass on that as well."

Nikolai got up, walked into the kitchen, and made himself a peanut butter and banana shake mixed with a raw egg and some low-fat milk and a glass of ice cubes. He ground it all up with his blender then walked into his bathroom to shower up. Thoughts of Tina popped into his head while showering. The turmoil of their relationship was just a complete train wreck. The fact that he began dating her while they worked together at the cable company despite the fact that she was six years older than he was and that she was married at the time didn't help either. Flashbacks of the months of talking on the phone for an hour at a time and meeting in secret places made the relationship more exciting for sure, but still a train wreck. Not again, he thought.

Now out of the shower, he was brushing his teeth, shaving and trimming his mustache and eyebrows. He began thinking back to the decision Tina made to leave her husband and how they dated, then quickly moved in together, into the same damn house she lived in with her husband! He was always feeling weird about living in the same house and even bedroom as she did with her former husband. She instantly introduced him to her dad, who practically adopted him. Then the turmoil of her mis-spending the money they brought in together and the vicious arguments of the squandering of the funds. Then of course, her sneaking around behind his back with his coworker and having it reported back to him caused him to do the same and the eventual breakup. Even the breakup went badly because she came back to him repeatedly while she was dating other guys, even while he was dating other women!

He remembered sitting with his deputy sheriff girlfriend while he was in the academy. Blow-drying his hair, he was remembering that he was more of a boy toy to the freckle-faced redhead deputy than a boyfriend, and had to laugh about the incident when they were sitting beside one another inside the Burger King restaurant on Tyler Street in Riverside, across from the Tyler Mall. They were sharing lunch as Tina walked inside with her girlfriend solely because she had seen his '69 El Camino in the parking lot. She walked by the two of them like she never even saw them, and ordered a large slushy drink. As she and her girlfriend walked by Nikolai's table, she turned and poured the entire slushy all over the deputy sheriff. Of course, Nikolai was soaked as well, and he just sat there trying to keep the deputy calm with a half smile and half scowl on his face. The deputy tried to get up and climb over him. He stopped her advance as he knew if he let her up there was going to be an epic ass whooping. Tina's lips were trembling as she screamed at the drenched deputy, "You're just a whore, you know that, just a filthy, dirty, man-stealing whore," and stomped off with her girlfriend in tow. It was funny to him at the time, like the pot calling the kettle black.

Nikolai stood up and helped the seriously peeved deputy slide out of the booth where they were sitting. With a snarl on her lips, looking up at him she said, "Well, that was fun. Is that the woman you told me about that you lived with and you had all the drama with?"

Nikolai walked with her toward the restroom and said shamefully, "Yeah, that would be her." The two parted ways and walked into their prospective restrooms where they attempted to wash up and rinse off from the dousing of 44 ounces of sticky cherry slushy off themselves. They both walked out almost at the same time, then both laughed at one another and Nikolai said "Well, I guess we're gonna have to go back to my place and shower up. I can wash our clothes as well."

The freckle-faced deputy smiled and said, bearing a wicked evil grin, "Yeah, we're going to have to find something to do while the laundry is going!"

Nikolai laughed at himself in the mirror as he applied hair spray over his mop. Even though they had their ups and downs, he couldn't help but think fondly of his time with Tina. They were not exactly the best for one another, nor were they the worst.

He walked out to the living room and found Diamond Dave sitting on the couch watching *Smokey and the Bandit* of all things, right at the spot where Sheriff Buford T. Justice walked upon the three young men stripping Sally Fields's car, which she abandoned when Burt Reynolds iconic Trans Am pulled up. Nikolai and Diamond Dave burst out laughing as the sheriff blurted out, "Hold up on that car wash, gentlemen!"

He sat down on the couch, and Diamond Dave could see he was pensive. Dave turned off the television and asked him what was on his mind. Nikolai told him what he had learned about Ricky Hassler. Diamond Dave shook his head and replied, "Man, I knew there was gonna be nothing but trouble with that fuckin' sand rail the minute we saw that shitty frame and welding job on the role cage system.

Not to mention, the fact that he laughed you off when you told him to get rid of that shitty single lap belt safety belt garbage it had and replace it with a five-point harness. I may not have any love for the guy, Nikki, but I would never wish something like this on anyone. How is Tina, have you heard?"

Nikolai sighed. "Haven't heard, I am hesitant to even reach out to find out, given our history. I want nothing to do with opening that door again."

Diamond Dave laughed out loud. "Yeah, brother, amen to that. Enough with the crazy, now let's get in the gym. I've had enough of this sittin' around crap, and we can get some sustenance afterward!"

The two men got up, changed into their workout gear, locked the front door of the house, and Nikolai unlocked and opened the garage door. Diamond Dave walked over to the GTX, got in, and turned the ignition over. The starter made that unmistakable hyena laughing sound as it turned over, but the joke was done when the Mopar came to life.

He put the car in first gear, squealed the tires as he left the garage, and Nikolai closed the garage door and locked it, basking in the sound of that wicked 426 Max Wedge! He got in the passenger seat, and Dave slowly pulled onto the street, then sidestepped the clutch and accelerated, causing the rear tires to go up in smoke and the rear of the Mopar to pitch sideways.

He slowly backed off the accelerator, and the car

righted itself, and he shifted into second gear, chirping the tires. Nikolai was fumbling through Dave's cassette tapes to find the perfect tape and found it, Scorpions *Blackout*. He plugged it in and turned it up!

Nikolai and Diamond Dave ripped through a vigorous workout, talked about life, and Nikolai thought about how tough this whole thing must be on not only Hassler, but his parents, his girlfriend, and of course all of his friends. They skipped dinner and got a protein shake instead and headed home. It was 10 p.m. when they got back to the house. Diamond Dave started to back the GTX into the driveway and stopped the car abruptly and looked over at Nikolai. He had a wicked evil grin on his face and said, "Nikolai, I just had a great idea. We're gonna throw on some clothes and head over to that place at Universal City Walk called... B.B. King's, yeah. I heard that place is jumpin' all the time, so, open the garage, and I'll put the sled away, and we can take your El Camino, whadda ya say?"

Nikolai was wide awake. He smiled and opened the door to the GTX and looked over at his half-crazed buddy. "You got it, mang, let's do this!"

Nikolai ran into the house as Dave parked the GTX. They changed into jeans, polo shirts and headed out.

They arrived at B.B. King's at 10:30. The place was not packed. There were a few women sitting at the bar and scattered tables with some folks, and as they walked in, George Thorogood and The Delaware Destroyers were making their way on stage.

Diamond Dave and Nikolai sat at the bar, Nikolai was smiling ear to ear. He loved George. As they walked up, Nikolai yelled at the singers, "Man what a lucky night for us, our favorite rockers, a Friday, and a light crowd! Glad to see you guys."

George Thorogood looked down at Nikolai, kneeled, and shook his hand. George smiled and with his gravel and gritty voice said, "Nice to meet some legit fans, you look like a Marine, you in the military?"

Nikolai shook his hand and laughed and said, "No, man, I never had that honor. I am a cop, however."

George stood up. "Oh yeah, which department?"

"LAPD."

George laughed. "Well, cheers to you, man. Are you from California?"

Nikolai laughed. "No, man, I am from New York originally. Poughkeepsie to be exact."

George squawked back, "Well, man, I'm from Delaware. What do you wanna hear.?"

Nikolai stood up, raised his huge arms above his head. "'Bad to the Bone,' baby!"

George ran his pick over the guitar strings and asked him, "What's your name, brother?"

Nikolai told him, "Nikolai!"

George addressed the microphone. "Welcome to B.B. King's, friends and neighbors. This first riff is dedicated to our new friend, Nikolai!" He began with the well-known riff and started singing, Bad to the Bone together!

The group went on with four more songs, they took a break, and Nikolai offered to buy George a cocktail.

George jumped off the stage and sat at the bar stool next to Nikolai and said, "I'll have a bourbon, my friend," and lit a cigarette.

Nikolai, Diamond Dave, and George were laughing, talking about street rods and where they grew up, and Nikolai told the bartender to bring each of them one whiskey, one Scotch, and one beer! The bartender said alright, what kind! Nikolai laughed. "Won't matter mister, just bring what comes easy."

Nikolai began singing the next verse:

"Want to tell you a story

About the house-man blues" and went on from there.

George laughed as the bartender returned with a tray of liquor, and as they each downed the first shot of whiskey, George said, "Man, you're not bad. How about you come up on stage and sing that shit with me?"

Nikolai raised the glass of Scotch the bartender brought them. The three men clinked the glasses and downed the Scotch and Nikolai said, "Well fuck, man, I'd be honored!"

They jumped up on the stage. George Thorogood spoke into the microphone, "Ladies and gentlemen, tonight and tonight only, we will be singing with…" George stuttered and looked at Nikolai, who got the hint and spoke up.

"Nikolai Drew!"

The band chimed in, and they began singing, George started the first portion, then Nikolai chimed in with the second, and they sang the third together. This went on for the entire song, and the crowd was laughing and singing along. Nikolai felt reborn and had chills as he sang with the legendary performer. When it was all done, Nikolai jumped off the stage and had a bourbon with Diamond Dave as the clock chimed one a.m., and the two men decided it was time to head out, so they split the tab and headed home.

Nikolai always regulated his alcohol so he didn't get drunk. He drank a glass of water between every cocktail and always sipped so as not to get hammered. Nikolai turned the ignition of the '69 El Camino, and as it thundered, Diamond Dave put on Nikolai's favorite Van Halen tape. They both started signing together as David Lee Roth was singing "Hot for Teacher!"

On the way home, Nikolai's pager was going off with a 911 at the end of the police dispatch phone number. He was shaking his head, and Dave asked him what was going on. Nikolai showed him the pager. "Well, it's the dispatch number with a 911 at the end. I've been drinking, so I am not goin' in. I'll return the call when we get home."

When he and Diamond Dave got home, they opened the garage, put the El Camino away and went inside while Dave secured the garage door. He picked up the cordless phone, called the number, and heard Dispatcher Huff's voice on the other end. Nikolai asked him what was going on.

The dispatcher told him that a woman named Tina was looking for him, something about nearly dying in a sand rail accident with an old friend of theirs, and that she had left her number asking that Nikolai give her a call. Nikolai wrote the number down and thanked the dispatcher for the call. He ran his fingers through his hair and thought to himself, *Now what the hell do I do!*

It had been two years since he had spoken to Tina. He figured he had better call her and get this over with. He was bound to run into her at some point and didn't want the grief of her being pissed at him yet again for not calling her after this scene.

He looked at the piece of paper, turned the cordless phone on, and heard the dial tone, then punched in the number that was given to him by dispatch.

One ring was all it took, and Tina picked up the

phone. Her voice was cracked, and it was clear she was crying. "Hello," she said.

Nikolai spoke. "Hey, Tina, got your message, what's going on?"

Tina went into the story, explaining how the group was out in Palm Springs with their rails, Jeeps, and dirt bikes and parting pretty hard. She told him that she had been drinking pretty heavily and got in the sand rail with Hassler. They took off, spinning donuts and then sped off really fast, and the next thing she knew, they hit a big dirt berm and the rail shot into the air. She said it twisted sideways and then rolled over like six times, and the next thing she knew, people were standing around her as she lay on the ground. She said that Hassler was unconscious in the rail, upside down and bleeding from the head. She said it seemed like hours before paramedics arrived, and almost immediately there was a medical helicopter that took both her and Hassler to Loma Linda Hospital.

Nikolai was silent. Tina, crying, said, "All I could do was think that I needed to call you, Nikki, so I called your mom, and she gave me the number for your precinct. Funny how you are always the first person I think of when I am in trouble, isn't it?"

Nikolai's first response was to say something spiteful, like, "Yeah, because all you hang out with is sanctimonious, narcissistic losers who only think of themselves" but thought better of it. Instead, Nikolai asked, "What are the doctors saying?"

Tina got choked up. "The specialist said that it's too early to tell. The swelling is too bad. They have his head in a device that keeps his head straight and are going to monitor him.

"He has severe injuries to the C-5 and C-6 vertebrae, which could cause him to be a quadriplegic. He had to be intubated as well, but think he should be breathing on his own, but again, it's all way too early to tell." She was sobbing on the other end of the phone.

Nikolai asked, "What about visitors?"

Tina, still sobbing, said, "Only family members, Nikki, but I will get ahold of you if anything changes. How do I reach you? I don't want to call the police station again. That was uncomfortable."

Nikolai paused for a moment thinking to himself, *Shit, this is what the hell I was trying to avoid*, but continued. "My pager number is 818-867-5309. Just shoot me a number with a 411 or a 911 depending on the severity, and I will get right back to you, okay? Thank you for reaching out, Tina. I am really glad you are okay."

She paused, and Nikolai could almost hear her smile on the other end of the phone as she said, "Oh, thank you, Nikki. All I could think of was to get ahold of you, honey."

Nikolai hung up and lay down, thinking, *Well,*

that was fun! He turned on his radio to the jazz channel that was soothing and allowed him to sleep, and all he could think about were all the nights cruising market street, or going to the dance clubs where there would be a group of them hanging out together and how Hassler would somehow always pick a fight and how it would end up that Nikolai or Walker Hayes were doing the actual fighting. He had enough of the group at one point. Who wouldn't with a group that liked to call themselves "The Soap Opera" as most all of them had dumped their partner and started dating others' partners more than a few times, and frankly, the gene pool and drama pool had become a bit much… He finally drifted off to sleep.

CHAPTER
FOURTEEN

Nikolai woke up a little later than usual. It was noon, and he popped up in the middle of a bad dream. He was almost sweating and dreamt he was back in a relationship with Tina again. It was so vivid, he found himself looking around for evidence of her presence. There was none! A sigh of relief.

He put on his robe and slippers and walked out to the kitchen. There was a note from Diamond Dave saying he was off to a job interview with Black and White Tow Company. Nikolai chucked to himself. Well damn, that was quite a leap. Diamond Dave had *no* tow experience.

He poured some coffee out of the cold pot that Dave had left for him, slid it into the microwave oven, and as it was heating up, he walked back into his bedroom to retrieve his pager from his nightstand.

As he walked back to the kitchen, he looked at the pager screen and noticed three pages, two he didn't recognize, and one from Bedo's desk with a 411 at the end, indicating he had some information he wanted to share. Nikolai removed his now warmed up coffee, grabbed the cordless phone from its charger, and called the number. It rang quite a bit. Nikolai was just about to hang up when he heard someone pick up, panting, saying "Bedo" loudly.

Nikolai laughed. "What the hell, Detective, you take up running suddenly, you might wanna take it easy. You're liable to give yourself a heart attack."

Bedo responded in true fashion. "Shut your ass, fuckstick! Thanks for calling in. I decided to do a little digging and got a search warrant on the two pagers from that double homicide. I reached out to Motorola and faxed the warrant over to their legal department; they are gonna do their best to get the details back to me as quickly as possible, God only knows what that means."

Nikolai paused for a moment. "That was a great idea. Where did you come up with that?"

Bedo told him, "Well, I was thinking, it's like anything else you want to search right? So I called Motorola to try to access the information on who had paged these two for the last two months and hit a brick wall. They transferred me around until I finally got ahold of their legal department.

"Fortunately the gal that is working in the unit

used to work for San Francisco PD, and she told me how to get around the nonsense and that was with a warrant. I am hoping that we can figure out who these two were mingling with, and who knows, maybe we will sniff out a murderer in all this crap! I will keep you posted."

Nikolai's voice was excited. "If you need help calling numbers, let me know, happy to help."

Bedo assured him that he would, then went on saying, "By the way, the chief put out a memo today that the officer of the quarter luncheon with all the local businesses is happening in two weeks. You're getting a Medal of Valor at the luncheon. There will be other plaques awarded, but yours will be something special." He laughed out loud. "I have a medal I'd like to give ya, fuck head!"

Nikolai told him off. "You're full of shit."

Bedo laughed again. "I wish, dipshit. You're gettin it, and all the people there are gonna be kissin' your little rookie ass!"

Nikolai's pager went off again with the same number as one of the ones from earlier that day. "I gotta go, Detective. I'll be in to deal with your BS later!" He hung up and decided to call the number.

The voice on the other end answered quickly, "Senator Matt Michael's Office, may I help you." Nikolai introduced himself and stated that he had received a page from this number.

The woman on the other end recognized the name.

"Officer Drew, thank you for calling back. We understand that you are receiving a Medal of Valor in a couple of weeks, and Senator Matt Michael wants to also honor you with a proclamation, so I just wanted you to be aware and let you know we appreciate your service and look forward to seeing you."

Nikolai responded in a curt fashion, "Ma'am, I am not receiving any such award, and I will not." Suddenly the line went dead, Nikolai said hello repeatedly and to no avail. He was going to need to deal with the chief on this matter in person, he thought to himself.

Nikolai decided to go into the station early so he could have a conversation with the chief about this award nonsense and figured he would work out afterward. He put on his workout gear and walked out front to unlock and open the garage door. He slid behind the wheel of the '69 El Camino, fired it up, and pulled out of the garage, onto the driveway. Leaving the car running, he got out, closed the garage door, and locked it.

He then took the drive into downtown so he could get this crap out of the way. He arrived at Parker Center on North Los Angeles Street and took the elevator up to Chief Belknap's office. He approached the chief's secretary and asked if he could get in to see him for a moment.

She asked him to have a seat, and she would see if he was available and asked Nikolai for his name.

When he told her, she smiled kindly and said, "Oh, yes, Officer Drew, your name has been coming up a lot these days." A few moments later Chief Belknap walked into the waiting room and escorted Nikolai down the hall into his office. He closed the door and offered Nikolai a seat in the black leather playpen couch that was positioned in front of the chief's desk. Chief Belknap asked what he could do for him.

Nikolai began and was clearly frustrated. "Sir, I am here about this Medal of Valor thing, I really want no part of this."

Chief Belknap smiled, put his hand on Nikolai's shoulder, and asked, "Why is that son? Your actions almost a year ago are amazing and worth discussion and frankly, worth recognition."

Nikolai looked the chief in the eye and continued. "Look, sir, I don't believe in receiving an award for taking the life of another human being, dirtbag or not. It's just not right."

The chief smiled. "Alright, Nikolai, I will tell you what, we need to do this ceremony. It's part of what we do, not only to celebrate what you did, but also to celebrate that you survived a violent attack. But it's more than that. It's a dog and pony show for the local business owners with the Police Action Committee. This event raises funds for the department and helps us acquire new equipment that we may not have been able to afford otherwise. So, I propose this, show up, take the award, shake hands, and talk about what happened with folks, then before you leave, hand the award back to me, and I will lock it away until such a time that you decide you'd like it. Can you do this for the department, son?"

Nikolai understood what the chief was saying. It made sense to him at this point. He nodded. "Yes sir, I will do my bit. You can hold on to whatever is given. If this will help the department, you can count on me, sir."

The chief showed Nikolai out. Nikolai thanked the chief's secretary and took the elevator down to the lobby level, walked out the elevator, and returned to his car and made the journey to his police station, parked his car, and made his way inside.

He had plenty of time today, so he decided that he was going to warm up with a battery of running a mile, firing six rounds, and repeating this four times. He made the watch commander aware of what he was doing, then set up his gear. Nikolai removed his newly acquired Sig Sauer P-220 .45 handgun, four magazines, and his cleaning kit. He got tired of carrying that Smith and Wesson model 645 Semi-Automatic handgun. Damn thing was accurate, but way too heavy. The Sig was much lighter because it had an alloy frame and was an inch shorter in barrel length. He was still waiting on the holster to arrive from Safari Land so he could get qualified with the weapon and carry it.

The indoor range was totally secure, so all he

needed to do was exit the station side door, run his mile, use his key to get back in the building, then unlock the range to get in as well. This was something he timed and kept track of. His best time was a seven minute mile, and every time, he hit his mark all six times, center mass. Today he was going to tax himself a little further. He wanted a six-minute mile flat and was going to hit the target center mass with three shots, then hit the head of the target with three rounds. Nikolai loved to challenge his physical abilities regularly, but also his breathing techniques in live shooting scenarios because one never knows when something like this may happen again.

He hung a sign on the range door that said "Range is in use" and stretched before his run. He walked out the front door and began running westbound on First Street. He picked up the pace as he ran northbound on Maclay, which was uphill. He made it to Third Street and turned right and headed eastbound and made it to Brand Boulevard and turned right, now heading southbound back to First Street and kicked it into high gear. He looked at his watch and realized he was almost at six minutes, so he picked up his pace. He arrived back at the station, unlocked the door, and ran to the range. He made it in six minutes and ten seconds. *Not good enough*, he thought to himself. He got to the range table and fired three rounds at the target's chest, then three at the head, hitting his mark every time. One could hardly tell he hit the target with three rounds in each location.

Nikolai ran back to the side door of the station and began his route all over again, this time picking up the pace even faster. He returned to the station in just under six minutes this time but could feel his heart racing. He opened the side door, jogged to the range, and reloaded the Sig Sauer, took three slow breaths, calming himself and squeezed off the six rounds. He again hit his mark perfectly. The third lap was easier. He had found his stride and made it back in five minutes and fifty seconds, relaxed his breathing, and executed the battery of shots, once again hitting his mark flawlessly.

He ran out of the station once again, now making his fourth mile and really pushing himself this time. He returned to the station in five minutes and forty seconds and ran to the range door. He again calmed his breathing and slowed his pulse and decided to change up the shooting battery. He unloaded the Sig Sauer with his left hand, placed the weapons barrel between his legs keeping an eye on the target, and slid the fourth loaded magazine into the weapon. Then, with his left hand, he fired with his left arm only, simulating that he had injured his right and now with the weak hand, fired the battery of rounds first at the chest and the last three at the target's head.

To his surprise, he missed two out of three rounds aimed at the head, grazing the silhouette. Not bad he thought, but decided he was going to simulate this regularly. Perfect practice makes perfect, he thought. He thought to himself how the weapon was so smooth out of the box. He also loved how there was no safety for the weapon, just a decocking lever. Having grown up around firearms, he always felt that a safety on a weapon, especially a side arm, would be nothing but trouble in a hostile situation. He had read so many reports of officers being in shootings and either getting themselves wounded, or killed because they drew a weapon with the safety on and didn't react quickly enough to make the weapon ready to fire. He wasn't going to be found in that position!

CHAPTER
FIFTEEN

Nikolai policed up his brass, took his side arm apart, cleaned it quickly and thoroughly, and returned all of his goodies to his locker. He then went to the gym and spent the next two hours training. When completed, he made himself a protein drink, took some amino acids, and then got in the shower. He had forty-five minutes before roll call. While getting his final prep work done, Sergeant Maddox approached him in the locker room. Maddox spoke at nearly a whisper so only Nikolai could hear. "Drew, there is a ride-along in the lobby, actor guy. Wants to ride along in order to get some experience as a cop for some show he has coming up or some shit. You willing to take him out with you?"

Nikolai laughed out loud, then asked, "Why me, Sarge?"

Maddox whispered again, "Because, you are a good sport, and the rest of these knuckleheads will just tell me to pound sand. Come on, help this guy out."

Nikolai agreed, smiling at the sergeant as he finished getting in uniform. Maddox walked into the lobby and met with the actor. He informed him that the officer taking him on the ride along would be out shortly, handed him a clipboard and some paperwork to fill out and sign. "Have this ready for the officer when he comes to get you."

Roll call was over, and Nikolai set up his unit first and then went to retrieve the guy in the lobby. He was hoping it wasn't some jamoke, but someone he could get along with and actually share some quality conversation with. As he walked into the lobby, he noticed the man standing there. He turned to face Nikolai, and he recognized him immediately; he was an A-List actor known for gangster roles he had portrayed.

We will simply refer to him as R. L. Nikolai shook his hand and introduced himself, and R. L. smiled and spoke. "Thank you for your time, Sir, I mean Mister Drew. I appreciate it."

Nikolai corrected him. "You can call me Nikolai, Nik, fuckhead, but not Mister Drew. You say that, and I am looking around for my pops, get me?" R. L. agreed. Nikolai held the door and escorted him around the station.

As they approached the break room, he asked R. L. if he wanted some coffee, which he declined. "I'm just anxious to drive around and learn a bit about your day to day life as a patrol cop."

Nikolai took a sip of his coffee and waived at R. L. and said, "Well, come along, do tell, what inspired you to want to go on a ride along?"

R. L. laughed. "Well, I am up for a role as a cop, and I need the inside track on what it's all about. My manager suggested I ride along with a police department for a few shifts and get a hang of the lingo and so forth. Your help is going to be very important."

Nikolai pointed out the back door to the waiting patrol car. He took in that it was a rather cold evening. R. L. looked at Nikolai and asked, "Are you going to bring a jacket along?"

Nikolai giggled. "No man, the chill keeps me awake."

He and R. L. both got in and sat down. R. L. put his seat belt on. Nikolai did not, and he pulled out of the parking space. Nikolai explained, "We're going out looking for arrests of any kind tonight. I particularly love narcotics, stolen vehicles, and gun busts. So, what I would like is for you to either stay in the car, or stand outside the door of the unit during a traffic or pedestrian stop, alright? I'll guide you the best I can as things evolve. Just stay by the car."

R. L. looked over at him and nodded and laughed. "Right on, can't wait."

Nikolai continued and held up four fingers with his right hand. "If I do this, it means we're code four, meaning everything is under control. At that point, you can ask me questions, fair enough?"

R. L. nodded in agreement again.

Nikolai went on. "Okay, last thing, if for some reason I get in a foot pursuit, you will stay with the car and wait for me to return or for my backup unit, get me. You do not follow along for any reason." Nikolai put the car in drive, pulled out of the patrol parking lot, grabbed the microphone, and put out, "1-Lincoln-27, show me 10-8 with a ride along." He put the microphone back in its holder, looked over at R. L., and with a half crazed look on his face said, "Fuck, I love this job!"

They drove around quite a bit. Nikolai was taking it all in, and R. L. asked him, "What are you looking for? You remind me of a Terminator by the way you are scanning all over the place."

Nikolai smiled. "It's hard to say. There are things that are not normal out here, a car driving with no lights on, a person walking in the shadows who darts when he sees us, could be anything, honestly, and I won't know till I see it. We're just hunting right now."

After an hour of driving around, Nikolai pulled into the 7-11 store located at 776 North Maclay, a regular coffee pit stop. He and R. L. got out of the car, and just that moment, a guy ran out of the door carrying a 12 pack of Coors Light.

In a flash of a second, Nikolai looked in the store to see the clerk lying on the floor and with a disgusted look on his face turned and began chasing the suspect, looked over his shoulder, and told R. L., "Stay with the car, mister!"

Nikolai had his eyes on the suspect as he ran diagonally across Glenoaks Boulevard from the 7-11, grabbed his handheld radio with his left hand. "1-L-27, be advised I am in foot pursuit of a 211 suspect male, Hispanic, 5'7", wearing plaid jacket running westbound on Glenoaks from North Maclay!"

Dispatch parroted the message and follow up with "Unit to back identify." Three other units put out the response. The suspect turned northbound, still running at full speed.

Nikolai put out on his handheld radio again, "27, be advised, I am not northbound on Hagar from Glenoaks, units responding, set a perimeter north and east of my location, also send a unit to check on the store clerk. He was down as I began running."

Nikolai was closing the distance between him and the suspect, Nikolai yelled at him, "Alright, fucker, stop running, or this is gonna get ugly, you hear me!" Nikolai went from being 100 feet behind to about 50. The suspect felt him gaining on him and threw the beer down. He then jumped on a 14 foot chain link fence that surrounded a school playground, scaled it, and as he went over the top, he dropped the 14 feet. Just as he hit the ground, Nikolai hit the fence and heard a tremendous snap, like the crack of a two by four piece of wood. Nikolai was now face to face with the suspect on the opposite side of the fence. The suspect's face was sheet white, his mouth wide open, and shrieking in pain.

"Fuck me, ese, I broke my leg!"

Nikolai looked down and observed the man's left leg dangling, swaying free, the foot was about two inches off the ground. It was obvious by the way the foot was swaying that he had snapped the bones in the calf clean in half, the fibula and tibula. Jumping off a fourteen-foot-tall fence in the cold night air was obviously the perfect scenario for a break such as this. Nikolai got back on his handheld radio. "Units be advised, I am code 4, control. I need an ambulance at my location, North Hagar just North of Glenoaks, I have a male about nineteen years of age with what appears to be a broken fibula and tibula. Can you also send a unit with bolt cutters to my location, I am going to need assistance opening the gate here in order to gain access to where the suspect is currently standing."

Dispatch responded, "Roger 27, advising paramedics now, unit to assist 27 identify."

Sergeant Maddox barked over the radio, "1-L-30 en route."

Within moments Sergeant Maddox arrived. He

exited his unit and went to the trunk retrieving his bolt cutters. He approached, shaking his head, "Go get your unit and ride along, I'll cut the gate open. This is one for the books, kid!"

Nikolai jogged back to the 7-11, and found Officer Fabriovetti with the clerk taking his statement and R. L. standing next to his unit patiently.

R. L. asked, "What happened, that sounded interesting over the radio?" Nikolai laughed and motioned him inside the 7-11. He got a cup of coffee for himself and the sergeant and again asked R. L. if he wanted one, which he declined.

He looked at R. L. and laughed. "So, what we have here is a beer run, typically a petty theft under 484 of the penal code.

However, because Joe shit, the rag man that ran from me, knocked the clerk down physically, it is now a robbery under 211 of the penal code because he used force during the commission of the crime. Now, here is where it gets interesting. When we get back over to where knucklehead is, who by the way tried to pull a Spiderman, scaled a fence and snapped his lower leg in half, we're going to check dumbass's pockets to see if he has any cash. If he doesn't, now we can add Burglary under 459 of the penal code because it shows he entered the building with the intent to commit a crime, get it?"

R. L. looked at him and shrugged his shoulders. "You're gonna have to explain that again when you have a moment in English. I have no clue what you just said."

Nikolai looked at R. L. with a confused look on his face, then at the clerk and Fabriovetti. "You alright, young man?"

The clerk smiled and said in his Indian accent, "He just pushed me down as he ran out of the store, I am okay."

Fabriovetti looked at Nikolai and said, "I'm almost done getting the statement and I'll try to get a copy of the security footage as well. I'll get you the info as soon as I am done here." Nikolai put two dollars on the counter for the coffee, patted Fabriovetti on the back, and thanked him.

He handed a coffee to R. L.. "Hold on to this for the Sarge please. Let's get back over there." As they pulled up, the ambulance was just arriving. The suspect was crying, eyes watering pretty wildly. Nikolai and R. L. got out of the unit. Nikolai took the cup of coffee from R. L. and handed it to Sergeant Maddox. Maddox leaned in and whispered, "This kid's pretty fucked up. Looks like he snapped the fibula and tibula clean."

Just then the paramedics walked up and assessed the suspect. The female of the two addressed Nikolai and Maddox. "This guy snapped this thing clean, we're gonna get a stretcher, but were going to need your help to get him onboard. It's not going to be pretty."

The male paramedic wheeled the stretcher over and placed it next to the suspect. Nikolai spoke to the suspect. "What's your name?"

The suspect looked at him with fear on his face. He was still in pain and said stutteringly, "Joaquin Rivera."

Nikolai looked at him compassionately and spoke in a low and calm voice. "Okay Joaquin, I am not talking to you as a cop, just someone who's trying to help you right now, you understand?"

Joaquin looked at him with tears in his eyes and said, "Yes sir."

Nikolai put his hand on his shoulder and said, "Okay, we're going to get you on this stretcher, nice and slow. It may hurt a bit, but I want you to hold on to my shoulder as tight as you want as we help you move onto this thing. Okay, on three." Nikolai and the female paramedic carefully braced the leg as the suspect sat on the stretcher.

He lay back, and as they all worked together to swing the leg onto the stretcher with him, he let out a bloodcurdling scream that was deeply unsettling. It triggered a visceral response from R. L., who had never witnessed such a thing. The look on R. L.'s face was flushed, like he was about to become physically ill.

They placed the gurney on in the ambulance. Nikolai checked the suspect Joaquin's pockets for his wallet, weapons, and for any cash and found nothing but the wallet with his ID, but no cash. That cinched up the burglary additional charge with the robbery. No doubt the District Attorney would drop one for the other, but they would let that get settled in the courtroom. Nikolai called into dispatch to run the subject in the system for warrants. While waiting for the return, he turned to Sergeant Maddox for consultation.

"Well, Sarge, he's clearly not going anywhere. He will be at the hospital for some time. The question is, do you want to eat it and take him into custody or write the paper and let detectives put together a warrant for another time.

Sergeant Maddox laughed. "You already know the answer to that, kid. We are not buying this dipshit's medical bills. Kick him and let Dick's write the warrant later. Great job however. Get the paper written and get back in the field, will ya!"

Nikolai released the subject to the paramedics and decided to stop back at the 7-11 store on Maclay. Fabriovetti was still there talking with the clerk, so they stopped. Nikolai and R. L. exited the vehicle, Nikolai got another cup of coffee and got the details from Fabriovetti.

"Apparently your douchebag came in, walked around for a few minutes. The clerk noticed he was acting strange and moved out from behind the counter. He noticed the suspect grab the 12 pack and start to run for the front door, so he stepped in the way and told him to drop the beer. The suspect grabbed him with his right arm that was free, threw him at the counter, and ran out the door. He fell to the ground, and that is when he saw you give chase. Here is his info for the report and the statement on the back." Nikolai thanked him and motioned for R. L. to head to the patrol unit.

As they drove off, R. L. looked at Nikolai with wide open eyes and said, "Dude, you are something else. You get all hyped up in this thing, and with a flip of a switch, you are kind as can be to the same douchebag that robbed the liquor store! How do you do that?"

Nikolai paused for a moment and responded, "I think it's instinctive. There came a moment when the dirtbag became a victim himself, albeit a victim of his own stupidity, but a victim just the same.

"I became empathetic to his circumstance and chose to calm him down and let him know that we were there to look out for him, even though we had to deal with his being a bonehead."

They pulled up to the station and went into the report room where Nikolai quickly wrote the crime and arrest report giving all the details about the incident and subsequent release due to the extent of the injury. It was now two in the morning, and Nikolai walked R. L. back out to the police parking area and asked cordially, "It's been a hell of a night, do you wanna call it a day, or are you in it for the entire shift? No pressure, it's your call." Nikolai was hoping he would take off. This whole taking a civilian for a ride along was a bit taxing.

R. L. smiled and told him, "Hell no, I am good to go. This has been very informative and frankly, entertaining."

They entered the patrol unit, and R. L. buckled up his seat belt just as Nikolai put the vehicle in drive, as they hit the street again, Nikolai picked up the mic once again and said, "1-L-27 is 10-8." They headed down Brand Boulevard to San Fernando Road and headed west into Pacoima. They hit Van Nuys Boulevard and turned left, and Nikolai turned off the unit's lights and flipped a switch on his control panel that also deactivated his unit's brake lights, which allowed them to drive around less visible. Nikolai looked over at R. L. and told him, "We're heading into the projects, brother, so keep an eye out. They really don't like us over here, and most patrol officers don't drive around here for fear of taking bottles, rocks, or worse."

R. L. looked at him and in a high voice said, "Worse, whaddaya mean, WORSE!"

Nikolai laughed. "Relax, man, they don't shoot at black and whites that often."

R. L. exclaimed, "That often!"

Nikolai turned onto Lehigh Ave. into the middle of the territory claimed by "Pacoima Trece" a gang linked to La Eme, better known as the Mexican

Mafia. This project was well known for drug sales, people driving in from everywhere to buy a dime bag of meth, coke, or heroin. As they pulled closer to Carl Street, six young men saw the police unit and ran in all directions. Nikolai parked the car, and one of the young men ran right toward him. Nikolai had not called out the stop yet. He grabbed the young man and threw him against the unit. R. L. was now out of the passenger side looking all around and in his head. He had no fucking clue what he was looking around for, or what he was going to do if he saw it!

Nikolai put the young man in an arm bar, and as he patted him down whispered, "Rico, what the fuck are you running from." He found out quickly, as he reached into Rico's right front pocket. He found three baggies tied tight each with two white rock substances consistent with that of methamphetamine in them.

Nikolai had dealt with Rico before, whose real name was Rollo Tomasi, but he liked to go by Rico, because it sounded tougher. He was just about to put the cuffs on him for possession for sales when dispatch called out, "1-L-27, respond to the area of First Street and Hubbard regarding a possible pedestrian versus train."

Nikolai mumbled under his breath, "Fuck me! Well, Rico, today is your lucky day, I am not bustin' you for possession for sales today, but, cabron, you owe me one, you understand." Not a peep out of Rico, so Nikolai tweaked the arm bar a little harder and asked again in his low raspy voice, "You owe me one, comprende, amigo?"

Rico squealed, "Yes, man, yes, fuck, thank you, okay!"

Nikolai released him and at the same time removed his stainless steel Spyderco knife from his pocket and cut the bags open and dumped the rocks onto the ground and crushed them with his boots, making sure there was nothing to salvage. He looked at Rico and told him, "Get the fuck outta here, Rico. I just saved you a year in the can. Remember, fucker, you owe me one."

Nikolai and R. L. got back in the car. He turned on the lights and activated the brake light disconnect and sped to the location he was dispatched to. R. L. looked at him smiling like a cheshire cat. "What the fuck just happened, and what did you whisper to him?"

Nikolai told him a little excited, well, we had a felony arrest of a little fucker I have dealt with a lot. He just got a hall pass because we got dealt a pedestrian versus train, which means a dead guy or gal. This takes priority. I whispered in his ear that he owed me a favor, and he knows it's a big one."

In a matter of less than three minutes they arrived at the location. The train was stopped completely blocking every street from Brand to Maclay to Hubbard, which was a disaster because commuters were going to need to get through these major arteries to get to work in the next couple of hours. That meant they needed to move quickly. When they arrived on the scene, Nikolai activated his overhead amber lights and parked his unit at the cross arms, which were still down flashing and the bell ringing. He looked at R. L. and told him, "Stick with me, but don't say anything, just follow along."

The locomotive was about a quarter mile west of Hubbard, the direction the train was traveling on the railroad tracks that paralleled Truman Street. Nikolai and R. L. walked down the tracks and observed the engineer of the train walking toward them with a flashlight. R. L. tripped and fell. Nikolai stopped to help and observed next to R. L. the bloody upper torso of a body with one arm and no head. It was a bloody mess. He helped R. L. up, and it was then that R. L. realized what he tripped over.

R. L. exclaimed, "Is that what I think it is."

Nikolai commented, "Yes, don't look at it man." They kept walking.

The engineer walked up and told Nikolai, "The guy looked right at the train as it approached and leaped in front, man, stupid fool, I performed protocol and hit the brakes, and here we are.

Nikolai looked at the engineer with sympathy in his eyes. "I get it man, these are not fun for anyone. How many cars are you pulling?"

The engineer, shaking his head, replied, "110.

This is a hot mess. We have to stop everything until this is dealt with."

Nikolai asked him to get his credentials so that he could file a report. The engineer walked back toward the train to get the information. Nikolai walked back toward his unit and got on his handheld radio. "27 to 1-L-30, can you meet me at my location, Hubbard near First Street please?"

Sergeant Maddox replied immediately, "27, I am already here, standing by."

Nikolai picked up the pace with R. L. returning to where the cars were parked, and as they came across the dismembered torso, R. L. stopped, looked down, and realized that this is what he tripped over. A sudden wave of nausea came over him, and he turned his head and began to vomit profusely. Nikolai paused and put his hand on his shoulder and said empathetically, "Yeah, I get it man, it's a lot to take in. Come on, keep movin'." They made it back to Hubbard and met the sergeant, who was parked next to his unit.

Maddox smiled. "Well, there, you look like you could use some water, or a Jack and Coke!" and handed R. L. a bottle of water he had in his unit. Maddox was a Vietnam era Marine so none of anything much bothered him. He went on speaking with Nikolai, "You gotta get this unfucked, and I mean quick, mister. Traffic is gonna become a shit-show right quick and in a hurry if you don't! You have a plan?"

Nikolai smiled. "I always have a plan, Sarge, you know that. I have the conductor getting me all his credentials and his BNSF contact info and where to ship the report. You already notified the coroner, and I am about to identify remains and clear the tracks of them after I document and photograph them so I can get this train on its way, sound good?" he said in his best Marine Corps impression.

Maddox gave Nikolai a sadistic grin. "You shoulda been a Marine, son, God dammit, you are squared away! Make it so."

Nikolai told R. L. to stay with the unit while he went about the mess of dealing with the remains. He put on some thick rubber elbow-high gloves and got the Instamatic camera he carried with him out of his war bag, which was all neatly placed in the trunk of his cruiser. He went about his business of looking under the train for missing body parts. Fortunately, there were none beneath the train, just along the right side of the train and all within about fifty yards of one another.

The conductor provided him with all his information, and Nikolai carefully documented it all on a three by five inch interview card, as well as the BNSF incident number and information where to forward the report. He dismissed the conductor who quickly got the train moving, all within twenty minutes of Nikolai's arriving on scene. Nikolai noted where he found all the body parts with photographs and measurements, but was unable to locate the head of the victim. This was puzzling. He looked all along the train tracks to no avail. He finally started getting creative and decided to look over fences on the south side of the tracks, the opposite side of where the train had hit the subject. The hunch paid off. He looked into an open dumpster at the far west end of the Arco Station which was at the northwest corner of Hubbard and Truman, and there it was, face down in a bunch of trash! He photographed the location and went about the disgusting task of climbing into the trash can to retrieve the bloody mop. He climbed out of the dumpster with the head in hand and made his way over to the north side of the tracks and lay the mop with the other bodily remains. He then started sifting through the remains of the pants of the subject in an attempt to find a wallet or identification. There was none, and it appeared that the poor soul was homeless and smelled of alcohol. The head was intact, but the face was a bit battered from the collision with the train, Nikolai did not recognize the man. Unlike the coroner's investigator, he arrived within an hour of being called; must have been a slow night. Investigator Winslow was getting the stretcher and body bag out of the van and made his way toward Nikolai. They had worked together before. Winslow smiled cordially at Nikolai. "Good evening to you, Officer Drew." Nikolai returned the gesture and led

Winslow to the remains.

They lit them up with flashlights, and Winslow gave Nikolai a blank look and said, "Well, you don't disappoint, Officer Drew. You always make my job easy. Any special instructions for me on this one? Do we know who he is?"

Nikolai shrugged his shoulders. "Sadly no, sir, no identification whatsoever, and I scoured the area."

Winslow told him, "Not to worry. I'll print him and figure it out as soon as possible. Would you mind helping me with the heavy parts, and you can be on your way."

Nikolai handed the coroner's investigator a copy of the field interview card with the LAPD incident number, Nikolai's info, as well as the BNSF information he had acquired, and he helped the coroner place the parts of the deceased man into a body bag. They lifted the bag onto the gurney, and Nikolai even assisted the coroner in loading it up into the van.

Nikolai removed the bloody rubber gloves from his hands, wadded them up inside out and placed them in the back seat of his unit for disposal once he arrived at the station.

He and R. L. loaded up into the police car, and Nikolai drove them back to the station so he could write up the report. On the way back R. L. was chatting. "You, sir, have one fucked-up job, but I have learned a lot today. Do you mind if I ask what days you're off, and would you mind if I rode along with you again?"

Nikolai laughed. "Be my guest. Perhaps you can tell me more about you on the next ride along." R. L. laughed and agreed. Nikolai dropped R. L. off at the front of the police station so he could get to his car and get home. He pulled into the station and went about writing up the report, laying out the details of the unknown male suicide by train. The report was completed in less than an hour, including the evidence report and photographs booked into evidence. He turned everything in and while pouring a cup of coffee, Sergeant Maddox walked in the back of the station.

Maddox barked at Nikolai, "Where is your girlfriend, mister?"

Nikolai laughed. "I dropped him off on the way in. Report's in your inbox, Sarge. Let's hope the rest of the shift is peaceful. shall we?"

Putting the request to the law enforcement gods seemed to work because the rest of the shift was quiet, Nikolai took his unit to the top of the parking lot of Holy Cross Hospital, his favorite spot to watch the sunrise over the valley. He sat on the hood of his car and sipped coffee and basked in the joy of watching the transition of city lights washed out by the sun seeing the Valley as beautiful instead of the wretched hive of criminal activity that Nikolai experienced daily.

His mind shifted to the double murder investigation and all of the information that was yet to be revealed in this case and found himself immersed in what the complexities would turn up. All that aside, he felt blessed to wear the badge and enjoyed striking fear into the hearts of men who strike fear in the hearts of men. It felt good to him to be the seventh generation in the line of centurions.

CHAPTER
SIXTEEN

The graveyard shift ended, and Nikolai found himself waiting for Detective Bedo to arrive at the police station that morning. He sat at Bedo's desk, leaning back in his chair with his feet on the detective's desk. He nodded off and found himself awakened by the heavy jarring of Detective Bedo shaking the chair where he was sitting. Bedo laughed as he barked at Nikolai, "Get the fuck out of the captain's chair mister!"

Nikolai got up, yawned and looked at his watch. It was 0845. Bedo was late. He looked at the bright-eyed detective, who was taking a sip from his typical Big Gulp Coke from 7-11, no doubt his first stop before driving into the station house. Nikolai sarcastically commented to Bedo, "Jesus, man, you scared the shit out of me."

Bedo replied sarcastically, "Well, that's what you get sleeping at a man's desk!"

Nikolai gives him a sarcastic look. "This double murder is really under my skin. Do you have anything new on the pager warrant?"

Bedo gave Nikolai an evil grin. "Yes, as a matter of fact, I do. Let's go for a drive." That was Bedo's code for not wanting to share anything in public that might spoil the case.

They got into Detective Bedo's unmarked unit and drove out of the parking lot. As they drove, Bedo began the complicated tale. "Well, here is what I know so far. This guy has been getting pages for the last year and a half from a ton of numbers, but two stand out. One is an 818 number from the Van Nuys District Attorney's Office, 103 up until about three months ago. Then, suddenly, the number changes to the San Fernando District Attorney's Office. I know these numbers. They are to the main desk, and the calls would get transferred from there."

Nikolai was really puzzled. "So, this guy was like an informant to the D.A. or something?"

Bedo slapped the back of Nikolai's head. "I think it's much more complicated. There are no working cases with this guy or the swap meet. I think, my boy, that what we have is a relationship between the victim and a female Deputy District Attorney. I have a contact in Human Resources and am going to find out which female DAs have relocated to the San

Fernando Office around this time period. Imagine what we can uncover!"

Bedo returned to the station parking lot and backed his unit in and reminded Nikolai, "Remember, kid, nothing about what I tell you to anyone. This is getting quite interesting. I will keep you in the loop as information comes in."

Nikolai saluted the detective, got out of the unmarked unit, and walked around the outside of the police station to the lot where his '69 El Camino was parked. As he made his way to the El Camino, his pager went off. It was the ex again. He decided to go back into the police station and call her rather than waiting to get home. This way he could cut the conversation short if it went sideways.

He dialed the number pressing 9 first for an outside line. Tina answered the phone. "Hello," she said emotionally.

Nikolai responded, "Hey, Tina, just got your page. I'm still at work, so this may be a short conversation."

Tina said solemnly, "I understand, Niki. It's about Eddy. He's conscious. I just got word that he is paralyzed from the waist down. He is not able to move his arms much. They have him in a special traction device so that he can't move his head. They are hoping the nerve damage isn't permanent. Honestly, I have no idea what all that means, just that it's bad. Anyway, his girlfriend is there with him, and other visitors are now able to see him."

Nikolai was at a loss for words. He didn't really know how to feel or what to say. "I understand, I will make some time to get down there as soon as I can."

Tina was silent for a moment. "Will you let me know when you are going? I will try to be there at the same time. It would be nice to see you again."

Nikolai got a weird feeling in his stomach. The last thing he wanted was to get involved in another relationship with her, so he had to make sure he was direct if and when he saw her. "Sure, I will let you know. I have to go. The sergeant needs me. I will check back with you soon."

He hung up, and just then his pager went off again. This time he didn't recognize the number. He picked up the phone again, dialed 9 and dialed the number that came over the pager, a 909 area code. A gruff male voice answered, "Walker Hayes."

Nikolai laughed. "Hey, fucko, what is goin on?"

Walker was brief. "Well, brother, Eddy is conscious. Doctors are saying he's paralyzed and say it's too early to tell how bad or how permanent it's gonna be. A few of us are gonna go by to see him around four o'clock, for moral support. You free to meet us down there? You know where he is, right?"

Nikolai thought for a moment. "Yes, man. I know where. I will find a way to make it. You can count on me."

Walker replied, "You're a good man, Niki. See you later today."

They hung up. Nikolai stood up and retreated to the El Camino. He paused for a moment, thinking of what the next move was going to be. He got in the car, turned the key in the ignition, and started the car. He let the engine warm up for a minute or two and realized the next move was to head out to Riverside, take a nap at his mother's place, then shower up, head to Loma Linda to see Eddy, see the gang and go back to the valley to suit up for work. This wouldn't be the first time he had to function on little or no sleep, and it probably wouldn't be the last. He turned on the radio, grabbed his Dire Straits tape, and fast forwarded it to "Sultans of Swing"!

As he drove toward the freeway, he was immersed in the lyrics and started singing along with the tune. The energy he felt from the guitar riff and the lyrics always gave him a great feeling!

As he headed down the eastbound 210, the guitar riffs of Mark Knopfler relaxed him as he headed home to Riverside.

No one was home when Nikolai arrived at his mother's place on Saffron Court. The cul de sac was a source of peace for Nikolai. Every time he pulled onto Saffron Court from Mac Arthur and California, he was reminded of all the years of hanging out working on street rods with his high school buddies! The neighbors loved having the knuckleheads hanging around: Lou, F.J. Martin, Louie, Bill, Earl Bartel, Johnny B, Craig, and H.P. and of course Jake,

Hassler, and Walker Hayes! They were roughnecks, but a goodhearted bunch. Nikolai parked the '69 El Camino at the curb in front of the duplex, locked it up, and walked to the back half of the unit where he unlocked the door, walked in, and lay on the spare bed where he often slept. His mother always had a spare room, Oreo cookies, and milk waiting for Nikolai's next visit.

Three o'clock came way too fast. The alarm went off, and Nikolai sprung to his feet and got in the shower. Within twenty minutes he was dressed and ready to go. He thought about calling someone to let him know he was on his way, but honestly, he hoped no one but Eddy would be there. This visit was about him, after all, not a homecoming.

Nikolai arrived at Loma Linda Hospital in Redlands and made his way to the Intensive Care Unit where Eddy was likely located. He addressed the charge nurse who pointed to where Eddy was resting. He painted a smile on his face and walked in to find Eddy lying on the bed, wearing a steel halo fastened around the top of his head and rods leading down to a harness that was on his shoulders. For a moment Nikolai saw himself in the bed. His shooting could have easily left him like this, or worse, he could have been killed. He had never told anyone of the circumstance he himself had dealt with. He was not proud of what had happened and simply didn't want the attention, good or bad.

He snapped out of his deep thought. He started to see the others in the room, Eddy's mom, his sister (who Nikolai had dated a couple times before he even knew Eddy) Eddy's girlfriend who was sitting in a chair with a solemn look on her face, and damn, Tina was standing next to her consoling her. The emotions of the moment were subsiding as he assessed all of the people of the past, the most sincere of the bunch being Eddy's mother. She looked woeful and weary. After all, her son was in a critical and devastated position, his body broken and no one really knowing was to come of him.

Nikolai grabbed a chair and sat next to the bed with Eddy. He looked at him and smiled and said sarcastically, "Well, this a fine mess you've gotten yourself into!"

Eddy smiled. "Don't make me laugh, you idiot. Could turn me into a fuckin' vegetable! Thanks for coming, brother. I guess you heard all about it, yeah?"

Nikolai smiled, but the look in his eyes couldn't be dismissed. Eddy knew he was truly hurting for him. Nikolai thought for a moment and replied, "I heard the short story, I figure we will wait till you're out of this rig and bed, and you can tell me all about it over drinks, how's that?"

Eddy laughed. "That sounds like a winner, man. Did you drive all the way out here from Los Angeles?"

Nikolai nodded his head yes. "I drove to my

mom's place, took a nap, then headed here. I have to work tonight, but wanted to get here to see you."

Eddy looked at him with soulful eyes. "Much appreciated, Niki. It's been a revolving door here since yesterday when I was allowed friends as visitors."

Nikolai smiled. "That's what it's all about, man. In all seriousness, what can I do for you?"

Eddy told him to get closer. Nikolai lowered his head so he could hear Eddy whisper, "Get the soap opera the fuck outta here, will you please? Jesus, man, they are seriously causing me to wanna end it. You'd think I was dead for Christ's sake."

Nikolai burst into laughter as he sat back down! Eddy laughed. "Hey, fuckhead, I am serious!" Nikolai spent about an hour visiting with everyone and finally made his exit. As he walked out to his car, he was followed hastily by Tina. She was bandaged up and bruised from the rail accident, but she still looked like a naughty Sally Field, Nikolai thought to himself. He tried to ignore her, but she kept getting closer, finally reaching him a few cars away from where he had parked the El Camino yelling, "God damnit, Nikolai, would you stop for a minute and talk to me?"

Nikolai hung his head and stopped walking. All he could think to himself was this was shit he didn't need. Tina stood about 5'2", a full foot shorter than the musclebound Nikolai Drew. She had an hourglass frame, long brown hair, green eyes, and pouty lips.

She seemed sweet enough, but this godforsaken woman had more baggage than a New York Bound 747 passenger plane; she had cheated on her former husband, Nikolai, and all the other men she had been with. Nikolai's disdain for her ran deep, but he remained polite. Tina gave him a hug and told him how nice it was to see him. Nikolai looked down and said, "Well Tina, you too." His gag reflex was kicking in, if he were Pinocchio, his nose would have grown two feet from that whopper!

Tina's attention turned to the '69 El Camino, and she pointed at it as she walked over toward it. "I see you still have this thing. It looks good with the center lines. Are these the same tires and wheels off your '67 Chevelle?"

Nikolai smiled and nodded yes. Tina continued. "It was sure a stroke of luck that my dad found this for you after your '69 Chevy pickup got stolen." Nikolai's frustration started to come out. This was a big source of frustration for him. "Yeah, lucky, after trading my perfectly good Camaro to your brother for that beat to hell truck, then spending countless amounts of money on her just so she could get stolen out in front of the condo you were staying in Riverside. One more money pit, not including the monumental shit storm you drove me into while we lived together." He raised his hands in frustration. "Ya know what, I'm good, love your dad, love the El

Camino, and glad I am in a good place these days. I have to split. I have a long drive back to L.A."

Tina's eyes were watering. "We both have our story, Niki. I still think there was more good than bad. Hey, I am living in Pasadena now, literally three doors down from David Lee Roth. We should have dinner or something soon, let bygones be bygones?"

Nikolai unlocked the driver's door of the El Camino and opened it. He smiled at Tina. "I have no issues with you, Tina. Let's just leave it how it is, let sleeping dogs lie to coin another cliché. Nice seeing you." He got in the car, shut the door, and simultaneously started the El Camino. He didn't allow her to warm up, he just put it in Reverse, and backed out of the parking space. He waved at her as he drove off and left the radio silent for a bit. The drive was gonna be a long one. He got to the spot where the 10 freeway met the 91 interchange. He was debating which direction to go, Riverside for a brief visit, or just take the 10 freeway toward Los Angeles. Just as he was about to head to L.A., his pager went off. He looked at it, praying it wasn't Tina. Thankfully, it was the back line to the Detective Bureau with a 16 after the number, meaning 16 David for Detective Bedo. He turned the car toward Riverside and figured he would stop at his mother's house so he could call in.

CHAPTER
SEVENTEEN

Nikolai stepped on the gas and managed to get to his mother's house in less than twenty minutes. He trotted into the house and dialed the number. Bedo answered, and Nikolai told him he called as soon as he could.

Bedo went on. "Well, kid, we have narrowed down the personnel changes at the D.A's office to two people. Guess who one of them is?"

Nikolai thought for a moment and laughed. "Please tell me it's Fancy Pants Lense!" (Lense Seaman was a patrolman who repeatedly got under everyone's skin because he was always running around telling everyone how bitchin' he is, kinda like the character in one of Barry Sadler's songs - Garet Trooper.)

Bedo laughed. "Give it a rest with that dipshit,

will ya. I am talkin about your friend, Deputy D.A. Chang."

Nikolai was now intrigued. "Who else?"

Bedo laughed. Another D.A. but not a person of interest. Word from on high is that Chang is extremely controversial and likes to play the victim card since her husband was murdered in the late '70s. She's also known for being a real climber, using any man or woman she can to get what she wants. So, we have some digging to do, seein' how this is all circumstantial at this point. We need to get something solid if we want to pin this on her."

Nikolai pondered that thought for a moment. Bedo barked over the phone, "You there? Don't forget, comin up this Friday is your big night, fucko, so get your acceptance speech ready."

Nikolai laughed. "Fuck me! Alright, I am in Riverside, and I have to work tonight. It's five o'clock and gotta get on the road. Catch ya later."

Nikolai hung up and got out of his mother's house. He started the El Camino and decided to stop off at Naugles on Magnolia by the Tyler Mall. He cruised down Magnolia and passed Tyler Avenue. He hit his left turn signal and turned onto Banbury Street and immediately pulled into the Naugles parking lot and stopped three cars back from the drive up window. It was at that moment that he flashed back to years ago riding in the passenger seat of Eddy's black 1979 Z/28 Camaro.

They were in this very drive thru line, the T-tops were off; it was two in the morning, and Eddy was driving Nikolai to get some food, Nikolai had left his '67 Chevelle at the Carl's Junior down the street where all the gear heads were parked. Cruising was still a thing, and they had relocated the cruise spot away from Market Street as Market was smack dab in the middle of the area where Riverside Police Department's station house was located. They wanted a steak and egg burrito so they teamed up to drive to Naugles. There was a car in front of them that for some reason wasn't moving. Eddy got a little impatient and gave two quick blasts on the horn.

The passenger and driver of the late '70s white Vega began flipping them off and slowly began driving forward, just slow enough that it took a few minutes for them to get to menu/speaker where they would order their food. The Vega finally moved forward, and Eddy ordered their usual steak and egg burritos and would go back to Carl's Junior where their buddies were waiting with beer. Eddy pulled forward, and the guys in the Vega were still being rather loud and flipping them a middle finger. Eddy got up in the seat out of the T-top and flipped the men off and told them, "Take your mom's car home before she grounds you bitches!"

Well, that didn't bode well. The attendant handed them their food, and they drove forward. While waiting for their order, a rather long-haired gangly gentleman in his 30s started walking toward Eddy's car, swinging a six-foot length of chain around and was sort of staggering. Nikolai couldn't make out what he was saying but recognized that this was going to end up with Eddy's Camaro taking a beating if he didn't do something and Eddy was way too close to the drive-up window to get out. Nikolai got out of the car and made his way to the gangly thirtysomething. It was obvious at this point that Nikolai was much bigger than the gangly assailant. Nikolai spoke directly to the man. "Look, brother, this is not a road you want to travel. Two things are gonna happen, I am gonna take that chain from you, and then it's gonna end up somewhere you aren't gonna like. So, pack up your shit and head home before you get hurt." By now, the other much shorter and heavier driver of the white Vega got out of the car and was walking toward Nikolai.

He was also a little drunk and barely uttered his threat, "You're gonna do what, Pretty Boy, bore us to death? There's two of us, and your little buddy is clearly not backin you up."

Nikolai clenched his right fist that was by his side and started to turn away. "You're right, you're right, fellas. Clearly you're much tougher than we are. I'm just gonna get back in the car and we will take off," The two drunk men were now feeling overly cocky and just as they started to lunge toward Nikolai, he closed the gap between them, grabbed the chain held by Captain Gangly, and punched the man across the bridge of his nose. The crack was rather loud, and the man fell to the ground, blood all over his face. Nikolai grabbed the chain and threw it over the fence into the Magnolia Drive-In area and started to move quickly toward the shorter, heavier driver of the Vega.

By now, Eddy was pulling out of the drive-thru and yelling at Nikolai to get in the car because the attendants had called the police. Nikolai checked on the gangly assailant to make sure he was going to be alright. He was moving, but in pain and had vomited all over himself. He got in the Camaro, and they sped off back toward Carl's Junior where they had quite a laugh over the entire incident, Nikolai spouting how Eddy's alligator mouth once again overrode his jaybird ass and Nikolai had to clean up!

Nikolai snapped out of it in time to see that two cars had moved forward. He moved up and got himself a Diet Coke for his drive to the Valley. He was thinking to himself how he hoped Eddy would be able to walk again and start some of the shit he was known for in the past. He paid his forty-five cents at the window, collected his large Diet Coke, and made his way down Magnolia to La Sierra Avenue, turned right, and then turned left onto Arlington Avenue. He cruised slowly past Crestlawn Cemetery and thought of his grandfather and grandmother who were buried there and proceeded around and down to Sixth Street.

He finally made it to Hamner Avenue and took that all the way to the 60 freeway and headed west, all the way to the 57 freeway, which eventually got him to the 210 freeway, a straight shot into Los Angeles. The two-hour drive was monotonous. He decided to go straight to the police station and get a workout in so he could relieve some of his pent-up frustration after that entire round-trip adventure. He always kept a workout bag behind the seat of the El Camino just in case. He pulled into the parking lot, grabbed the bag from behind the seat, secured the car, and walked into the back door of the police station. He got suited up and warmed up with some stretching before he began working his back. The entire workout was rather a blur. He was feeling an array of emotions dealing with the fact that he was seeing his friend lying in a hospital bed, helpless. He didn't know whether he should be pissed at him for being reckless or sad for the entire situation. He settled on feeling a little of both. Life is just like that though. One minute you're riding high. The next minute, you're facing a crazed gunman who is so desperate to get away, he will kill anyone in his way to do so. Then there was Tina. Her ability to send him packing on a guilt trip was absolutely ridiculous! Before he knew it, Nikolai was dripping in sweat and had literally exhausted himself hitting back, biceps, and abs literally back to back with no rest. He completed a two-hour workout in just over an hour. He decided to get in the shower, put his street clothes back on, and get something to eat.

It was now 8:45 p.m., so he decided to head over to the IHOP on Truman Street.

It had just opened, and he thought it would be a good time to check out the bill of fare. He pulled into the parking lot and backed his El Camino into the parking spot closest to the door. There weren't a lot of cars in the lot.

He walked in, and the hostess escorted him to a table, gave him a menu, and let him know a waitress would be right with him. He looked through the menu but remembered someone telling him that IHOP made a wicked plate of spaghetti and chili. For some reason that sounded like the thing to do, so he closed the menu and waited for a server. Almost immediately a woman walked over to the table and introduced herself as Kandee and asked if he would like to hear about some of the specials.

Nikolai looked up at the woman. She was tall in her flat, comfortable shoes, about 6 foot. She was slender and had her reddish brown hair up in a bun, and her name tag said the name, just like she said it, "Kandee." She was biting her pen as she gave him a wicked look.

He smiled and replied, "Um, no, Kandee, I would like an iced tea, and I am ready to order, I hear you folks have a wicked plate of spaghetti and chili that isn't on the menu. Is this true?"

The waitress thought about it for a moment. "Let me ask the cook, and I'll bring you back an iced tea."

The waitress walked over to the kitchen window and asked the cook, "Sir, do you have the ability to make spaghetti and chili. We have a guest that is requesting that?" He didn't hear the rest of the conversation, however. She returned to his table, iced tea in hand, and let him know that the cook could indeed prepare that for him.

Nikolai smiled. "Well, that is perfect. I will take that, thank you." She took the menu and walked away, looking back at Nikolai, biting her lip.

Nikolai was wearing jeans, sneakers, and a white t-shirt. The shirt was an extra large, but looked small because of the size of his frame. The waist of the shirt was loose because of his small waist, but the shoulders, chest, and arms were bulging through the material. The waist was loose enough that one couldn't see the .45 Sig Sauer tucked in the back of his pants. He added some Sweet 'n Low to his tea and shook his head in disbelief at the waitress name "Kandee."

While waiting for his food, a different waitress walked by and giggling asked him, "Are you married? My girlfriend Kandee was curious and didn't want to ask you herself. She's shy."

Nikolai looked around to see if he could see the tall waitress. She was nowhere to be seen. He held up his right hand and said, "Nope, not attached."

The girl scurried off, Nikolai was thinking to himself, *Good Lord, it's like I am back in high school, what next?*

Ten minutes went by, and Kandee brought a refill for Nikolai's iced tea. She had all the signs of a school girl in heat. She had her hand on her hip, she was flipping the hair that dangled by her ear, and asked casually, "I will have your meal out shortly, what is your name?"

Nikolai was smiling politely and responded, "Nikolai Drew."

Kandee went on. "Is that Russian?"

Nikolai was always flustered by this question, but responded politely just the same. "No, actually. The name originates in ancient Greece!"

Kandee laughed as she twirled her hair. "Really, Greece!"

Nikolai laughed again, almost sarcastically, "Yup, Ancient Greece, like a thousand years ago during the time of Marcus Aurelius."

Kandee walked away, laughing. "Marcus Aurelius, who the hell is that?"

Nikolai whispered under his breath, "Jesus, I am surrounded by a mental case!"

Moments later Kandee reappeared with a plate of spaghetti and chili and a fresh glass of iced tea and mentioned to Nikolai, "So, Nikolai, I love Greek food. If you are ever interested in going out, you know, for some Greek food, Nikolai. By the way, what do you do for a living?"

Nikolai smiled. "That sounds fun, Kandee. How should I let you know if I want to go out for some Greek food? I work in sanitation."

Kandee looked at Nikolai with a bewildered look on her face. "Sanitation?

Nikolai laughed and replied, "Yes ma'am, you know, I dispose of people's trash!"

Kandee rolled her eyes and, while looking around in an attempt to be cautious, handed Nikolai a folded up slip of paper. "This is my pager number and my home number, but please don't say anything to anyone. It's against company policy for us to date customers or fraternize in any way."

Nikolai smiled, put the piece of paper in his pocket, and began working on eating his pasta pondering the thought, what the hell was it with waitresses' attraction to him anyway! As he ate, his mind wandered back to this double homicide he had been working on. He was going to get ahold of the coroner that tipped him off to the DNA philosophy and see how difficult it was to get a sample of the stuff so he could test it against what was found at the crime scene. Nikolai finished and paid his check at the cash register and left a good tip for the waitress. It was now 2200 hours, so he headed to the police station and decided to use the massive dose of carbs from the spaghetti to push through a heavy workout before his shift began at 2345 hours.

Nikolai finished up the workout, showered up, and got suited up. Roll call concluded, and Nikolai set up his patrol unit with all his gear. He pulled out of the parking lot, and instead of driving to the 7-11 store at 146 Hubbard for a cup of coffee and conversation with Davinder, he turned the opposite direction headed to the coroner's office. The radio silence was deafening. It was going to be a quiet night, he thought. He pulled into the coroner's parking lot, parked, and made his way to the back door. He was hoping one of the late-night ghouls was around that may be able to answer a question or two about DNA. He knocked at the door rather loudly and waited a few moments. There was no response, so he rapped even harder this time.

A few moments went by, and when no one opened the door, he began to walk to his patrol unit. Suddenly, the back door of the building opened up, and an elderly woman poked her head out rather cautiously. She breathed a sigh of relief when she saw it was a police officer. She opened the door all the way and greeted Nikolai with her right hand out, "Hello, officer, what may I do for you?"

Nikolai shook her hand and introduced himself. "Hello, ma'am, Nikolai Drew, LAPD. I have a few questions for you, if you have a moment. What is your name, by the way?"

She smiled at Nikolai and said, "I'm Winny Corvelli, hun."

Nikolai smiled. "I've been working with Baxter Mane on the Papadopoulos double homicide case."

Winny walked Nikolai into her office and offered him a seat. Nikolai sat down, and Winny went through her files. "I have been here longer than anyone. Baxter is a great guy, but his knowledge is a little raw." She smiled and removed a file from her cabinet and continued. "What is it you need, love?" She opened the file.

Nikolai started chatting, hoping what he was about to say made sense to the elder investigator. "Well, this may sound crazy, but there were three different blood samples located at the scene. There were two found on the male victim."

Winny smiled. "Yes, I know, I discovered that. What is your question, hun?"

Nikolai continued. "Well, I was curious about how DNA can be collected? I have several subjects I am looking at that may be good for this murder. Can you tell me the best source of obtaining DNA from a suspect so that I can test it against the blood we found on the victim?"

Winny smiled again. "That is a great question, hun. The easiest way is to simply get a warrant!"

Nikolai laughed. "Yeah, well I don't have anything solid enough to allow a warrant. I have to be a little more, let's say creative."

Winny pondered. "Well, anything left in public that the person has drunk out of, or had in their mouth, like a cigarette for instance. Just as long as you saw them put it down and they had no expectation of privacy, meaning they abandoned it."

Nikolai stood up and shook Winny's hand. "That is what I was hoping for, Doc. Thank you for your help."

Winny escorted Nikolai to the rear door and let him out. "Come back anytime, Officer Drew." Winny said.

Nikolai had a clear path to finding something that may lead them to a suspect in this case. He pulled out his notebook and wrote the information down and returned it to his breast pocket. He couldn't wait to share the information he learned with Detective Bedo when he saw him the next morning.

CHAPTER
EIGHTEEN

Tuesday morning, when Detective Bedo arrived at the Detective Bureau at 0700 hours, no one was there yet, and he liked it that way. He didn't even turn on the lights, just the light at his desk top. He walked quietly to the break room and snuck a cup of coffee from the patrol division side of the building. He felt like a burglar, low-crawling in an attempt to avoid getting caught, even though he was merely trying to avoid having a conversation this early in the morning. He poured the cup of coffee, quietly, so quiet no one even heard him place the coffee pot back on the hot plate. He turned, walked down the hall toward the Detective Bureau. He made it to the hallway then turned into the bureau, and just when he thought he escaped clean, he felt a hand on his shoulder.

He stopped, his shoulders dropped as he held his

cup of coffee, and his head fell forward in defeat. "God damn it, Nikolai," he said in a low voice. "I swear to god, kid, you have the bedside manner of a chainsaw murderer. Keep it quiet and follow me to the dungeon. I don't want anyone knowing I'm here."

Bedo used his key to unlock the door into the Detective Bureau. Bedo went to his desk, and Nikolai went to his coffee area and made a pot of coffee. While he was doing so, he shouted out to Bedo, "You know, fucko, if ya just made your own pot of coffee, you wouldn't get caught up in patrol bullshit this early, and no one would ever see you."

Bedo had his feet up on his desk sipping his coffee and replied sarcastically, "Yeah, well I would have to wait ten fuckin minutes, and I'd be a grumpy fuck if I had to wait. Besides, what would you find yourself doing if I took away your job, Boot!"

Nikolai sat down next to Bedo's desk and smiled. Bedo barked at him, "It's way too god damn early for this shit, kid, spill."

Nikolai leaned forward and told him about his conversation with the coroner, "Last night I was bangin' this case around in my head, so I went by the coroner's office and spoke with Winny. She told me that if I want to narrow down who the suspect is, all I have to do is get something like a water bottle, a cigarette, or something with saliva or blood on it, and she can match it to what we found at the murder scene."

Bedo was still enjoying his coffee and laughed out loud. "Yeah, saliva or blood, how are you gonna do that without a warrant, genius, because we have nothing of substance that will justify a warrant."

Nikolai expounded, "Well, see, it's like this. Winny told me that if someone drops a water bottle, a cigarette, a pen, or anything that they abandon, there is no expectation of privacy, and I can collect it as evidence for testing. I merely have to have a clean chain of evidence on the item."

Bedo responded in a sarcastic tone, "Well, you better be careful here, fucko. You're fuckin' around in uncharted territory here. You fuck this up, and not only will you torch this very promising career you are embarking on, you might just get yourself prosecuted along the way or worse, killed! By the way, I heard about your ride along with that actor guy, R.L., that sounds like a total shit-show."

Nikolai replied, "He's actually a really cool guy. He had a lot of questions and liked my persona."

"Persona, don't get all sophisticated on me, Nancy! Anyway, Victor told me the guy really took a liking to you. Just don't get swooped in by these jugheads. Most of them live on another planet, okay."

Nikolai walked out, brushing Bedo off. "Yeah, yeah, don't get swooped in, these jugheads live on another planet. Got it, detective!"

Nikolai headed down the hallway. It was the end

of watch, after all, and he needed to get out of his uniform and head home. He walked into the locker room, and as he finished cleaning up his gear and getting into his street clothes, he was approached by reserve officer Victor Denofrio.

Denofrio walked up behind Nikolai and grabbed him under the armpits and tickled him. Nikolai spun around laughing and addressed the 5'6" reserve officer. "Victor, what the fuck is wrong with you, man!"

Victor laughed and exclaimed, "More than I can possibly share with you, brother. Hey, I got a call from R.L. this morning. Apparently he was truly impressed with you after riding with you."

Nikolai laughed. "Well, that was a wild shift. He got to see a lot, probably more than he expected."

Victor expounded, "Well, he told me he plans to ride with you again. Feels like you are the model he wants to use for the cop character he is getting ready for. He also had a great idea. Thought you should get into doing extra work, thinking it may lead to something cool for you. Well, I told him that you were already in the system with *Call the Cops* and had been for months but no love yet."

Nikolai laughed again. "All good, man. It really isn't my thing anyway."

Victor punched him in the shoulder again and shook it in pain. "Damn it, man, the pay is good, and who knows, you could end up getting a speaking role and get your SAG card or who knows. With your physique, you might even land some bodyguard gigs!"

Nikolai thought about that for a moment. "What the hell is a SAG card?"

Victor shook his head. "Screen Actors Guild, man. If you get a speaking role, you get to enter the guild. More exposure and even more work. Anyway, long and short of it is that he is going to put a word in for you personally."

Nikolai smiled with a wicked grin. "Fine, man. I remember what you said. If they call, don't fuck it up. They won't call again."

Victor laughed. "Well, you're a natural character. You will fit right in. What is going on with the councilman, anything new?"

Nikolai didn't want to stress him out with details. "Nothing yet. If something comes of that, I will let you know, but relax, I won't burn you."

The two men parted, and as Victor walked away he said loudly, "Remember, if they call you, don't fuck it up. You won't likely get a call back, and that would be a shame!"

As Nikolai started to head toward the back door of the police station he heard the shriek of the chief's secretary come over the intercom speaker. "Officer Drew, please come to the chief's office. Officer Drew, please come to the chief's office."

Nikolai stopped, slumped his shoulders, his chin

dropped forward, and he ran his hand through his hair then turned slowly in defeat as he made his way down the long hallway to the chief's office. He walked up to the chief secretary's window and was alarmed when she wasn't sitting there. The chief was going through a filing cabinet. Chief Belknap noticed Nikolai and stopped what he was doing and approached the window. The chief smiled at Nikolai and said, "Hey kid, I am just makin sure you're coming to the dinner event on Friday. It's only a few days away, don't let me down."

Nikolai smiled. "I will be there, Chief, I assure you."

The chief barked back, "Bring a date. It's gonna be a good time."

Nikolai walked away and headed to the parking lot. *A date!* he thought to himself. He didn't have time to take anyone on a date. His mind flashed for a moment toward his ex, Tina, then he shook his head thinking to himself again, *Don't you even think about it, dipshit.*

He unlocked the driver's door of the El Camino and plopped down in the driver's seat. He closed the door, turned on the ignition, and thought pensively for a moment. He turned on the radio, and the band Queen was singing the song "Hammer to Fall." Music always got Nikolai in a good mood. He put the El Camino into drive, tapped the steering wheel, and pulled out of the parking lot. He pulled to the intersection of Brand Boulevard and Truman and looked catty-corner to his left and saw the Bank of America at the corner and remembered he was in need of some cash. He pulled into the parking lot, got out of his car, and walked inside. He hated Automated Teller Machines. He always preferred that human contact. He stood in line, thinking of the song he was just listening to, holding his wallet and checkbook in his hands. There were several people in line, but he didn't mind. He looked up and realized that the person in front of him was that waitress from IHOP. He was pondering trying to remember her name. He turned out of her view in hopes that she wouldn't see or recognize him.

Too late, the redheaded 5'11" waitress was looking around in the bank and took a double-take at Nikolai, who was three inches taller than she was and looked at him and smiled. "Hey there, how are you? Fancy meeting you here and how is the sanitation work going?"

All he could do was think to himself, *Fuck me, what is her name!* Then it hit him. "Oh hey, Kandee, didn't see you there." He looked away rolling, his eyes like that was the dumbest thing he'd ever said. *Good job Mister Master of Observation!*

Kandee continued. "So, are you planning on paging me, you know so we can get some Greek food, you know, if you are still interested, but if your not, that's ok too"! All of this blurted out of the redhead's mouth quickly like she had been on methamphetamine or had drank three pots of coffee.

Every time Nikolai was about to answer a question, she hit him with another, then another. He looked at her and finally got in a word edgewise. "Drink a little coffee this morning, did ya?"

Kandee's lip wrinkled as she made frustrated eyes at him. "So, you gonna ask me out mister trash man? I know you want to. You told my coworker you thought I was cute!"

Nikolai laughed as the line moved forward. He was thinking, *Only two more people to go!* He looked down at the redhead who was clearly a little smitten with herself, probably more than she was with him and said, "I did *not* tell anyone that I thought you were cute. I may have thought it, and the only way she got that hint is if she's a clairvoyant!"

"So, you don't want to ask me out?" she asked with a disappointed look on her face.

Nikolai stuttered a moment. "That's not what I said. First of all, I am not in sanitation; well, I do take out the trash, but in truth, I am a cop. Does dating a gun slinger concern you? Ya know, cuz most people don't like law dogs?"

Kandee laughed, "We knew you were a cop when you came into the restaurant. I love a man in uniform, especially when they are built like you!"

Nikolai grinned, "Tell ya what, I have an award

dinner I have to go to this Friday night, starts at six. Would you like to join me?"

Kandee replied, "A little forward aren't you, award dinner?"

Nikolai scoffed, "Forward, you asked me to ask you out! And yes, an award dinner, law enforcement thing, but hey, if you have other plans and don't wanna go, I totally understand."

Kandee pulled out a piece of paper and pen and wrote down her address and pager number then handed it to Nikolai. "This is my address and my pager number 'Again', in case you lost it the first time! I live with my parents in Glendale. Pick me up at 5."

Nikolai panicked and asked, "You live with your parents? How old are you anyway?"

Kandee had an opening at the window and walked to the clerk and looked back, "Relax officer, I'm legal!"

Nikolai also had an opening and approached the clerk. "Can I get a hundred dollars in five dollar bills please."

She accessed his account information and started counting the money in front of him. Just then Kandee walked up behind him, pinched his butt cheek, and whispered in his ear, "See you Friday night, officer!"

Nikolai took the hundred dollars in fives and slid it in his checkbook. He went about this little routine every month, or as he needed cash. Every day before his shift, he would take out a five-dollar bill and place it in his uniform shirt breast pocket, and that was his spending budget for his meal for that day. If he made lunch and took that to work, he would be able to save the five dollars and put it away for a rainy day. This was a little ritual he learned from his mother's husband. This discipline had been something he had used for the last couple years when funds were tight.

CHAPTER
NINETEEN

Nikolai walked into the gym. He was keyed up and knew he would never be able to shut his eyes, much less get any sleep. He walked into his new favorite place, Wright's Gym, and began warming up. He heard a yell come across the gym from the locker room area. He couldn't miss the Italian slang from his buddy Carbone. "Hey, you fuckin bastard, you look like a fuckin seagull stretchin its wings over there. Next thing you know, you're gonna lift your leg and fall asleep!"

The two men made their way toward one another and clasped each other's right hands, thumbs intertwined and fingers wrapped over each other's thumbs as if they were going to arm wrestle. They pulled on one another's hands then hugged like the brothers they were.

Nikolai smiled at the Italian. "You're in here late, ya fuckin Dago!"

Carbone laughed. "Yeah, well it's a slow day and needed to blow off some steam. I'm workin' back and bi's today, you wanna team up?"

Nikolai shoved his shoulder. "You bet, meatball, just don't slow me down. I gotta work the yard tonight, and then I'm off Friday night and have to go to that police officer dog and pony show award dinner for the Los Angeles Political Action Committee."

The two men went about their workout. It was a grueling three hundred repetitions of each body part super setting abdominals between each set. They walked out to Carbone's car, panting and trying to pretend they each were not exhausted in that typical act of bravado often demonstrated in the workout areas where would-be gladiators spent so much time.

Carbone composed himself. "I need to get some hours in this month for my reserve officer requirement. Would you mind if I ride along with you tonight?"

Nikolai laughed. "You are always allowed in my car, ya fuckin wop, as long as you promise not to shoot me again!" Just then Nikolai's pager went off. It was a 213 number with a 411 at the end. He looked at Carbone. "Hey man, I have an urgent page, do you mind if I use that fancy car phone you have to make this call?"

Carbone smiled. "Sure, you're gonna owe me though. That shit ain't cheap!"

They sat in Carbone's Mercedes 450 SL convertible. Carbone handed him the phone and told him, "Just punch a one, then the area code and number, then hit send!"

Nikolai followed the instructions and looked at Carbone with a look that meant, *I'm not a fuckin idiot.*

A woman answered the phone. "Ingrid speaking."

Nikolai replied, "Yes ma'am, Nikolai Drew here, I received this number on my pager?"

Ingrid responded, "Yes, Mister Drew, I am reaching out to see if you are still interested in doing walk on work?"

Nikolai was confused for a moment, and then it registered, Victor's connection for studio work. All he could remember was him saying not to fuck it up. He replied, "Absolutely ma'am, thought you had forgotten about me."

Ingrid giggled. "No, Mister Drew, we haven't had a lot of work lately, but, we have some openings coming, so be prepared. We will be in touch."

Nikolai had written down the information with a pen and paper that Carbone gave him and got off the phone quickly so as not to cost the man a small fortune.

Carbone hung the phone up and commented, "What the hell is that all about?"

Nikolai told him about the ride along with an A-List actor and how it turned into a potential gig as a movie or television extra. Nikolai didn't talk about it being Victor Denofrio like he had been asked, he caught himself before spilling the beans.

Carbone laughed. "You bein a yes man to some director, that's gonna be a laugh! I'll bet a hundred bucks you get fired before you get done with the photos!"

Nikolai flipped him the bird as he got out of Carbone's Mercedes. Nikolai drove home, unlocked the garage, opened the door, and backed his El Camino into its spot. Diamond Dave's hot rod was gone. He closed the garage door, locked it, and walked into the house.

He took a shower then walked out to the kitchen to get some water and picked his pager up off the kitchen counter as it was vibrating and discovered three pages from a 213 number that he didn't recognize, a Los Angeles area code.

He picked up his phone and dialed the number. A woman answered, "*Call The Cops*, Bianca speaking."

Nikolai was caught off-guard because he had just had a call from them, but responded, "Hello, Bianca, Nikolai Drew calling. I received a page from this number."

The woman was so nice Nikolai thought. She said, "Well yes, Mister Drew, I am calling to let you know that we have a part for you. It's a walk on for a

TV show called *Jake and the Fatman.* You need to be there at 9 a.m. on Monday morning. Can you make that date, sir?"

Nikolai thought about that for a moment. Off at 8 a.m., twenty minutes drive time, "Yes ma'am, I can make that happen."

Bianca continued. "Alright, Mister Drew, you need to bring a long-sleeved uniform with no patches and tie, no hat. You have a minimum of four hours commitment, meaning if you are there for one hour, you get paid for four, but it could go longer. Do you have a pen for the address?"

Nikolai grabbed a pad and pen and replied, "Yes ma'am, go ahead."

Bianca slowly stated, "You need to arrive at Burbank Studios, 3000 West Alameda Avenue. You will drive up to the guard shack and identify who you are and what show you are working on, and he will direct you to where you go next. Did you get that, sir?"

Nikolai had it all written down. Burbank Studios, 3000 West Alameda Avenue, Jake and the Fatman, Monday at 0900 hours, and he confirmed to Bianca that he in fact had the information. She hung up, and Nikolai found himself actually excited about what just happened. Who knows what could come of this, he thought. How cool that a call from R.L. must have jump-started something.

CHAPTER
TWENTY

Seven p.m. came way too soon. Nikolai woke up, moved his legs off his bed, and ran his hands through his thick brown hair. It was still Thursday, but yet, it was really Friday for him. He got up, put on his workout clothes and a ball cap. He walked out to the kitchen and poured a cup of cold coffee and slid it into the microwave. He removed fruit from the freezer, poured in a half a cup of nonfat milk into the blender, then added a cup of protein and a spoonful of peanut butter and turned on the contraption! As it blended the magic healing elixir Nikolai removed his cup of coffee from the microwave and took a sip. He turned off the blender and poured the drink into a glass and slowly sipped it between sips of his coffee. The silence was soothing. He was waking up and now thinking in depth about what his day was going to be like!

The ride along with Carbone was going to be fun. Having a phenomenal partner who truly had your back was priceless. The prospect of getting involved in Hollywood was intriguing to him, but he wasn't giving it much thought. It would be or it wouldn't be. Then the date night with Kandee. He wasn't sure if it was a good idea to indoctrinate someone on a first date to a function like he was about to expose her to, but he thought, what the hell, taking her would ensure he would actually go, because honestly, he was ready to pull a no-show, even at this moment.

Nikolai walked into his room, made his bed, picked up and inspected his war bag and walked out the front door, locking it behind him. He unlocked the garage, lifted the garage door, and paused realizing that Diamond Dave's Mopar was still not around. Puzzling he thought, but not surprising given his new job and all.

Nikolai threw his war bag on the passenger seat of the El Camino, fired it up, and pulled out of the garage. He got out and was just about to shut the garage door when he heard the familiar roar of Diamond Dave's 426 Max Wedge arriving into the neighborhood. He paused a moment, and Diamond Dave pulled into the driveway, backed down the driveway and into the garage. He shut the ignition off to the thundering Mopar and got out of the car. "What's goin on, Nikolai!" he said as joyfully as always.

Nikolai smiled and responded, "Brother, you wouldn't believe all the shit goin on these days! How have you been?"

Diamond Dave grinned. "Well, John Willis with Black and White Tow got back with me, and I am now a full blown tow truck driver! After a couple days of training, I am having more fun than I ever thought possible!"

Nikolai high fived him and replied, "Well that didn't take long! You're flyin high, my friend! Congrats!"

Diamond Dave looked elated and satisfied. "What about you, man, give me the skinny!"

Nikolai just didn't have time. He had to get to the police station and get in some cardio before starting work. "Let's catch up over the weekend, brother. I have to get some shit done before the shift starts. We will get caught up over drinks!" Nikolai got into the El Camino and drove off.

Minutes later he arrived at the police station, removed his war bag, and walked into the back door. He put his war bag in his locker and retrieved his Sig Sauer P-220, four magazines, and a couple boxes of ammunition and walked to the back of the station to the firing range. Nikolai placed the lanyard with the police station key around his neck, laid his weapon on the shooting bench with the slide back with the ejection port open, and began loading the weapon's magazines with seven rounds each. The "Black

Talon" ammunition was Nikolai's favorite because the 230 grain bullet came out of the muzzle at around 830 feet per second. This was subsonic (under 1,000 feet per second), which means it would not over-penetrate. Because of the unique construction of the projectile, a petal shape, it created a massive wound channel, and upon striking the target, the kinetic energy would likely stop the most aggressive of subjects. This was extremely important when dealing with violent assaulters, especially if they were under the influence of drugs. If the moment of truth came around again, Nikolai wanted to be ready, and he practiced with his ammunition of choice so he was prepared in a live scenario.

Nikolai finished preparing the magazines and ran out the back door of the station just outside the range. He secured the door and began running south on Brand Boulevard to Truman Street where he turned west. He was going to push it a little today and run three miles to Hubbard, back down First Street into the front door of the station back to the range and fire seven rounds from the weapon. In record time, he returned to the station in eighteen minutes, fired the seven rounds with precision, putting all seven into the center ring of the target at twenty-five feet away. He decided to take another run, this time one mile and would push himself even harder and fire another seven rounds. His goal was to get his heart rate up so that when he fired, he was simulating the effects of adrenaline running through him. Practice, after all, made perfect, but he was taught by his father that even better was that perfect practice made perfect results!

Nikolai ran out the back door of the station this time north on Brand to Third Street. He was singing cadence as he ran,

"Everybody's doin it right (Hard work, work)
Hard Work, that's what they say (Hard work, work)
Hard Work, to earn my pay (Hard work, work)
Hard Work, do it every day (Hard work, work)
I get up 'bout a quarter to three (Hard work, work)
Gotta go and earn my pay (Hard work, work)
Put my boots on and lace 'em up (Hard work, work)
I got another day's work (Hard work, work)
Hard Work, that's what they say (Hard work, work)
Hard Work, I earn my pay (Hard work, work)
I put on my ruck and move on out (Hard work, work)
Gotta go make the call (Hard work, work)
Im bangin' on the doors in the morning (Hard work, work)
Get up and let's go to work! (Hard work, work)
Hard work, you pack up the chutes (Hard work, work)
Hard work, you loading 'em up (Hard work, work)
It's a Hard Work manifest! (Hard work, work)
Hard work, you gotta do it right (Hard work, work)
Hard work, and here we go (Hard work, work)
Well son, I'm ready to rock (Hard work, work)

Hard work, I'm earning my pay (Hard work, work)
Hard work, that's what they say (Hard work, work)
Hard work, we're movin on out (Hard work, work)
We gotta go and do the job (Hard work, work)
Load 'em up on the airplane (Hard work, work)
In the early morning rain (Hard work, work)
Hard work, that's what they say (Hard work, work)
Hard work, lead me here (Hard work, work)
Hard work, turn it up (Hard work, work)
Hard work, fired up (Hard work, work)
Everybodys on the plane (Hard work, work)
Gotta sit 'em sit 'em on down (Hard work, work)
Hard work, the engines are on (Hard work, work)
Hard work, the mission is GO! (Hard work, work)
Hard work, that's what they say (Hard work, work)
Hard work, I do it for play! (Hard work, work)
Hard work, I earn my pay (Hard work, work)
Hard work, we're on the go (Hard work, work)"

He turned onto North Maclay and headed south back to the station and arrived just over five minutes later. He was winded as he hit the range, immediately retrieved his pistol, loaded the magazine, dropped the slide, feeding the deadly round into the chamber. He aimed at the target's center, took a breath, slowly relaxed, and held and slowly squeezed the trigger five times then raised the weapon's muzzle to the head and squeezed two more. The slide locked back as it will when you expend all of the rounds from a semi-automatic handgun. Nikolai kept the weapon pointed at the target for a couple extra seconds then removed the magazine, set them both on the bench and returned the target with the automated, chain-driven device. He grinned as he noticed the perfectly placed holes in the paper where he had struck the target dead center in the chest and noticed that the two rounds to the head overlapped one another making an oval rather than a single circle. Nikolai had been shooting since he was five years old, and his father was a perfectionist. Even though he hadn't seen him in several years, he knew he would be proud that his son was a distinguished expert in shooting.

Nikolai took the weapon apart, cleaned it vigorously, and lubed the slide rails before putting the weapon back together. He reloaded the magazines and went to the locker room. He quickly took a shower, shaved, and began the process of putting his uniform on. He was standing in front of the mirror in his slacks and boots and t-shirt blow-drying his hair when Carbone walked in. He stopped, looked at Nikolai, and snidely commented, "What's up, pretty boy. Jesus, man, focus less on the hair and eat something will ya, you look anorexic!" Carbone, much like most weightlifter types, would tell others that they looked skinny or would ask in a way that seemed sincere things like, have you lost weight, in order to get their counterparts to feel insecure.

Nikolai just continued about his business,

smirked, and emitted a simple four-word response: "Go fuck yourself, Carbone!"

Nikolai finished suiting up and made his way to the dispatch center so he could chat with the dispatch officer about his day and review the daily log. Just then, Cindy walked into the dispatch area and relieved Huff. She smiled at Nikolai. She always acted like she had a crush on him, even though she was damn near old enough to be his mother. She also hated most cops, she had an edge to her, but she liked Nikolai, probably because he always got her coffee and snacks during the shift and didn't hit on her like some dumb ass jock douche in high school.

Nikolai smiled back at her. "Well. Cindy, looks like it's gonna be a wild night!"

She laughed. "Why's that? Looking at the log, swing shift has been dead, no activity, like it's a tomb."

Nikolai laughed. "Well, young lady, that's the reason! They've been sleepin on the job. Now it's time to go shake the trees and round up all the nuts!"

Carbone walked up behind Nikolai and jabbed the back of his knee with his knee knocking him off balance a bit. "No bigger nuts out here than ole Nancy and me, Tina!"

Nikolai shoved Carbone against the dispatch console in retribution and asked Tina if she wanted a coffee.

Cindy smiled again. "Why yes, Officer Drew, that would be wonderful!"

Nikolai retreated to the break room across the hall and poured a cup of coffee in Cindy's favorite cup, which was always stored in the cabinet above the microwave. He returned it to her, and she thanked him with a nod and closed the dispatch door. She closed the gap between them and said, "Hey, there's a change happening on the shift tonight, I wanted to let you know so you didn't get blindsided." She looked around to make sure she wasn't heard. "You know the name Tuko, yes?"

Nikolai smiled. "Oh yeah, rumor has it he's a piece of work."

Cindy told Nikolai with a serious look on her face, "He's far more than a piece of work, Drew. He's a full blown dirtbag. This guy never backs anyone up. If he ever gets there, it's long after the shit has hit the fan. He's also a reprobate and the kind of guy that is always trying to get dirt or make up dirt about others to make himself look good. He's all about himself, never doing any of the work, but always trying to take the credit. Just watch your back. Oh, word has it that he has a girlfriend around Harding and Eighth Street, which is out of his beat area."

Nikolai smiled. "I promise I will, young lady!"

He opened the dispatch door, propped it open, and walked into the squad room where role call is held. He sat down in the back row and sat in the last seat on his right side. Carbone walked in and sat down next to him, placing two cups of black coffee in front of him and Nikolai. Nikolai raised the cup and took a sip, and a few moments later the rest of the shift members walked in and took their seats around the room. The last one to enter was Tuko. He was a regular looking guy, nothing special and always smiling like a hyena, and about as trustworthy. He always seemed to be trying too hard to be everyone's buddy.

Sgt. Maddox walked in, and Nikolai perked up a bit. Sgt. Brodie was a wing-ding, often called Sgt. Nutty and was barely tolerable. Nikolai loved Maddox. He was a "by the book" Marine who served during the Vietnam era.

Maddox looked around the room. "Alright, men, Sergeant Brodie has been struggling with graveyard since having his kid, so, after nagging me for what seems like an eternity, I traded day shift with him and will be working the rest of this rotation with you nutty batch of fucktards. Also joining us is Officer Tuko, who swapped shifts with one of you knuckleheads, and he too will be with us the remainder of the rotation. You all know me, you all know what I expect. Work together, back each other, and don't cause me any headaches!"

He barked out unit assignments and looked out at Nikolai with a sarcastic look on his face, "Officer Drew, I am assuming that because you have the WOP sitting next to you that you two would like to ride together this evening?"

Nikolai looked at the sergeant and replied, "Sir, guy just wandered over here and sat his silly ass next to me. I am happy to do whatever you like, sir, take him along, leave him here, or stuff the little bastard in the trunk. Your call."

The room erupted in laughter. The salty sergeant leaned on his podium, head hung down, brooding. "Well I hear he nearly shot your leg off. You two fucktards pull any of that shit on my shift, and I will have you both walkin a foot beat in the Alaskan Territory where there is nothing more than penguins and igloos, got me? Don't ever call me sir. I work for a livin', and you don't see any god damned lieutenant bars on my uniform, do ya!"

Nikolai replied, "Yes, Sergeant Maddox, whatever you say, Sergeant Maddox!"

The room dispersed. Nikolai asked Carbone to grab a shot gun and told him to meet him at the unit. Carbone snapped to attention and saluted. "Sir, yes sir."

Nikolai stopped for a moment, hung his head down, and shook it as he continued walking to the back parking lot where the units were stored thinking to himself, *It's gonna be one of those nights!*

Nikolai got the trunk squared away. It was surprisingly in decent shape since his last shift. There were only a few things missing: a blanket, a box of flares, and the first-aid kit was a complete mess. All in all, not bad. Carbone walked out and loaded the 12 gauge shotgun and placed it into the shotgun rack, careful not to load a round into the chamber.

They got in the car and as they pulled out of the parking lot, Carbone grabbed the microphone, pressed the button, and broadcast, "1-adam-22 is ten-eight, the double deuce is on the loose!" He hung up the mic and laughed. "Fuck, I love this job!"

Nikolai drove to 776 North Maclay and pulled into the 7-11 parking lot. The two men got out of the car, Rageet was working the counter, ,and as always waved as the officers walked in and greeted them with the customary, "Hello, buddy!"

Nikolai greeted the man and poured a cup of coffee. Carbone had no interest in coffee. Nikolai walked up to the register and dropped a dollar bill for the coffee. Rageet tried as always not to take it, but Nikolai again refused. "So, Rageet, anything new going on? Anyone I need to give some special attention to."

Rageet smiled. "No sir. Ever since you caught that robber and broke his leg, no trouble with gang bangers here."

Nikolai spit coffee out of his nose. "Hey, man, I did not break that man's leg. He jumped down from a twelve-foot fence and snapped it when he hit the ground. Don't be saying things like that. You're gonna get me a baaaaaaad reputation!"

Rageet apologized. "I am sorry, Drew, that's what I meant, my English is still just so, so."

Nikolai and Carbone got in the unit and headed to the south side of the city, the home of the Shakin Cats. As they drove onto Kalisher Street, Nikolai turned off the headlights and hit the blackout switch on the Motorola control head. This switch made it so there were no brake lights when you applied them, nor were there backup lights. He also turned the dimmer down on the radio and scanner so the lights were not so visible inside the unit. All the windows were down in the unit so they could hear. Nikolai backed the unit into a business driveway, and the two men rolled up the windows and got out of the car. They turned on their hand radios very low so as to not draw any attention. They were now in the heart of gang territory walking a foot beat where most people would be afraid to drive a car. They walked around the entire area. It was a ghost town other than a couple drunks making noise at Las Palmas Park. They got back to the car, and as they got in, Sergeant Maddox pulled up. Nikolai pulled out of the driveway and alongside of the sergeant's unit. "Hey ya, Sarge," Nikolai said.

Maddox replied, "Gentlemen, I see you're out low crawlin', I like it! Anything exciting goin on out here?"

Carbone chimed in, "Not a damn thing, Sarge, but hey, the night is young!"

THE BLUE HARD LINE

Maddox smiled. "Carry on, gentlemen, don't get your tit in a ringer!"

They parted ways, and Nikolai turned on the lights and deactivated the tail light kill switch and went back to the hunt. It was now 0130 hours and bored out of their minds, they decided to walk another foot patrol. Nikolai blacked out the unit in the alley north of San Fernando Road at San Fernando Mission Boulevard and parked. He and Carbone got out and began walking the front end of the shops scouting as there had been reports of rooftop burglaries throughout the San Fernando Valley. They walked all the way down to Brand on the north side of the street heading east then turned around and walked back down westbound. As they crossed Maclay Street, Carbone caught a glimmer of light in the window of the Cortez Brothers Jewelry Store. They carefully peeked through the steel security gates into the building and noticed a rope ladder hanging from the ceiling and flashlight activity in the office at the very back of the store.

Nikolai got on his handheld radio looking around above to see if he saw anyone or anything. "1-A-22 control, be advised, we are code 6 at 1244 San Fernando Road on a 459 in progress. We have two inside and a possible third on the roof. Give me units on the west and east end of the location, one at Mission and the other at Maclay. Be advised, we believe there is a third on the roof, respond blacked out and quietly please."

Nikolai told Carbone to keep an eye on the front door and keep his radio low and let him know he was going to get up on the roof.

Carbone asked, "Why didn't you ask for Air Support?"

Nikolai smiled. "Because, I wanna catch him by surprise, mister. Besides, we wouldn't get an airship for 30 minutes. This would be over by then!"

Nikolai ran around the back of the building. He didn't see an address or any names of businesses on the back wall. *This is a shit show, can't find anything back here*, he thought to himself. A topic for another time. He stumbled upon a ladder leading to the roof that had a steel door that was standing wide open. These are locked at all times, and he found the lock cut and lying on the ground. He quietly climbed the ladder. He was in a seriously compromised position and hoped that if there were a third suspect on the roof that he would be occupied watching the hole that the other two climbed into to enter the jewelry store.

He got to the top of the ladder, unholstered his side arm, and quickly peeked over the wall and back down. There was no one there. He climbed slowly over the wall onto the roof and crouched down as he walked across the roof line. Radio traffic was heard faintly as units arrived in the area. He heard Sergeant

Maddox call for him, and Carbone told him that Nikolai was on the roof looking for a third suspect.

As Nikolai made his way west toward the jewelry store, he observed a third suspect crouched down by the large hole they had cut into the roof. There were tools, an axe, hammers, crowbars, and the like. Nikolai made his way to the suspect and was just about to make his move when the man turned, saw him, and ran across the roof of the buildings.

Nikolai ran after the man and removed the hooks holding the rope ladder and threw it down the hole to thwart any efforts by the two men in the building from climbing back up. Now they had to exit the building, which would likely not be easy. Nikolai removed his radio and broadcast, "Units be advised, I am in foot pursuit across the southside mall roof approaching Mission Boulevard. Suspect is a male, 5'7", wearing all black clothing."

Dispatch responded by parroting the information put out. The suspect jumped over a wall, and Nikolai was quickly at that location. He started to jump and realized that the drop was about twelve feet, quite a fall, but he had no choice. He turned backward and grabbed the wall extending his arms to shorten the drop, and fell about six feet and resumed his pursuit. He was getting closer to the suspect, and suddenly, the man veered to his left and started to scale down the wall, which was a twenty-five foot drop. Nikolai looked over the wall as the man tried to make his way and then lost his footing and fell. Nikolai heard the awful snap of bone as the man landed on his feet. The man gave out a scream that could be heard for blocks as he fell to the ground. Nikolai had heard that kind of thing before.

Nikolai saw a figure step in frame. It was Sergeant Maddox. He looked down at the fallen subject and commented in his normal sarcastic way, "Well, that little move of yours turned to shit, didn't it!" He got on his handheld radio. "1-L-30 control, gonna need a medic at the southwest corner of the south side of the San Fernando Mall. We have a male Hispanic, twenty-ish, with what appears to be a broken ankle, I will be standing by."

Sergeant Maddox yelled at him, "You wanna get your rooty poot ass off that roof mister and get down here and clean this mess up!"

Nikolai saluted the sergeant. He looked around and found another ladder leading off the roof on the back side of the mall. He started down and found yet another steel cover near the bottom of the ladder, which necessitated him working his way down and making the final drop, which was about eight feet down. He walked east back toward the jewelry store and radioed in. "1-A-22, can you notify the store owner and ask them to respond, please. We still have two inside the building."

Dispatch responded, "Roger that, sir, it's already

done. Store owner was twenty minutes out, ten minutes ago."

Just then, the door of the jewelry store burst open, and two men ran out. They saw Nikolai, who immediately leaped and clotheslined one of the men, knocking him to the ground on his back. Nikolai restrained and handcuffed the man and got on his handheld radio, "1-A-22, be advised, two suspects just exited the rear of Cortez Brothers Jewelers, I have one in custody, the other subject fled eastbound in the rear alley. I see him heading toward South Brand."

Carbone and Officer Farzaralli walked around the back of the building, and both men stared at the back door waiting to see if there was anyone else inside. Carbone looked at Nikolai. "Well, you look like shit. What is with the guy on the roof?"

Nikolai was in the middle of working the suspect for information as he removed the suspect's wallet from his right rear pants pocket. He held up a finger as to suggest "hold for a moment." Looking at the identification he found, he said, "Okay, Cidricedos, is there anyone else inside the store? Who is your partner that ran off, where is he headed?"

The man looked at him, puzzled, and replied, "No hablo Inglés."

Nikolai looked at Carbone and Farzaralli with a look that clearly said "well that's bullshit" on his face. He asked the man again, "I know you speak English, fucko, so, why not help us so we can help you. Is there anyone else in that building?"

The man still had a bewildered look on his face and replied, "No hablo Inglés, señor!"

Farzaralli slapped the suspect upside the head and said, "Hey, Nikolai, ya know what a Mexican and a cue ball have in common?!"

Nikolai said, "I have no clue, but I am sure you're gonna tell us!"

Farzaralli smiled and said, "The harder you hit 'em, the more English you get out of em!"

The suspect's eyes got big, and his mouth dropped, and he laughed nervously. Nikolai smiled at the suspect and said, "Gotcha, fucker! Now look, tell me if there is anyone else in the building!"

The suspect, ashamed that he laughed, knew he was caught. He looked down at his feet and said, "There is no one else in the building, just me and that idiot Carlos who ran from you. Gilbert was on the roof as a lookout!"

Nikolai said, "Well, if Carlos is such an idiot, where was he going?"

The suspect chuckled. "Well, he is heading where I parked my El Camino. Problem is, I have the keys in my pocket, and it's a long fucking walk back to Tujunga."

Carbone asked the suspect, "What color is the El Camino, and where did you park it?"

The suspect motioned with his head. "It's parked over off Celis and Brand, it's black primer eh."

Nikolai picked up his radio and broadcast, "Units in the area be advised the suspect we are looking for is heading toward the area of Brand and Celis. He's looking for a primer black El Camino, and he goes by the name of Carlos."

Nikolai looked at Carbone and asked, "Do you want to hold onto our amigo here for a moment, and I will go get the unit, or would you like to go?"

Carbone smiled. "Well, Nancy, I didn't know you cared! I'll go get the car. I'll be right back."

The suspect looked at Nikolai, puzzled. "Did your parents hate you or something ese?"

Nikolai looked at him, confused, "No, why would you ask that?"

The suspect replied, "Well, who names their boy Nancy. That's just fucked up, nothing personal!"

Nikolai hadn't even realized that Carbone called him that. He looked at the suspect in disgust. "That dickhead is being funny. Nancy Drew, get it?" He pointed at his name badge.

The suspect had a puzzled look on his face and replied, "No, I don't get it, how is that funny, eh?"

Nikolai replied sarcastically, "Never mind!"

Sergeant Maddox sent the other subject off to the hospital with another officer and made his way to where Nikolai was holding the one suspect at the back door of Cortez Brothers Jewelers, and Carbone pulled up at the same time.

Sergeant Maddox commented, "Well that was one hell of an Obs, you two. I would prefer you weren't galivanting in foot pursuits across rooftops, God damn it, but what the hell, the only injured party is the dirtbag. Did you clear the building yet?"

Nikolai placed the suspect in the back seat of his unit and replied, "No, Sarge, you wanna go with me, and we can leave Carbone with the suspect?"

Sergeant Maddox smiled at him. "No, kid, you two go have fun with that. I'll watch spiffy here till you get back."

Nikolai got on the radio to alert dispatch. "1-A-22 to control, be advised we are going into Cortez Brothers Jewelers to clear the building, stand by one."

The dispatcher replied, "Roger Adam 22."

Within a few minutes the two men returned to the rear of the building. Nikolai got on the radio, "1-A-22, be advised, the building is clear. We are code 4 at this location."

Dispatch responded, "Roger Adam 22, reporting code 4 at Cortez Brothers Jewelers."

Nikolai looked over at the sergeant. "So, where is broken ankle boy, Sarge?"

Sergeant Maddox replied, "He's probably at Holy Cross right now getting looked at. I sent Fricassi and Hooper down there to supervise. If he has good ID, they will cite him so he doesn't cost us for the medical, ya know, since he's not a violent criminal. If he doesn't have ID, he's off to Twin Towers." Los Angeles Sheriff's twin towers facility was where criminals injured during a crime were booked as they had facilities that can handle them.

Nikolai asked sarcastically but in the nicest way possible, "Hey, Sarge, where is Tuko. We haven't heard from him all shift?"

Sergeant Maddox gave him a dirty look just as one of the Cortez brothers arrived at the back door. Maddox exclaimed, "He's probably not adjusted to the graveyard shift yet, some find that a bit of a challenge, and well, let's be honest, he left the last shift because he pissed off everyone on the shift. Don't be spreading that shit. Just keep your eyes open."

Nikolai greeted the man and walked him inside the building. Julian Cortez turned on all the lights and began assessing the damage. He looked at Nikolai and asked, "How did you get alerted to this, officer?"

Nikolai replied, "Well, sir, my partner and I were walking a foot beat around the mall and saw a faint light in the very back office here in the building. We noticed the rope ladder hanging from the roof in the middle of the store, and here we are. We got two of the three subjects so far. The third is still outstanding. Can you tell if they got anything? The suspect we caught running out the back door had nothing on his person."

Julian Cortez looked all around the building. The only thing that looked disturbed was the lock cut off the steel bar that secured the back door, and it appeared that someone was trying to pry the safe open. "Well, we lock up all our jewelry in these three safes at the end of every day. They tried to pry their way into each of them, but failed. These safes are fireproof and impossible to break into. This is the first time we have ever had to test them."

Nikolai took all of Julian's information for the report and thanked him for being so prompt.

Cortez shook his hand. "My brother and I are truly grateful for your keen observation skills, Officer Drew. We will be attending the award ceremony tomorrow night, we had heard about you, but having met you, well, now I am motivated to be there. Thank you again."

Nikolai and Carbone transported the suspect to the jail, pulled into the sally port, and secured their weapons in the gun lockers. Carbone removed the prisoner from the back seat of the patrol car and handed him over to the jailer. The suspect got out of the car and told Carbone, "I didn't forget you fuckers cracked that joke about the Mexican and the cue ball, fucker, that shit is racist!"

Just then, officers came over the radio stating that they had just apprehended the third suspect who was caught trying to get into the primer black El Camino and informed dispatch they were en route 10-19 with one, meaning they were on their way to the police station with one in custody.

Nikolai met the officers at the sally port and took the prisoner from them and handed him over to the jailer. The officers walked into the station and began writing their supplemental report about what they witnessed and how they caught the suspect.

The jailer asked Nikolai, "What are the charges going to be?"

Nikolai thought for a moment, then told him, "Straight burglary, brother. We have a third guy down at Holy Cross Hospital. I am going to go check on him, and I'll let you know what the scoop is. Do you want anything to eat or drink while I am out and about?"

The jailer responded quickly, "No, I already had something, and I have coffee, but thank you, Nikolai."

Nikolai motioned to Carbone to follow him. They went to the sally-port, collected their weapons and drove out. Carbone asked Nikolai where they were off to.

Nikolai told him that they were headed to Holy Cross to check on their prisoner with the broken ankle to see what his status is.

They arrived a few minutes later at the Emergency Room area of Holy Cross and parked behind Farzaralli's unit. They walked in and standing in the hallway was the fiery redhead English nurse, Melanie Ketchmire.

She looked at him with a devilish look on her face and with her English brogue said, "Well if it isn't Officer Nikolai Drew, the Captain America of the LAPD. You must be here to see that broken fella that the other two uniformed men wheeled into my ward?"

Nikolai smiled. "Yes ma'am, we are. Can you lead us to them?"

Melanie said, "Well of course, lad, but, it comes with a favor. You have to come get me before ya leave as I have a question to ask you."

Nikolai bowed and said, "Gladly."

The two men were led to the exam room at the end of the hall. Nikolai shook the two men's hands, "Hey Farz, any word on this character yet?"

Farzaralli pulled him outside and left Hooper and Carbone with the suspect. "Yeah, he's got ID on him, and he's clean. I just talked to the sarge, and he told me to write him a ticket for 459 P.C. Problem is, I left my cite book at the station, can you help me out?"

Nikolai smiled. "Absolutely, brother!" and escorted him to his unit, grabbed his cite book and tore off the next one in line and handed it to him. Nikolai asked him how the ankle was.

Farzaralli told him, "It snapped bad. Best we cut him loose rather than buying that injury, know what I mean."

They walked back inside and he left him to citing the man, and as they headed out, Nurse Melanie was waiting. Carbone walked to the car, and Nikolai walked to the side area of the hospital where the staff often smoked. Melanie lit a cigarette and crossed her arms. "Well, I haven't seen or heard from you in quite a while, are you all healed up now?"

Nikolai responded, "Yes ma'am, absolutely, thank you!"

Melanie continued. "Well, how is your head with all of it then? You handling it alright, Niki?"

Nikolai smiled. "I am. I am fully dialed in and recovered."

Melanie became indignant. "Well then, you have my phone number, you ass. You owe me dinner or drinks at least. Don't leave a girl waiting now, Niki!"

Nikolai smiled. "I promise, Mel, I will call you, and we can set something up. You can count on it. Can't wait to sit down in a nonformal setting with you!"

They parted ways, and Nikolai got in the car, backed out, and headed back to the police station. Carbone looked puzzled at him. "Well, what was that all about 'Niki'!"

Nikolai replied, "Old debt. She was the nurse who gave me my physical when I was hired, and then, she helped me when I was wheeled in after the shooting. There is a spark there, but I am just not ready for anything serious with anyone. She is way intense and looks at me like I'm a meal, if you know what I mean?"

Carbone laughed, and moments later they arrived at the station. They went inside, and Nikolai began writing the arrest report and asked Carbone if he would mind grabbing him a cup of coffee and all the information on the men in custody.

Carbone went about the business of collecting everything and returned shortly with what was requested. Nikolai picked up the phone and called into the jail and asked the jailer for the booking numbers for the two that were brought in. Carbone peeked in on the jailer, who was fingerprinting the first subject. He overheard the subject telling the jailer about the cue ball story.

Carbone spoke up. "Hey, dirtbag, no one here is racist. The officer was testing you to see if you were lying about speaking English or not, and you failed. If you would like to file a complaint, I'll get the sergeant in here right now so we can get the paperwork started."

The suspect looked over at him while he was being fingerprinted. "I ain't filing any complaint. You cops all stick together and lie for each other all the time."

Carbone laughed and replied, "Your call."

The suspect spoke up again. "I am hungry. Can I have something to eat?"

Just then Nikolai stepped in, overhearing the

suspect asking for food and replied instantly, "Sure, there isn't much open, but I will get you somethin'."

Nikolai and Carbone walked out, and Nikolai asked Carbone, "Hey, run over to McDonald's and grab him and his partner a cheeseburger, some fries, and a Coke. Get me two of those with no onions and a Diet Coke, okay?"

Carbone snapped back, "Anything for you, man, but we aren't a luxury hotel. Why get that dirt bag anything?"

Nikolai looked at him and said, "Because he's hungry. We never deprive people of food. Karma's the boomerang you never have to throw, brother. Whether we do something shitty or nice to someone, we get it back in return, ya dig?"

Carbone walked off. "Yeah, fuck head, I dig, and that saying wasn't cool in the '70s when the hippies were sayin' in either!"

Fifteen minutes later Carbone returned with the requested food and set it on the report room table next to Nikolai. Nikolai smiled and thanked him, got up, and walked the food and drink to the cell where the suspect was being held with his partner in crime. He slid the food and drinks through the hole at the bottom of the cell door designed for delivery to prisoners and rapped on the cell window. "Hey Cidricedos, special delivery, as promised. Like I said, there isn't much open. but we can always count on McDonalds."

Cidricedos picked up the food and held up his Coke cup like he was giving Nikolai a sign of respect for getting him and his partner something to eat. Most wouldn't have never given it a second thought.

Within an hour, the report was done, and Nikolai walked up to the dispatch area and dropped off the folder in the watch commander's incoming file for approval. He stopped in and asked Cindy if she needed anything.

Tina was an excellent dispatcher. She smiled at Nikolai and used her index finger to get him to walk closer to the desk. She spoke quietly so only he could hear her, "That dipshit Tuko has been AWOL the entire shift. No radio contact, nothing. You may wanna check in on him. Even the sergeant hasn't tried contacting him."

Nikolai nodded and walked out the back door of the station with Carbone. He pulled his handheld radio from its holder and broadcast, "1-A-22 to 1-L27."

There was no response for nearly thirty seconds then, "27 go ahead."

Nikolai replied, "27, clear for a meet, 146 Hubbard?"

Tuko replied, "Roger 22, see you in two."

Nikolai and Carbone got to the 7-11 on Hubbard first and backed their unit in. Nikolai and Carbone walked in and greeted the clerk. Davinder was always friendly, and they got two cups of coffee. Nikolai left a dollar bill on the counter and the two men waited by the rear of Nikolai's patrol unit. Tuko arrived shortly after and got out of his car. His uniform looked like hell, and he was yawning.

Nikolai smiled at the senior officer. "So, you doin alright out here on your first night?"

Tuko smiled back. "Yeah, it's gonna take a minute, this graveyard thing isn't easy to acclimate to. You'll figure that out after you've been on the job a while. The best shift is day watch, if you ask me. Gives us the ability to live a regular life."

Nikolai was done with this conversation. He got all the answers he was looking for. It was obvious that Tuko was out hiding somewhere sleeping in his car while the rest of them were making shit happen. He never asked about the arrests, which meant he had no idea anything went down.

They all parted ways. As they drove around Carbone spoke up. "I didn't speak up because I know as well as you do that fucker was off sleeping or fuckin' off. He didn't even ask about the burglary. Probably had no idea anything went down, fuck that guy!"

Nikolai replied, "Yeah, man, I get it. Let's not share this with anyone. It just makes us look bad, you know what I mean. Just hope this guy doesn't get himself or one of us killed in the process."

The rest of the shift was pretty quiet. As the shift ended, all the men were in the locker room changing clothes. Sergeant Maddox addressed everyone. "Well, gang, that was a great shift. I was not sure about being back out here on graveyard again, but this was a great surprise! See you all tomorrow. Wait, not you, Drew. You have to go to that dog and pony show tomorrow night, right?"

Nikolai looked over at him. "Yes indeed, unless you wanna swap places with me, Sarge?"

Sergeant Maddox snapped in a typical Marine Corps. Drill Instructor fashion, "Fuck no, mister. You go forward and have fun with that crap. I'll be sleepin' and eventually getting up and gettin ready for our shift! Meanwhile, don't let it go to your head!"

Carbone and Nikolai walked out the back door of the station where their cars were parked, and Carbone shook Nikolai's hand. "Well, cumstain, it was a blast hangin' out with you! See you on the next one!"

Nikolai got in his El Camino and fired the machine up and headed home. He performed his regimen, backed into the driveway, unlocked and opened the garage door, backed the El Camino into the garage then walked out, closed the door and secured it before walking into the house to go to bed. He was exhausted and frankly a little sore from the day. He got undressed and climbed into bed, closed his blackout blinds over his bedroom window, and turned on his seascapes music. In seconds he was out like a light.

CHAPTER
TWENTY-ONE

Three p.m. came quickly. Nikolai woke up, rolled his legs off the bed, and stood up. He stretched, put on his sweatpants and slippers, and walked to the kitchen to pour himself a cup of cold coffee. Diamond Dave would always leave coffee for him so all he has to do is heat it up when he gets up. He slid the cup into the microwave and heated it up. He walked to the living room and turned on the stereo and was instantly hit with the song "Wasn't That a Party" by the Irish Rovers! Catchy toon, he thought. He retrieved his coffee and took a sip. He then removed the high-speed blender, "The Juice Tiger as promoted by Jack LaLanne." He couldn't believe he paid a hundred dollars for this thing! He began filling it with the nutritional supplements that not only kept his body recovering from the onslaught of training he put himself through, but it also helped him stay healthy from the day to day nonsense that humans put themselves through.

He was contemplating the events of today. He needed to get in the gym, do his laundry, and clean up the kitchen, and looking around, he realized that he didn't need to clean up much around the house. Diamond Dave had already seen to that! Nikolai finished his protein shake. It was now 4 p.m. and he had to get ready for his dinner engagement this evening. He hated having to wear a suit and couldn't believe he invited Kandee to this party. It did serve its purpose, however. He was now obligated to pick her up and promised the chief he would be there. He got in the shower and began the process of getting ready. He did, after all, need to drive to Glendale to pick up Kandee, then to Burbank to the "Castaway Restaurant" for the event.

When he arrived at Kandee's place, he parked the blue and gray primer '69 El Camino with center lines in front of the large and impressive home. He got out of the car and put on his suit coat and walked to the front door. A tall older gentleman opened up the door before Nikolai could even knock. He stuck out his hand, and Nikolai grabbed it sternly. The man introduced himself. "My name is Don. Nice to meet you, Nikolai, Kandee has told us all about you, or at least as much as she knew about you anyway. She's still getting ready and will be down shortly." Don looked at the 1969 El Camino in disappointment as he closed the door and offered Nikolai a seat in the formal living room. As they sat down, a woman walked into the room.

Nikolai stood up and gently shook her hand. "Good evening, ma'am. You must be Kandee's younger sister?"

The woman giggled and sat down next to her husband, smiling at Nikolai. "No, I'm her mother, Linda. It's lovely to meet you Nikolai. Is that name Russian?"

Nikolai laughed as he responded, "No ma'am. My mother always loved the name and wanted my name to sound romantic and edgy."

The woman continued. "So, Nikolai, how long have you been in law enforcement, and tell us about your parents."

Just then Kandee walked down the stairs and saved Nikolai from her parents' rendition of the Spanish Inquisition! She grabbed his hand, pulling him off the couch, and told her parents, "We gotta go, folks. We are running late for Nikolai's big ordeal. She rushed him out the door. He opened the passenger door to the El Camino, she slipped in, and they took off.

Kandee apologized. "Sorry about the parents. They are prudes and love to embarrass me."

Nikolai scoffed. "Doll, they didn't bother me, I like who I am. Besides, they are just being protective of you and want to know what guy is sweeping their daughter off for the evening. Can you blame them for being inquisitive?"

She then asked him, "So, what usually happens during events like this. Are you getting an award or something?"

Nikolai replied, "I have never been to one, so it's as big a surprise to me as it will be to you. As for an award, yeah, you could say that."

Kandee got all giddy, clapping her hands together. "What kind of award? Did you save a drowning baby or something like that?"

Nikolai didn't go into it. He wasn't really thrilled about talking about it. He simply responded in a somber tone, "Yeah, something like that."

They arrived at the Castaway and were greeted by a valet. Nikolai didn't have a problem leaving his car with them. He never kept any paperwork with his address in the car or any weapons. He took the ignition and door key portion of the ring off and handed it to the guy and escorted Kandee inside. He checked in at the ballroom door, where the chief's secretary was smiling and informing everyone who checked in what their seating assignments were going to be.

She looked up and smiled at Nikolai and handed him two pieces of paper. One read steak, the other seafood. She informed him that he would be sitting at table 1 with the chief. He smiled and escorted Kandee to the table, and the chief, who was alone was sitting with the department's attorney, Paul Payne. They both stood, shook Nikolai's and Kandee's hands, and they all sat down.

Chief Belknap smiled and said, "Well, I am glad you decided to come this evening, Nikolai, it's a big deal!"

Nikolai politely responded, "I wouldn't miss it, Chief." Inside, he thought to himself, *Shit, now there's no way I can duck out of here early.* Suddenly Nikolai felt a wet finger in his ear and recognized the distinct odor of cigarettes and Brute 33 behind him. He moved his head and stood up.

It was Detective Bedo and his wife. He was dangling a cigarette out of his mouth and shook Nikolai's hand, saying, "Relax, kid, don't be so jumpy."

Nikolai looked puzzled. "I thought you said you hate these things and never go?"

Bedo smiled and pulled out a chair for his wife, who as circumstances would have it would be sitting next to Kandee.

A waitress came by the table to take a drink order and asked which meal each person was going to have. Nikolai asked Kandee what she would prefer, steak or seafood? She smiled. "Why don't we just share some of each, I love them both!"

Nikolai liked that idea, no nonsense. Jovial conversation took place, and Bedo's wife asked Kandee how long she and Nikolai had been dating.

Kandee giggled nervously, "Oh, this is our first date. What was your first name again?"

Bedo's wife repeated her name. "Melissa. You're in for quite a night. These awards ceremonies are quite the dog and pony show."

Kandee smiled. The evening began with first a small speech from the President of the Los Angeles Police support committee thanking everyone for coming. The President of the Police Union got up and recognized all of the dignitaries, the local Senator, Assemblyman, and of course all five of the representatives of the City Council and of course the Chief of Police. They gave out several awards for conduct above and beyond the call of duty, not only to some of the police officers, but the Community Service Officers and a couple of the dispatchers.

The President of the Police Officers Association motioned to the Chief of Police, and as he walked up to the podium, POA President Lou Picarone introduced the chief. The two men stood next to one another. The chief began to speak, "Before I bring up this award recipient, I need to call up Senator Bob Bonda and Assemblyman Nick Kaige. They request to be here for this presentation."

The two men approached carrying large plaques and stood next to Chief Belknap and Officer Picarone. The chief continued. "It is with great honor that I call up Officer Nikolai Drew to receive a Medal of Valor for displaying extraordinary courage under fire last year. Nikolai, please come up and join me at the podium."

Nikolai was flushed as he walked up. The chief placed a specially made Medal of Valor around his neck and handed him a plaque as well as a felt box containing a medal he could wear on his uniform. He then introduced the State Senator, who presented him with a plaque that symbolized the gratitude of his district for his courage. Next, the Assemblyman Nick Kaige presented him with a similar award, a certificate from his office recognizing him for service above and beyond the call of duty.

Chief Belknap saved the best for last, and called up Los Angeles Mayor Tom Bradly. Bradly approached the podium and presented Nikolai with a ceremonial Key to the City and praised him for his conduct under fire. The chief closed by speaking of Nikolai's roots in law enforcement and his love of the city and the people he had sworn to protect and asked Nikolai to say a few words.

Nikolai didn't enjoy public speaking. He had a lot of experience doing it, but the thought of talking about himself made him uneasy, and he didn't care for chest pounding.

"Ladies and Gentlemen," he began, "esteemed colleagues and friends, standing before you today, I feel an overwhelming sense of gratitude but also a deep sense of humility. To be recognized with the Medal of Valor is an honor I never sought, and I accept it with the understanding that this award is not just about me, but about the immense responsibility we all bear as law enforcement officers. The actions that led to this moment were not ones of heroism in the way we often imagine it. There was no glory in that moment—only a choice made in a split-second, in the midst of chaos. A choice I pray no officer ever has to make. I did what I was trained to do, what my duty required of me, to protect the lives of others. Taking a life, even in the service of justice, is never something to be celebrated. It is something to be carried, and I carry it every day. I accept this medal not as a mark of distinction, but as a solemn reminder of the weight of the badge we wear. Thank you."

Nikolai made his way back to the table, Bedo got up and politely excused himself and escorted him to the bar. He asked him to pick his poison, it was on him. Nikolai thought for a moment then ordered, "I'll have a Manhattan on the rocks with Bulleit Bourbon please."

Bedo had a straight bourbon, and when their order was ready, Bedo raised his glass to Nikolai. He laughed and said, "How long did it take you to write that fuckin' speech. Jesus, kid, you sound like a statesman."

At that very moment, City Councilman Javier Melendez with his Deputy District Attorney counterpart Mai Chang came and loudly told Nikolai, pointing at his face, "Enjoy your celebration, Drew.

It's gonna be your first and last one. You're gonna be a civilian by this time next week!" He was clearly intoxicated, and Deputy D.A. Chang was notably embarrassed.

Police Officer Association President Lou Picarone caught on to what was happening, as did the Association Attorney Paul Payne. The two men walked over to where Nikolai was standing. Bedo escorted everyone into the hallway, and they chatted quietly trying to figure out what the hell that was all about.

Nikolai brought them up to speed on the story regarding Melendez's rant at a secretive power brokers meeting at a colleagues house where Melendez basically threatened the chief's job and how he had been cavalier at the gym the next morning and was sharing the information with one of the reserves that he lifted weights with. Paul Payne patted Nikolai on the shoulder and reassured him, "Don't worry, kid, you survived that shit-show of a shooting. We will get you through this.

They all parted company after commiserating. Nikolai went into the hall bathroom, used the facilities, washed his hands, and walked back out to the main hall. He saw Mai Chang smoking a cigarette and holding a glass of white wine. He tried to walk quickly past her, but she stood in his way. "I wanted to apologize for Javier, Officer Drew. He has been drinking, and he can be a little bit of a hothead when he has a few. Please don't take it personally. Here's the reality, Officer Drew. If you're the bad cop that Javier thinks you are, I and the District Attorney's office will merely prosecute you to the highest level of the law."

Nikolai didn't quite know how to react to that. Deputy D.A. Chang dangled her cigarette and fumbled through her purse, grinning at Nikolai and presented him with a business card.

She pulled a pen from the purse and wrote something on the back and then handed it to him. "This is my card. My pager number is on the back. If you have trouble with Javier, give me a call. I read about your heroic escapade." She touched his arm lightly and continued. "I personally think we need more officers like you, not less." Nikolai got a chill from the way she touched him and the way her eyes looked black as a shark's as she looked into him. It was eerie, he thought. She put out her cigarette and walked down the hall and back into the banquet area.

Nikolai started to walk away, and then the words of the coroner resonated in his head about DNA and what he could collect as a sample for testing. He retrieved the cigarette that Mia Chang had put out. He walked back into the men's restroom and grabbed a paper towel, wrapped the butt in it carefully, and placed it in his suit's inner pocket.

Bedo walked out of the banquet room and engaged Nikolai. "You okay, kid?"

Nikolai smiled. "I am. You're not gonna believe this, but I just got ahold of Mia Chang's DNA."

Bedo developed a wicked evil grin. "How did you manage that?"

Nikolai told him what happened. Bedo had him give him the cigarette butt, and told him, "Finish up your date. I will stop by the station on my way home and book this into evidence for testing and make sure we get this going ASAP. This is a huge break, Nikolai. Well done!"

Nikolai and Kandee walked to the front of the restaurant, and he handed the valet his ticket. The man pulled the El Camino up, and Nikolai opened the door to let Kandee in. When he got in the car, he was a little rattled by the councilman's threat and the bizarre feeling he got from the Deputy D.A. and girlfriend, Mia Chang.

As he drove toward her home, she talked about how the dinner event was very classy and was intrigued about the awards he received. She asked, "So, that was quite a speech. I had no idea you had gone through that"

Nikolai thought for a moment, then responded, "It's not something I am proud of. My family doesn't even know about this."

Kandee continued. "Wow, you don't think you should tell them?"

Nikolai replied quickly, "No, they don't need to know what happened. it will only cause them to worry about me, and for what? They, my mother especially, are worried enough. This kind of thing only makes it obvious that it could happen again or worse, I end up dead. They don't need that."

Kandee nodded her head in understanding. "I never really thought of it like that."

He returned Kandee to her home. He got out and opened the car door for her. She leaned in to give him a kiss. He returned it, and she almost sucked his tongue out of his mouth. He thought that was a good sign. He did feel some sparks, after all. He ushered her off to the front door. He didn't escort her, mostly because he wasn't in the mood to be cornered by her parents again.

He drove home and arrived at midnight. He needed to stay up till the sun came up, or at least till five o'clock so he could readjust to the schedule and be ready for the next graveyard shift the next day. Nikolai unlocked the garage, backed his El Camino inside, and noticed that Diamond Dave's Mopar was nestled in the garage as well. *Not like him to be in this early on a Friday night*, he thought! He closed and locked the garage door and walked in the house and found Dave watching television.

"What the hell ya watchin', man," Nikolai asked.

Dave laughed and replied, "It's *Porky's*, brotha, love this damned movie!"

Nikolai grabbed a deck of cards, his Planter's peanut jar full of quarters, and set it on the coffee table. He noticed that Dave was drinking a light beer, so he asked him to pause the movie and said, "You in the mood for some poker and bourbon while we watch this thing?"

Dave responded happily, "Hell yes man, let me get my quarters!" The two men always played quarter poker. It kept the game civil.

The two men laughed and enjoyed many hands of poker, changing games at the dealer's whim, meaning the dealer changed every time someone lost, so it changed the game every time.

One game was two card gut poker, another was Five Card Draw, deuces wild, the next was seven card poker with one-eyed jacks and deuces wild. This went on till nearly three a.m. They were watching *Top Gun*, and about half way through, Diamond Dave had enough. He packed it in and went to bed while Nikolai did his best to stay up till five a.m. but only got to four. He took the dirty dishes to the sink, washed them up, dried them, and put them where they belonged, then turned off all the lights and television and went to bed. He turned on his favorite seascapes music and drifted off to sleep.

CHAPTER
TWENTY-TWO

Monday morning came way too fast, Nikolai had made sure that everything he needed to do was completed so he could leave right after the shift ended so he could get to Burbank Studios. He initially hated the idea of this kind of work, but he was honestly starting to get excited and wonder what it was going to be like.

0800 hit, and Nikolai was practically running out the back door of the station. His gear was already in the El Camino, and he got in and started the car. It sounded so good as it idled! He was just about to put it in drive when there was a knock at the driver's side window. It was Bedo! He rolled the window down.

Bedo kneeled by the door so he could talk with Nikolai. "Well, the lab has the cigarette butt, if something comes of it, we are going to need to move quick to get a warrant and hit the house, which means, I have a judge on standby that will keep it quiet so she doesn't know we are coming. You in?"

Nikolai smiled and shook his hand from inside the car. "In for a penny, in for a pound I always say. You can count on me, Detective! Now, excuse me, I need to run. How long before we know anything?"

Bedo stood up, leaned down to the window. "Hard to say, I was initially told ten days, but the severity of the case has them working on an accelerated pace. Have a great day, kid."

Nikolai arrived at the back gate of Burbank Studios with twenty minutes to burn! He pulled up to the guard shack and gave him his name. The aged guard was jovial and kind of reminded him of Ernest Borgnine. He opened the gate and told him where to park. Nikolai pulled in, and as he parked the car and got out, he put his uniform over his shoulder and saw Danny Glover of *Lethal Weapon* walk by him. *Is this a good omen?* he pondered.

As he approached the door marked Stage 13 and opened the door, the security guard there asked for his name. Nikolai gave it, and he checked it off. He entered the room and was addressed by one of the staff, a cute young brunette, probably twenty, he thought that was holding a clipboard. She introduced herself. "Hi, Nikolai, I'm Natlie. Your job here today is to walk on as we direct or stand in a certain place as we direct, but you will mostly be a police officer going about his business, understand?"

Nikolai nodded. She then guided him to a dressing room area where he could put on his uniform. He looked around the room as he undressed and got dressed in his long-sleeved uniform. He got finished and started to walk out of the room and was nearly run over by William Conrad. Startled, he backed up and excused himself.

The man was about 5'8" tall and weighed about 260 pounds and was jovial and addressed him. "Son, you don't need to excuse yourself. This is close quarters drill around here. We gotta share what space we have. You a walk on?"

Nikolai confirmed that he was and went on, "William Conrad, you are a legend sir. I used to watch you on *Cannon* when I was a kid with my mom."

Conrad smiled. "Well, that's nice of you to say, but I'm just a fossil glad to be workin'. Call me Bill. What's your name?"

Nikolai introduced himself. "Nikolai Drew, Bill, nice to meet you."

Conrad smiled. "Well, have fun today, let's see if that Penny kid can show up on time."

As luck would have it, Joe Penny did show up on time. The director and cameraman were getting set up, and suddenly Victor Denofrio walked on and started working on the sound equipment. They did a couple rough blocking sessions.

Nikolai stood at a door off stage and waited for his cue to walk over to the water cooler to get a glass of water, then over to a filing cabinet and act like he was looking for something.

Suddenly the director called out, "Ready camera, roll sound, everyone in your places. Action!"

Everything was deathly quiet. Everyone moved seamlessly and then Nikolai noticed for the first time, there was a guy holding huge cards plain for William Conrad to read. He was going along very cleanly, and then the cue came for Nikolai to do his thing. He walked with purpose to the water cooler, filled up his cup with water, then across the room to the filing cabinet, opened the drawer and milled about the empty files, then he heard the director yell, "Cut!" He watched the scene on the camera listening to the sound from Denofrio's headset for a few minutes then barked again, "Print! Well done, everyone, next scene."

This went on for three hours, then the director called for a break for lunch. They all went out to the door of the studio where a caterer had set up a spread that had everything from fruit to salads to sandwiches. Penny and Conrad grabbed various items and sat down at their own table, and the rest of the hands filled their plates and sat down. Denofrio got a salad and sat next to Nikolai. They ate, and Denofrio elbowed him and said, "Well, how do you like it so far?

Nikolai smiled. "Well, it's pretty cool actually. William Conrad actually talked to me and told me to call him Bill. I have to ask, however, what is with the guy holding up those massive cards in front of Bill?"

Denofrio swallowed his bite of salad and nodded. "Aaaaah, good catch! Well, Will doesn't memorize a script, never has. He reads it, gets ready for it, but always reads the script from that thing you saw, which is what we call a cue card."

The two men went back to work, and the next several hours of the day were much like the first few. By the time five o'clock hit, the extras were no longer needed and were excused. Nikolai collected his clothes and walked out to the El Camino. As he was placing his items in the car, Victor approached him and pinched the inside of his lower thigh, which caused Nikolai to turn around and nearly punch the man. Victor laughed and flinched. "Jesus Christ, Nikolai. Relax, man!"

Nikolai laughed and pushed him back and exclaimed, "That hurt, fucker!"

Victor seemed quite pleased with himself and asked Nikolai, "So, what was your experience like. Did you dig it?"

Nikolai smiled. "Yeah, Victor, this was pretty cool. If I get a call back, I will definitely be here!"

Victor turned around and walked back toward the building. "Oh, you'll be getting a call back alright, brother, you can count on that!"

Nikolai made his way out of the studio lot and headed home. He was pretty exhausted and needed to get some shut-eye. He arrived at his house in no time at all, backed up the driveway, unlocked and opened the garage door and noticed that Diamond Dave's Mopar was nestled in its regular resting spot. He backed his El Camino in, grabbed his clothes and walked out the door of the garage, closed it and locked it.

He walked inside the house and found Diamond Dave prepping steaks and smelled the heavenly odor of baked potatoes in the oven. He also had asparagus out on the cutting board, and Diamond Dave was listening to a Waylon Jennings album.

Nikolai took in a big breath through his nose. "Man, that all smells good! How did you know I'd be home?"

Diamond Dave smiled. "I didn't, just figured I'd put yours in the fridge for when you did get home. Now you're here, so give me a hand prepping the asper-grass will ya!"

Nikolai threw his gear in his bedroom and walked back in the kitchen and began cutting the bottom of the stalks of the asparagus off. He then soaked them in a mix of olive oil and soy sauce then dumped some black pepper over them and wrapped them in tin foil. They walked out to the back yard and began working over the two steaks on the grill and laid the tin foil on the upper part of the grill. The grill was on high, so they let them sit for two minutes on each side to sear them, then turned the grill down to medium and let them cook for a few more minutes on each side till they were perfect. The asparagus took a little longer, so while Dave went in to finish the prep on the baked potatoes and steaks, Nikolai tended to the asparagus.

They sat at the dinner table, opened a couple beers, and enjoyed the fruits of their labor! They didn't chat much, just listened to the music and enjoyed the dinner they made. When done, they worked together to clean up the kitchen. Diamond Dave looked over at Nikolai and asked, "You're off tonight and tomorrow night, right?"

Nikolai smiled and nodded yes, its 1800 hours, I would normally be getting ready for work! Dave went to the videotape storage area and said, "Well then, what movie are we watching tonight, my friend?"

Nikolai walked over to the storage cabinet, and they looked around quite a bit. They locked in on the same movie at the same time. Diamond Dave picked up *Johnny Dangerously* and laughed! Nikolai commented, "That's perfect. I'm gonna go change out of my street clothes and get us a beer. Get it dialed in, brotha!"

Nikolai got back a few minutes later and handed Diamond Dave a beer and sat on the couch and relaxed as the comedy spoof on gangsters from 1984 began. Dave looked over at Nikolai. They clinked their beer bottles, and Dave said, "Man, I have to tell ya, it's great to just relax and hang out watchin' a great movie with a great friend!"

Nikolai raised the bottle back up and said, "Cheers to that, my friend. May the good times never end!"

Neither of them made it through the full movie. Nikolai woke up on the couch. It was 0230 hours, and there was nothing but snow on the television. He got up and woke Diamond Dave up, then turned off the television. They turned off the lights, and the two men went to bed.

Nikolai must have been tired because the next thing he knew, it was 0815 hours. That meant he had been sleeping for about twelve hours. Totally unheard of for him. He got up and found the pot of coffee still hot and Diamond Dave gone. Nikolai poured himself a cup of coffee and turned on the news. He then picked up the phone and paged his buddy Carbone. He figured he may be able to break away from his chiropractic practice to get a morning workout in. Ten minutes later the phone rang. Nikolai picked it up and said, "Talkin to ya cordless!"

Carbone laughed. "Hey, ya fuckin' dinkus, what is goin on?"

Nikolai was smiling. "What the fuck is a dinkus, ya Wop! I am off for a couple days and wanted to see if you wanted to get in the gym?"

Carbone replied, "I don't have anything till 1300

hours; that's one p.m., you undisciplined nasty thing! What do you plan to train?"

Nikolai looked at his notepad. "Looks like it's a shoulder and leg day, meatball, you in?"

Carbone shook his head and rolled his eyes. "I, I, I, I hate leg day. At least we can motivate each other. Meet at Wright's Gym in forty-five minutes?"

Nikolai responded, "You got it. You wanna wear the shirts and do-rags today? Keep our buddies sharp?"

Carbone laughed. "Fuck yeah, see you there, meet you in the parking lot!"

Nikolai got his ingredients dialed in for his protein shake and blended it up. While drinking the elixir, he put his workout gear on and put on the black shirt that had white iron on letters that said, "The All-White Brothers" and put on his do-rag. They did love messing with their two buddies at the gym who always wore matching shirts that said "The All-Right Brothers." These two knuckleheads had these shirts made in multiple colors and often wore them with crazy parachute pants. Carbone and Nikolai could not let this go without poking fun. Typical gym rivalry and shenanigans!

The two men arrived at nearly the same time at the gym. Carbone looked at Nikolai and said, "Man, ya gotta see this!"

He opened his trunk and pulled out a ghetto blaster, a large radio with a cassette player and put it on his shoulder like the kids do and hit the play button. Nikolai almost fell on the ground when "(You Gotta) Fight for Your Right (to Party)!" by the Beastie Boys came on.

Nikolai shook his head as they walked up to the front door and said, "This is gonna be fun, or we're gonna get totalled!"

They walked into the gym like gangster rappers walk in, and the Pendagrass brothers Carl and Pearl, otherwise known as the "All-Right Brothers" were there! They took one look at Nikolai and Carbone, walked over to them like they were gonna start some trouble, then started laughing out loud! The two men were laughing, and all they could say was, "Man, you guys crazy!" They all had a good laugh over the joke, then Carbone took the Ghetto Blaster back to his car and locked it in the trunk and returned to the gym. They began their workout by first stretching and warming up and started with their legs. They always started with legs because they each hated them the most and figured if they got them out of the way, they were least likely to skimp on that part of the workout.

In between the sets, they were working abdominals. The goal was always to get three hundred reps of each body part by the end of the workout. Meanwhile, Joe and Billy were on the bench press and engaging the manager, Tony, like they always do, some juvenile thing about being the strongest guy in the gym.

Joe, who everyone called Paulie like Rocky's stupid brother-in-law in *Rocky* was antagonizing Tony. Tony, being very secure and knowing better than to fall into the brother's juvenile trap, waved them off and ignored them.

When that didn't work, they went after Carbone. Carbone and Nikolai kept training and ignored them. Finally Joe started going after Nikolai, trying to get his goat. After a few minutes, Nikolai finally decided to reply, "Okay, Paulie, so if we do this, you'll shut the hell up about being the king of the gym or whatever it is?"

Joe gave Nikolai a dirty look, looking up at him the entire time and spouted off, "And don't fuckin call me Paulie, jackass!"

Nikolai smiled. "Okay, Paulie, so do your thing. We are all here. Show us what you've got!" Joe, or should we say Paulie, looked at the weight loaded on the bench, he counted up the weight. It was 450 pounds. He cinched up the kidney belt he had around his waist and lay on the bench. Billy was about to spot him, and Nikolai butted in. "Uh no, fucko, I'll spot him. This way we know there's no bullshit."

Tony was watching from behind the counter and walked over and stepped in. "Okay, you retards, if you gonna do this shit, I am gonna be the one to do the spotting for both of ya!" Joe moved the bar off and lowered it slowly to his chest, paused, and started to lift. His face was red, but he managed to complete the rep and set the bar back in place.

Joe looked over at Nikolai and asked, "You ready, kid?" Nikolai looked at Carbone and looked a little nervous. In truth, Carbone had never seen Nikolai lift heavy, so he didn't know what to expect. The look on his face, however, caused him to be a little nervous.

Nikolai took his position on the bench. He grabbed the bar and slowly lifted the 450 pounds from its resting spot. He slowly lowered the bar to his chest. He paused for a second and struggled. His cheeks were bulging from slowly letting his breath out. Tony was in position and just about to lift the bar because he felt Nikolai couldn't lift it; then all of a sudden, Nikolai smiled and knocked out three reps of the 450 pounds like it was nothing. He racked the bar, sat up, and looked over at Paulie and smiled, saying, "Alighty Paulie, no more of this fuckin' 'King of the Gym' bullshit!"

Billy and Joe just looked at each other, and Tony was also stunned. Carbone was laughing as they continued their shoulder workout and asked Nikolai, "How much do you weigh kid?"

Nikolai thought about it for a minute. "Somewhere between 325 and 330, depending on the day."

Carbone shook his head. "Christ man, how much can you actually max out on bench press wise?"

Nikolai shook his head. "Hell, I don't know. I just

lift to stay in shape, man, not to keep track or set any records. Hell, I didn't know how that was going to go, I usually get up around 400 and do twenty reps, so I figured I'd be able to get at least one. I thought I had a couple more in me." They were nearing the finish of their workout when Nikolai got a page. It was Bedo's extension with a 911 at the end. Nikolai excused himself and went to his car, got some change, and called Bedo's number.

Bedo answered the phone. "Go for Bedo!"

Nikolai replied, "Got your page. What do you need?"

Bedo looked around to make sure no one was eavesdropping. "Get yer ass in here. Come in the back door; we need to chat."

CHAPTER
TWENTY-THREE

It was not 1300 hours when Nikolai arrived in the Detective parking lot of the station and backed his El Camino into the last parking space against the wall at the very back part of the lot so no one would notice he was there. He walked up to the Detective Division door and found it to be open. Bedo was sitting at his desk and stood up and hung up his phone when Nikolai walked in.

Bedo ushered him into the back office of the bureau and shut the door. The two men sat down, and Bedo looked at Nikolai. "You ready for this, kid?"

Nikolai smiled. "Yeah man, spill!"

Bedo continued. "Well, the DNA came back, Chang is definitely our suspect, but it gets worse, or better, yeah, better!"

"Holy shit, it's her? How can it get better or worse?"

Bedo smiled. "Well, they found her DNA at our crime scene, but they also found that the blood found in the vehicle her dead husband's body was found in is also a match for her! Apparently, the lab thought they had this before, but wanted to check the integrity of the evidence found at her husband's crime scene to make sure that it was still good, and it is."

Nikolai's heart was racing at this point. "Well, what the hell do we do now?"

Bedo stood up and walked to the door and then to the back door of the Detective Bureau. "Come on, I need a smoke and a soda. Let's go for a drive."

They got in Bedo's Detective unit and headed down First Street to 146 Hubbard, and all the while Bedo was talking. "I have a search warrant ready to go for her office and her home. I don't think we're going to find anything at the office, but the home is likely to be full of evidence. We are going to need to roll alone on this, no SWAT, no other cops, just you and me, kid. If the word gets to her that we are on to her, she will likely burn the place down and disappear."

Nikolai's heart was racing. "Okay, when do we go?"

They got out of the car and walked into the 7-11. Bedo got himself a Big Gulp Coke, dangling a cigarette as he filled it up.

He walked by the desk and slid Raginder a one-dollar bill, and they walked back to the Detective unit.

"When do we go, well, kid, we go now. You need to sneak in, get in some street clothes and a vest and your gear. and let's roll now!"

Nikolai looked at him and replied, "Okay, drop me off in front of the station. I will get in, get dressed and meet you at your car in less than ten minutes.

Bedo dropped Nikolai off at the front of the station, turned around, and parked in the Detective parking lot. He walked in and headed to the chief's office. The chief was sitting behind his desk but had guests. He couldn't risk taking the time out to let the chief know what was going on, so he walked back to the Detective Bureau, put on his bullet proof vest, his Detective windbreaker, and loaded up on ammo. He walked back to his car, opened the trunk, and grabbed his shotgun, making sure it was clean and loaded.

Nikolai walked around the side and stood beside Bedo. "I'm locked, cocked and ready to rock, Detective."

They got in the car and headed to Chang's home, which happened to be in the foothills of Sylmar. Bedo told Nikolai, "This is an older home, built in 1929. It has a detached garage in the back, and it is on a raised foundation with a basement. I have already scouted the location. We are going to first hit the house, cover one room at a time. I'll be searching the rooms as you cover me, got it?"

Nikolai replied, "Got it, what if shit blows up on us and we end up in a shooting?"

Bedo looked at him pensively. "We do what needs to be done, kid, then we call it in and roll the world. Let's hope it doesn't come to that."

Bedo parked two houses away from Chang's home. They walked up quietly and walked down the driveway to the back yard. There was no one there, no car in the driveway or in the garage. Bedo worked the doorknob of the back door. It was locked, but the door jamb was old and had lots of wiggle room to work his credit card in. Within seconds, the door was open. Nikolai covered Bedo as he went room by room, guns drawn. There was no evidence of anything suspicious. They went through every drawer, every closet, every aspect of the home. They drew a blank.

Bedo was scratching his head and looked at Nikolai confused. "Man, I know something is here, and we're missin' it." They walked out the back door, and off to the left, there was a set of stairs that led to a door to the basement. Bedo motioned to Nikolai. They walked down the stairs. The door was locked, and it had a bolt with a lock securing it. Bedo told Nikolai to run back to the car and get his bolt cutters out of the trunk.

Nikolai took the keys and ran back to the car, retrieved the bolt cutters, and then ran back to the house. Bedo took the bolt cutters to the lock and removed it. He slid the bolt back and tried the trick with the credit card on the door mechanism. It didn't work this time, so Bedo moved back slightly then with all his weight, he kicked the door by the handle and broke it open.

The room was pitch-black, Bedo used his flashlight to find a light switch. There wasn't one; there was, however, a long fluorescent light across the ceiling with a pull chain dangling from it. He gave it a tug, and the place lit up.

To the left was a street bike. Nikolai pointed at it and told Bedo, "Dude, this is the bike that ran from me the night I got the radio call for the murder/suicide!"

Bedo was at the far right side of the basement at a desk, and called to Nikolai, "Hey, Nancy, you better have a look at this!"

Nikolai walked over, shaking his head. "Why do you fuckers get off on calling me Nancy, like Nancy Drew? That is just fucked up, ya know."

Nikolai stopped. There was a six foot wide, four foot tall peg board mounted on the wall. There were a ton of pictures of people alive with pictures of them dead next to them with names and dates. The first was the picture of Mai's husband, and it escalated to the far right side of the board. The last three were Georgann Emerson, the woman Nikolai found in the drive-in movie theater building, alive and dead. Next was Councilman Melendez, alive, with a red X across the photo. The last photo was a huge shock. It was a photo of Chief Belknap. Written in red across the photo were the words, "You're Next."

Bedo pointed to a picture of Nikolai. It was an 8" by 10" inch photo, much larger than the others, which were only 5" by 7", and there was an outline of a red heart in the center and a question mark in the middle of it.

The two men looked around the room. There was a gun safe that was secured. Nikolai was looking atop the desk and discovered three journals, one in the name of Javier Melendez, James Patrick Belknap, and the last was Nikolai Drew.

Looking through the journals there were dates with incidents on them with footnotes. The author called Melendez a misogynistic narcissist, racist, and womanizer. Belknap's book had notes about cases dating back to Mai's husband. Those footnotes were all over the place with dates and questions. "Does he know something?" "I know he knows something!" There was another comment written that said, "There is no way he is as straight an arrow as he seems" with devil drawings and the like.

Nikolai looked at Bedo, and the two men had their mouths open. Nikolai said, "This bitch is a fucking serial killer, brother. We best lock her down and now."

Bedo removed his handheld radio from his waist and switched it over to frequency two. The detective bureau was always monitoring both. "13 David to David 50."

Lieutenant Quinten McHale was a thirty-year

veteran and had come up the ranks with the chief. He answered, "David 50 go."

Bedo told him that he needed him and two uniformed officers he could trust and where they were and told him that he would give him the details when they arrived and how he didn't feel it was safe to go into detail over the radio. He further asked him to have the black and white park around the corner and walk in so as to not arouse suspicion.

Ten minutes later Lieutenant McHale arrived, and a black and white arrived with him, parking around the corner as instructed. The lieutenant parked behind Bedo's plain car, and the three walked up on foot. Bedo waved them to where he and Nikolai were waiting in the back of the house. Nikolai stood with the two patrolmen, while Bedo briefed the lieutenant. Nikolai could see the body language displayed by the lieutenant showed stress. The two then walked down to the basement of the house.

A few minutes later the lieutenant and Detective Bedo emerged from the basement steps. Detective Bedo told one of the uniformed officers to get the evidence kit out of the trunk of his car. He motioned for Nikolai to follow him downstairs. Lieutenant McHale used his cell phone to page the district attorney directly and waited for the return call.

Bedo pointed out what to print and what to collect and what to document and expressed how important it was to do so precisely. This was going to be a massive case and he imparted that if they fucked it up, she would walk.

The uniformed officer brought the evidence kit below, and Nikolai began the arduous process of photographing and documenting and bagging it all. He had the two officers put on rubber gloves and get the motorcycle out of the basement, which was not the easiest of tasks.

Lieutenant McHale received a call back from the district ten minutes later. McHale told the DA what they were dealing with and asked him if she was still in the building. The DA told him he would dig in discreetly and call him back as soon as he had an answer.

There were nine victims on the murder board. In the desk below the board, Nikolai found nine ledgers with each of the victim's names on the covers and the details within were gruesome, detailing the hate Deputy D.A. Chang had for each one along with dates, incidents, and the way she dispatched them. Each ledger was bagged individually because they would need to be checked for prints individually. The murder board, well that was a different story. Nikolai asked Detective Bedo if they could get a Community Service Officer to bring the D.A.R.E. Van or something similar so they could keep it intact.

Being now 1450 hours, the men were nearly done collecting all the evidence. The Community Service Officer George Ramirez did in fact bring the

D.A.R.E. van to the location. Nikolai loaded the death board into the van, and the CSO delivered it to the police station and booked it into evidence. Black and White Garage was informed as well so they could transport the motorcycle to the police station and store it in evidence. It was quite funny when Diamond Dave showed up with a flatbed tow truck to pick up the motorcycle. Dave backed into the driveway and tilted the bed of the truck to its lowest point. He and the two officers wheeled it up the bed, and Diamond Dave tied it down in just a few moments. It was like he had been doing the job for years. Diamond Dave waved at Nikolai and told him he would catch him later.

Lieutenant McHale had finally received a call back from the District Attorney who informed him that Chang was at the San Fernando Superior Court House on North Brand in Department A for a hearing.

McHale smiled at Detective Bedo and Nikolai. "I know where she is, kids. I am taking the two uniforms with me. You two button this place up and do one final sweep for evidence. Ill page you with my ID number and 1015 when I have her in custody, got me?"

Bedo gave him a thumbs-up as the lieutenant walked away. Bedo said to Nikolai, "He looks happier than I have seen him in years, like a school kid. You grab the last boxes of shit out of the basement. We will need to get Chang to give us the safe combo when we get her in custody and come back. I am going to do one final sweep through the house, just to make sure we didn't miss anything. Secure that door the best you can, and let's get the fuck outta here!"

Nikolai collected the last box of evidence and walked it to Detective Bedo's unit and secured it in the trunk. He was starting to head back to the house on foot and saw Deputy D.A. Chang walking up her driveway with a gun in hand. Nikolai was about to call Bedo on the radio, but realized he didn't have time.

Nikolai ran quickly and quietly down the street. He saw Chang creeping along the side of the house making her way to the back yard. He saw Bedo walking from the front of the house toward the back door where he and Chang were about to intersect.

Chang walked around the back side of the house and pointed her weapon at Detective Bedo, who was walking toward the basement door. Nikolai had a moment before it would be too late. It was clear that Chang was going to eliminate anyone who got in her way. Nikolai saw her start to apply pressure to the trigger of the weapon. He walked up behind her, holstered his weapon, and in a flash, grabbed Chang by the wrist in a violent hold. The wrist turn out caused her extreme pain. The weapon went off firing behind her, Bedo drew his side arm and turned in an instant, relieved to see that Drew had Chang on the ground face first, placing her weapon in his waistband and handcuffing her.

Chang was losing her mind. "Get your filthy fucking hands off me, Drew. What do you think you're going to do, huh?"

Drew pulled Chang from the ground and whispered in her ear, "Oh, ma'am, we're going to prosecute you to the highest level of the law!"

Chang squirmed and gave Nikolai a dirty look over her shoulder as he and Bedo escorted her to the detective unit.

Nikolai sat her in the back seat on the passenger side of the car and buckled her in and sat next to her to ensure she didn't try anything violent. These detective units did not have a cage to protect the driver from rear passengers, so it was always important to put officer safety first in these circumstances.

Bedo got on his handheld radio. "13 David Control."

Dispatch replied, "13 David go."

Bedo continued. "13 David, be advised, officer Drew and I will be transporting a 10-15 female from Sylmar to 10-19, clear for starting mileage?" (Officers are required to inform the dispatcher of their starting mileage and location when transporting a female anywhere for any reason to protect them from liability.)

Dispatch replied, "Roger 13 David, clear to copy."

Bedo continued. "Starting Mileage is 21453.2"

Dispatch replied and parroted the information.

Ten minutes later they arrived at the police station and Detective Bedo radioed dispatch that they were at the station and gave their ending mileage. Dispatch acknowledged.

Meanwhile, Deputy D.A. Chang was totally quiet all the way to the station. They pulled into the sally port, and Nikolai exited, removing Chang from the back seat. Nikolai and Bedo secured their handguns in the sally port gun locker. Nikolai held on to the weapon he took from Chang and walked up to the dispatch desk to relieve the dispatcher so she could search D.A. Chang thoroughly before she was booked. Nikolai was grateful that it was Cindy Anglin that was working. She would never give him a hard time about helping out in a female search.

Anglin walked in the jail and shared pleasantries with Detective Bedo. She entered the room where the Deputy DA was detained and began rifling through her pockets, waist band, shoes, and even her bra and between her legs to ensure she didn't have any other weapons in her possession.

Meanwhile, Lieutenant McHale and Chief Belknap were walking down the main corridor of the police station toward the jail and saw Nikolai manning the desk. They made a sharp left turn and walked into the Dispatch Center and closed the door behind them. The chief smiled, and Lieutenant McHale was grinning ear to ear.

Chief Belknap began, "How the hell did you find her and where the hell is Bedo?"

Nikolai smiled. "I was putting evidence away, and she was sneaking up on the house trying to get the drop on Bedo, who was in the backyard buttoning up. She had a gun drawn and was so intense on taking out Bedo that she never saw me coming. I put her in a wrist turnout and armbar and the gun went off. I had her cuffed quickly, and that was all she wrote."

Lieutenant McHale couldn't stop giggling. "Nikolai, do you have any idea how big this case is? Never mind. You are gonna hate it, but you're gonna get a huge 'atta boy from everyone again!"

The chief continued. "Is it true that she had a death book and photo of Councilman Melendez?"

Nikolai smiled and nodded his head up and down. "Yes sir, that fucker, I mean that guy is gonna owe you a huge apology."

Chief Belknap smiled. "No, Nikolai, he's gonna be kissin your ass for a long time to come over this!"

Desk Officer Anglin returned to take over the dispatch center, and Nikolai went back to finish up the report while Detective Bedo booked in all the evidence.

As the two men walked out the Detective Bureau door, Bedo put his arm around Nikolai and said,

"Alright, hero, you saved my life, so, we're gonna go celebrate. I'm gonna teach you how to order a good whiskey and teach you how to smoke a cigar so you don't look like a dickhead!"

Nikolai smiled and replied, "Alright, Detective, but I am not fuckin' smoking a cigar!"

"Oh, yes you are!"

"Ooooooooh, no I am not!"

"We'll see, but yes you are!"

THE END

APPENDIX

Law Enforcement Radio 10 Code
For Los Angeles County

10-0: Caution
10-1: Reception Poor
10-2: Reception Good
10-3: Stop Transmitting
10-4: Message Received, Understood
10-5: Repay Message
10-6: Change Channel
10-7: Responding
10-8: In Service
10-9: Repeat Message
10-10: Negative
10-11: Identify Frequency
10-12: Visitor(s) Present
10-13: Weather and Road Advice

APPENDIX

10-14: Citizen w/ Suspect
10-15: Prisoner In Custody
10-16: Pick Up Prisoner
10-17: Request For Gasoline
10-18: Equipment Exchange
10-19: Return(ing) To Station
10-20: Location
10-21: Telephone
10-21A: Advise Home I Will Return At:
10-22: Disregard Last Assignment
10-23: Stand By
10-24: Request Car-To-Car Transmit
10-25: Do You Have Contact With:
10-26: Clear
10-27: D.D.L Report
10-28: Registration Request
10-29: Check For Wants
10-29F: Subject Wanted / Felony
10-29H: Hazard Potential From Subject
10-29M: Subject Wanted / Misdemeanor
10-29V: Vehicle Wanted
10-30: Doesn't Conform To Regulations
10-32: Drowning
10-33: Alarm Sounding, Audible
10-34: Assist At Office
10-35: Time Check
10-36: Confidential Information
10-37: Identify Operator
10-39: Can () Come To The Radio?

APPENDIX

10-40: Is () Available For Phone Call?
10-42: Check The Welfare Of/At:
10-43: Call A Doctor
10-45: Condition Of Patient
10-45A: Good
10-45B: Serious
10-45C: Critical
10-45D: Dead
10-49: Proceed To:
10-50: Under Influence Of Drugs
10-51: Drunk
10-52: Resuscitator -53: Man Down
10-54: Possible Dead Body
10-55: Coroner Case
10-56: Suicide
10-56A: Suicide Attempt
10-57: Missing Person
10-59: Security Check
10-60: Lock-Out
10-61: Miscellaneous Public Service
10-62: Meet A Citizen
10-62A: Take A Report From A Citizen
10-62B: Civilian Standby
10-63: Prepare To Copy
10-64: Found Property
10-66: Suspicious Person
10-67: Person Calling For Help
10-68: Telephone For Police
10-70: Prowler

APPENDIX

10-71: Shooting
10-72: Gun Involved
10-73: How Do You Receive?
10-79: Bomb Threat
10-80: Explosion
10-86: Any Radio Traffic?
10-88: Assume Post
10-91: Animal
10-91A: Animal Stray
10-91B: Animal Noisy
10-91C: Animal Injured
10-91D: Animal Dead
10-91E: Animal Bite
10-91G: Animal Pickup
10-91J: Animal Pickup Collect
10-91L: Animal Leash Law Violation
10-91V: Animal Vicious
10-95: Need Id Tech Unit
10-97: Arrived At Scene
10-98: Available To Assign

APPENDIX

Law Enforcement 11 Codes

11-24 Abandoned vehicle
11-27 Urgent / DDL info via TT
11-28 Urgent Reg. Check via TT
11-29 Urgent / Check for wanted
11-41 Ambulance & Fire needed
11-44 Coroner's case
11-54 Suspicious vehicle stop
11-79 Accident w/ambulance en route
11-80 Major accident
11-81 Minor accident
11-82 Property damage accident
11-83 Accident - no details
11-84 Traffic control detail
11-85 Tow truck needed
11-86 Rolling car stop
11-95 Traffic Stop
11-98 Meet _____
11-99 EMERGENCY! Officer needs help fast. All units respond

APPENDIX

L.A. County General Codes

Code 1 Your convenience

Code 2 Urgent

Code 3 Emergency

Code 4 No further assistance

Code 5 Stakeout

Code 6 Out on a pedestrian contact or arrived on scene

Code 7 Mealtime

Code 9 Roadblock

Code 10 Wants Warrants Check

Code 21 Jail emergency

Code 30 Burglary Alarm

Code 33 Clear radio channel - Emergency traffic only

Code 666 Countywide emergency felony roadblock

www.ingramcontent.com/pod-product-compliance
Lightning Source LLC
Chambersburg PA
CBHW070610030426
42337CB00020B/3736